MW01542836

T-SHIRT

FOR ADOBE PHOTOSHOP® & ILLUSTRATOR® USERS

Revised and Updated for CS5

Dane Clement

T-Shirt Artwork Simplified, For Adobe® Photoshop® & Illustrator® Users
Dane Clement

Published By
Great Dane Graphics

Copyright © 2008-2011 by Dane Clement

Second Edition: April 2011

Notice of Rights
All rights reserved. No part of this book may be reproduced or transmitted in any form, by any means, electronic or mechanical, including photocopying, recording or by any information storage and retrieval system, without written permission from the publisher, except for the inclusion of brief quotations in a review.

Trademarks
All terms mentioned in this book that are known to be trademarks or service marks have been appropriately capitalized. Great Dane Graphics cannot attest to the accuracy of this information. Use of a term in this book should not be regarded as affecting the validity of any trademark or service mark.

Photoshop is a registered trademark of Adobe Systems Incorporated.
Illustrator is a registered trademark of Adobe Systems Incorporated.
Macintosh is a registered trademark of Apple, Inc.
Windows is a registered trademark of Microsoft Corporation.
Epson Scan is a registered trademark of Epson Corporation.

Warning and Disclaimer
This book is designed to provide information about creating artwork with Photoshop and Illustrator. Every effort has been made to make this book asa complete and as accurate as possible, but no warranty of fitness is implied.

The information is provided on an as-is basis. The author and Great Dane Graphics shall have neither the liability nor responsibility to any person or entity with respect to any loss or damages arising from the information contained in this book or from the use of the discs or programs that may accompany it.

THIS PRODUCT IS NOT ENDORSED OR SPONSORED BY ADOBE SYSTEMS INCORPORATED, PUBLISHER OF PHOTOSHOP AND ILLUSTRATOR.

THIS PRODUCT IS NOT ENDORSED OR SPONSORED BY EPSON CORPORATION, PUBLISHER OF EPSON SCAN SOFTWARE.

ISBN 13: 978-0-9820935-0-4
ISBN 10: 0-9820935-0-0

9 8 7 6 5 4 3 2 1
Printed and bound in the United States of America

www.greatdanegraphics.com

To my family
Maritza, Darian and Dylan

I love you.

Acknowledgements

First, I want to thank my wife Maritza, who's stuck by me for the last 20 years even though I have all of these crazy ideas that keep me working way too much. To her I want to say, thank you, I love you, and I promise not to keep working as much as I have been. I'll slow down just as soon as I finish...and then...oh yeah...that too!

Thanks to my beautiful daughter Darian and son Dylan who I love so much, for being there to make me laugh.

To my mom and dad for instilling in me a strong work ethic at a young age and encouraging me to do whatever I wanted to do in life.

I have to thank the best art director and assistant art director any creative company could hope to have. This book would not have been possible without the great dedication and help of my art director of almost 16 years, Missy Marino and assistant art director of the last 6 years, Joe Costello.

A special thanks goes out to one of the screen printing industry guru's and friend, Charlie Taublieb for taking the time to teach me how to separate black shirts back in 1992. I'm happy to say, I'm glad the days of airbrushing separations on clear mylar and then shooting them on a stat camera are all long gone!

My thanks to the team at the Imprinted Sportswear Shows for having me speak at all the shows for so many years. It was at these seminars that the idea for this book came to be. Meeting so many attendees that are hungry for knowledge is the reason I love to teach, it makes my day when I see the "light turn on" in their eyes.

To Sallie McDonlald for doing such a great job editing my "Cajun English" so this book reads as if a normal person wrote it.

Finally a heartfelt thanks to Tom Codute and SPSI for giving me an opportunity to further educate myself in the new and exciting world of direct to garment digital printing.

I'd like to thank you, the readers and seminar attendees. Without you, this book would not have happened. Thanks for your support and questions in emails, phone calls and after class discussions. Keep them coming, I want to know what it is you're interested in as I enjoy very much showing you how to do it!

Dane Clement

Dane Clement has been creating award winning illustrations and designs for over 20 years. In 1991 he started his own company Great Dane Graphics which specialized in the creation and separation of artwork for the screen printing industry. The knowledge he has acquired over the years has made him well sought out by screen printing companies worldwide to help get their art departments working smoothly and efficiently.

His expertise is shared in monthly articles for Impressions Magazine as well as in seminars throughout the year at Imprinted Sportswear Shows. He also participates as a judge for the Impressions Magazine Impressions Awards, and the SGIA Golden Image Awards.

After hurricane Katrina changed his business completely in New Orleans in 2005. Dane took a position at SPSI in Minnesota as an Application Specialist giving him an even greater knowledge in the expanding market of direct-to-garment digital printing. He has recently relocated closer to home in the New Orleans area.

T-Shirt Artwork Simplified was the brainchild of years of seminars, consulting, & speaking engagements and created directly from the common questions and problems discussed. T-Shirt Artwork Simplified is a 'real world' approach that will take your artwork to the next level in the never ending competitive business world.

With the growth of the textile industry and the number of people seeking the knowledge needed to take their artwork to the next level to help their companies grow, Dane has created artwork and training materials to do just that. With his line of Great Dane Graphics products - Raster Stock Art, Vector Clip Art, Photoshop Training DVD and his book T-Shirt Artwork Simplified, which has now been updated for CS5 users.

For more information on Dane and his products, visit
www.greatdanegraphics.com

In my 20 years as a member of the *Impressions* magazine editorial team, I've talked with countless T-shirt decorators who say their biggest challenge is dealing with artwork. Sometimes they are faced with making "something out of nothing" --given little to go on but a business card or rough sketch on a paper scrap. Or, they may want to raise their own bar by giving a customer's logo some added pizzazz, increasing their shop's reputation for being more creative than most.

No matter what kind of apparel decoration you offer, this industry shares the common factor that T-shirt embellishment begins and ends with art. Making that art great is up to you, so educate yourself. Doing so will ensure that you can have a competitive advantage over other shops by offering innovative and exciting designs using even the most basic of logos.

Dane Clement is considered one of this industry's masters of T-shirt artwork, and he has dedicated many years to sharing his insight with thousands of apparel decorators. Through dozens of tutorial articles in *Impressions* magazine, as well as the many seminars and workshops he has facilitated at the Imprinted Sportswear Shows throughout the country, Dane has helped both newcomers and experienced artists take their craft to the next level. He shares his knowledge with a passion and excitement for the industry, and *Impressions'* readers and ISS attendees give us with great feedback on how his techniques have helped them.

By Dane sharing his expert advice in this book, thousands of more apparel decorators will be able to increase their creativity and offer their customers quality artwork, rather than trying to compete on lower prices. And that's good business.

Marcia Derryberry
Editor in Chief
Impressions Magazine

Table of Contents

Introduction

The purpose of this book is to help answer the many art department related questions that I've heard for years and still hear year after year in my seminars. "I'm not an artist and I have to set up an art department for my business, where do I begin?" How do I create separations? What is the difference between raster and vector art? I don't know how to draw, how do I make better art? And many many more.

This book does not set out to teach you how to use Adobe Photoshop or Illustrator. It assumes you own the software and have a basic understanding of it. Even with a very limited knowledge of the programs you can still follow along due to the step-by-step nature of the lessons. What the book does do is teach you how to accomplish everyday tasks and problems you will come across in your business.

The techniques discussed here are by no means the only way to do things. These are the things I've been doing in my art department for the past 22 years that have worked for me, and I know they'll work for you too. Although I use Photoshop CS5 in this book, I've tried to make the lessons backward compatible as much as possible. Most lessons can be completed with older versions of Photoshop from version 7 to CS5. Adobe has moved a couple of things around, so you may have to look for them in the version you're using.

This book is purposely designed (at greater publishing costs!) with a spiral binding so that the book is easily read and used when both hands are on your keyboard and mouse. I must confess this idea comes from me doing exactly what you are attempting to do now, learn computer software while reading a book! In 1992 or 93, I'm not sure which, I was given a job on a Friday from an advertising agency. It was due on Monday! The job was to create juice labels, orange juice, apple juice and grapefruit juice. The labels were to wrap around large metal cans, half gallons or so. They gave me one printed photo of each fruit along with one sliced photo of each. I had to duplicate these photos all around the can. It had to be created in Photoshop, which I purchased the very same Friday! (This was before Photoshop even had layers!) So with book in hand, I proceeded to learn. After many hours and losing my place in the book so many times I can't even count, because it kept closing up on me as I tried to leave it on my desk and do something on the computer. I finally finished the job, on time and in budget.

I hope that printing this book in this way will save you much of the headache and aggravation I went through during that time. So much so, I remember it vividly to this day.

This book is designed for those wanting to begin to screen print or digitally print t-shirts. The book will educate and guide you through the complete art process from concept to printing out your separations. Dye-sublimation and any other decorative application printer will benefit from what's contained here.

The process and procedures that I discuss and show follow the same workflow for digital printing and screen printing. This is the most efficient and productive approach to getting quality work done quickly. After all, you don't make money creating the art. You make your money printing your goods.

It is designed for owners and managers who have limited art knowledge / experience but need a better grasp of the art process to better manage the business.

The book is also designed for the experienced artist, by providing comprehensive training that will allow faster and better art production.

The book will not and does not referee the never ending debate of PC vs. Mac. I'll leave that decision for you to make. This book assumes you are using or intend to use Adobe Photoshop and Illustrator. Remember, these programs are tools to produce art work better and faster than you would be able to without a computer.

If you are sacrificing quality and speed for lack of knowledge, this book will assist your improvement. If you do not have the computer equipment that will allow better and faster art production, this book will assist your decisions of keeping what you have or upgrading.

The one constant with art programs and computer equipment is that customers will gravitate to better art even over low price. Make sure you are not losing ground on your competitors in these areas. The book will give you a global perspective of your choices, without trying to also sell you programs or computer gear. Keeping your art room competitive is the missing link in otherwise successful print shops.

On the companion CD that's included with this book you will find full Photoshop files of some of the images used throughout the book as well as some QuickTime video's to help illustrate further some of the lessons contained in the book. There's our Great Dane Graphics Layer Styles included as well to get you making creative type treatments in your designs. You'll also find links to the separation software and RIP that I use every day, Spot Process / Separation Studio and AccuRip. Give them a shot, you can download them from my website http://www.greatdanegraphics.com. I know they'll work for you as well.

I hope this book teaches you the techniques and skills you need to get the art done quickly and correctly the first time you do it so you can enjoy a more profitable business experience.

Dane Clement

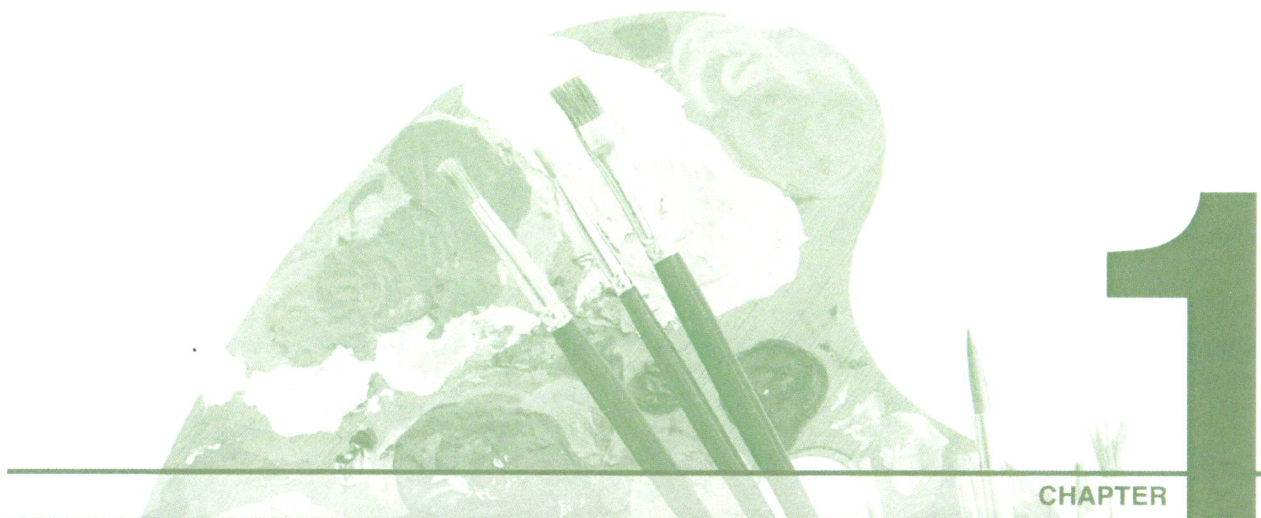

DESIGN BASICS

Design Basics

Great art sells, and it truly separates good companies from great ones. If you want to grow your business and be more profitable, then do what your competition isn't willing or able to do. The first thing that catches the eye of any consumer is the artwork. A focus on creating great artwork will separate your product from all the rest.

When the competition can't compete due to their lack of ability to create the quality artwork that your company produces, they will simply be left behind to watch your business grow.

Stop to take a look at any successful printer that you know. Take a look at all of the top printers in the marketplace today. The one common thread that they all share is great artwork. It is "the" major factor in their success. You simply cannot reach the upper tiers of success with inferior artwork. The success of your business depends upon your dedication and determination to create quality art. This will insure that you will have an appealing and marketable product that will surpass that of the competition.

This chapter is designed to help the "non-artists" in a shop. This group would encompass shop owners, sales staff, account executives, or new artists. The purpose is to help them understand what goes on in an art department. Examples of this would be explaining the procedures required to complete a design, or providing lingo to help them better communicate with the customer. It is imperative that the customer fully understands what the art department needs to produce quality work. This chapter will provide ideas that will help you know what to ask in order to guide your customer to a successful design.

Designing great T-shirt art is not as difficult as it might first appear as long as you keep a few simple design principles in mind. When working on a piece of art, you will first need to address certain questions. What will be in it? What is the subject matter? How much type will it need? What graphic elements do I have to work with? Do I have a photo or other illustration to use? It is important to know all these elements in order to arrange them together to form the composition of your design.

Screen Printing or Digital Printing

This book has been written for both screen printers and digital printers. The work flow is essentially the same. Artwork creation and creativity are the same for each. The only difference occurs in the final stages of getting ready to print. If you're a screen printer, you will need to create separations. If you print digitally, you may need to clean and adjust some colors. I teach it this way, because it just makes sense.

Composition

In order for a design to work, it must look unified. All the elements in the design must achieve a sense of unity and balance that is pleasing to the eye. If the elements seem separated or unrelated, then the design as a whole suffers. Some things that will affect your composition will be the size, proportion, and positioning of the elements to one another, as well as the colors you choose.

Focal Point

Focal Point is the point of emphasis in a design that initially attracts your attention. It is that thing that draws the viewer in and encourages him to get a better look. This is also known as the WOW factor. When a shirt is displayed on a wall or on a rack, this is what attracts attention. You can create this focal point through the use of size, placement, and color.

When using size to create a focal point, generally the most important item is the largest. As size decreases so does importance. However, it is important to note that this is not "always" the case, as shown in the second example below.

Focal point can also be created through the placement of the individual items within a design. Separating an item from the other elements will tend to get it noticed before the rest.

Finally, color can create a focal point. For instance, in a design where everything is the same shade or brightness, coloring the most important element in a contrasting color will attract the eye first.

It is important to keep in mind that while you can use each of these ideas separately to create a focal point, you will generally use more than one at a time.

Balance

The balance of elements within a design can also affect a design's composition. A design that is out of balance can be very disturbing to the eye. Two basic types of balance are Symmetrical and Asymmetrical..

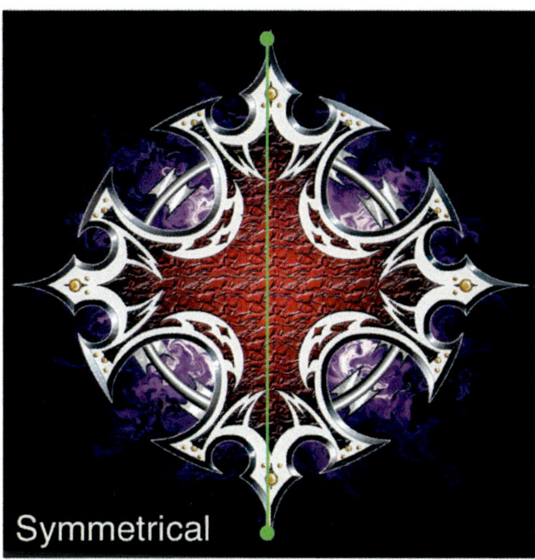

When trying to understand the idea of balance, visualize a vertical line through the center of your design. With symmetrical balance, whatever is on one side of the line will be "mirrored" on the other side. This way you will have equal "weight' on both sides of the line.

With asymmetrical balance, what is on one side of the line isn't necessarily on the other side. However, through the use of color, placement, or size, a visual balance can be acquired.

Image Size

Composition is also affected by the image size. When laying out a full sized design, I try to keep the size in proportion to 13"x15". This will help keep the width and the height of the design from getting too far out of proportion. The size may vary, but use these dimensions as a guide.

When considering what size to print an image, remember to keep the shirt size that you will be printing in mind. For instance, if you are going to be printing on kids shirts, the design shouldn't be too large. Otherwise, the design could end up under the arms or tucked down into pants. However, for a full size front or back design, usually bigger is better. Make the image fill the available space comfortably. For a left chest design, I usually keep the size around 3 1/2" to 4" inches.

Illusion of Space

Some other ways of creating interest in your design would be to create the illusion of space. Show depth in the image with the use of size, placement, color, and transparency. These images represent ways to do this. Notice the interest and movement in the Fat Tuesday image. This is created using transparent elements and simple fills of various percentages of color.

The Mermaid image creates the illusion of space and shows depth by using color, overlapping, and placement. Notice the elements in the background. The secondary information is created as a monochromatic element. It is all painted using various shades of blue. Then, when the main elements are placed in front (in full color), you notice those more. The eye will see the largest, most colorful element. The focal point then travels through the background and finally to the small fish (in full color) pointing to the only text in the image.

Cropping

Something you may want to consider when laying out your design is "how" or "if" you should crop the image or an element of the image. If you start with a very busy image, you may find that in order to get everything to fit on the page, all the elements have to be small. In order to make the elements larger, you can zoom in, cut off, or crop part of the image.

Notice in this Pirate image that the main element, the pirate, is cropped at the waist. This allows the ability to make him the largest part of the image, and thus become the focal point. When we look at this image, our brain can visualize the rest of the pirate. Because of prior exposure to pirate images, we know that he has legs or possibly a peg-leg. Just imagine how small and far back he would be if he had been placed full bodied in this image. Most often, cropping works to add interest to an image.

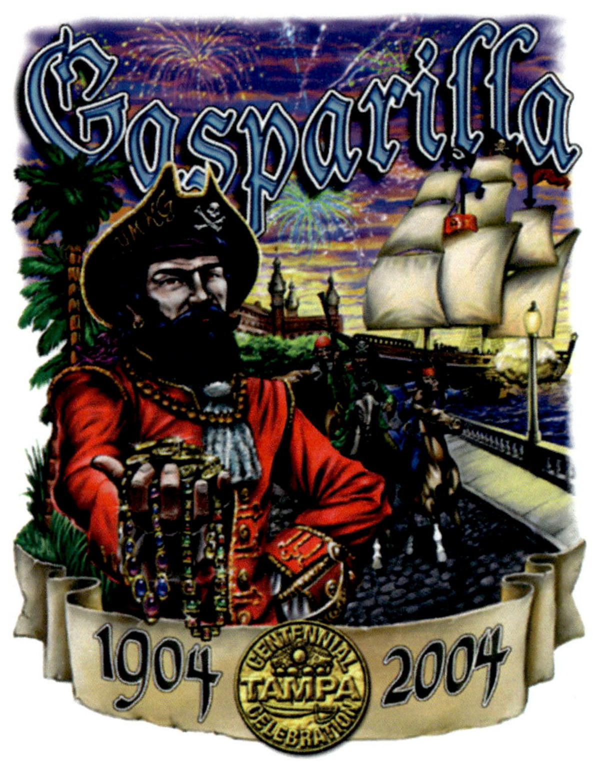

Tips and Tricks For Better Design

Type

It is your job to help the customer, by giving them some creative ways to deal with his type. Explain how they should add some flair by curving, distorting, or stretching type to add interest to a design. Suggest anything but simple plain ol' one color block type! It doesn't require any extra time to give it a little punch.

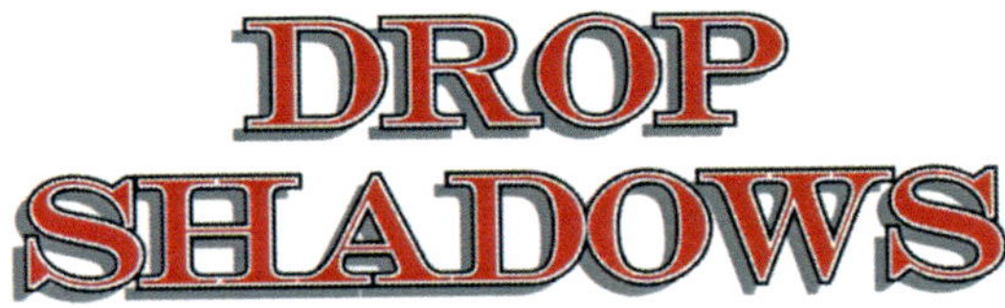

Add a drop shadow to create the illusion of depth..

Try reversing type out of an object. If you do this, be sure to use a bold font to prevent it from plugging up and losing the small detail when it is printed.

Textures

Add a texture to your object. Here are a couple of simple ways to approach it.

Draw your own shapes. These can be any shapes you like. A good option would be to colorize these shapes with different percentages of the same color in order to keep the number of colors down while still giving the illusion of multi-colors.

The blue color inside the letters are actually only one color, blue. The darkest color is 100% blue, while the other colors were created using lower percentages blue. We used 50%, 10%, 30% etc. and pasted them inside the shape of the other letters.

Use graduations of "spot colors" to create interest. This also gives the illusion that you are using more colors than you actually are by blending the two together and creating a third color.

Distortion Tools

Most drawing programs come with some fun filters and distortion tools that can create some interesting effects. Don't be afraid to try them out. However, don't just use a filter or tool because it's new and different. Be sure that it will work with your design or theme. You don't want it to look out of place.

Working With Color

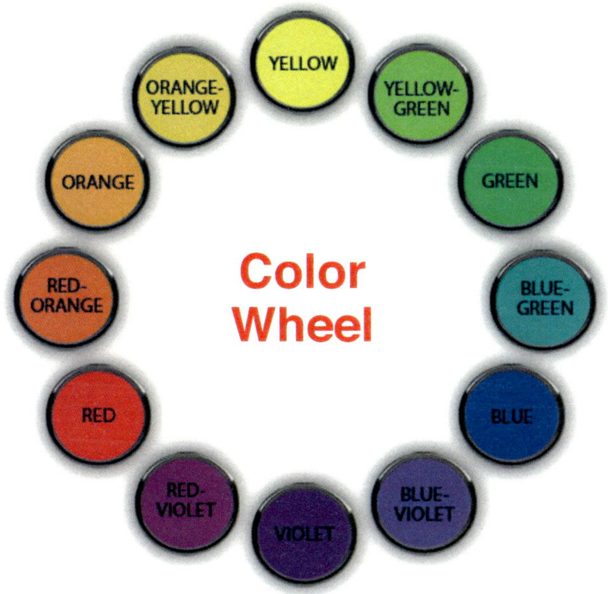

Working with color means different things to both the screen printer and the digital printer. Most people that own a digital printer, want to print color and lots of it. Why? Because they can, and it's easy. The printers are usually C,M,Y,K (Cyan, Magenta,Yellow, Black). Some have additional colors to help with the blending and the reproduction of organic colors such as flesh tones. These will usually have Light Cyan, Light Magenta as well. Some will have white ink to print on dark garments.

Digital printers can pull up any image or photograph they want, optimize it a little, and then simply print it! Screen printers don't have it quite so easy. There are a few determining factors that come into play for a screen printer. First, how many color heads or stations are on their press? They have to print films for separations. This translates to one film each for each color they want to print. Then the image must be burned onto a screen. Again (generally) one color per screen. Ink is added to the screen and one color is printed. This process is repeated until all colors are printed. Sometimes flash curing in between some of the colors is necessary. It is easy to see that there is a little more work involved for the screen printer to print color.

One advantage the screen printer has over the digital printer is the ability to print plastisol ink as a spot color. This ink will be much more vibrant on a shirt than the CMYK counterpart for the digital side. Using spot colors provides the ability to match a customers corporate color much more easily.

There is no way I can completely cover all aspects of color in this book. That would take a full book on it's own, and in fact, there are many books out there that do just that. What I "will" focus on are basic color schemes and techniques for use in your t-shirt or decorating business. This will be the "every day" stuff necessary to know to get the job done.

When designing an image, be sure to choose colors wisely. Don't just start picking colors randomly. You must have a purpose for the colors you choose. Be sure they will work together in the image. One of the first things to consider would be the color scheme. Some of the basic color schemes this book will address are Monochromatic, Complementary, and Triadic.

Monochromatic Color Scheme

A monochromatic image contains colors in one family. This includes different shades and tints of the same color. This color scheme is very easy on the eyes, especially when using blue. It normally has a soothing effect. The mood of a design can be set by the color chosen. Even though this scheme lacks the contrast and punch one might get with one of the other schemes, it tends to be the most elegant of the three.

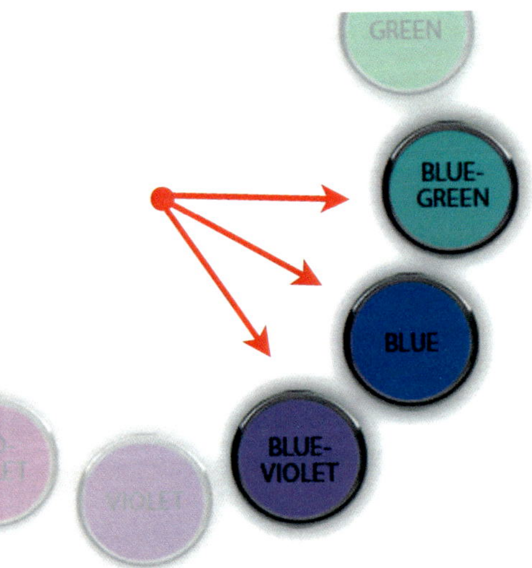

COLOR

Above is an example of a Monochromatic design. This scheme always looks balanced and visually appealing

Complementary Color Scheme

Complementary colors sit opposite each other on the color wheel (red/green, blue/orange, violet/ yellow). These colors always work well together, thus living up to the term complementary.

Think of the main colors you see at Christmas time... red and green. They work well together and are put together for that reason.

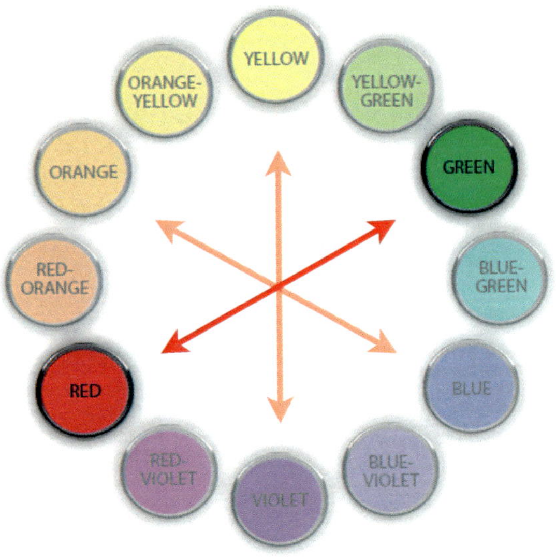

COLOR

Above is an example of a Complementary design. This color scheme offers the strongest contrast out of the three and will command the most attention from the viewer.

When using complementary colors together, it is important to be aware of the strength of each color. Having two complementary colors at full saturation can cause them to fight each other for the viewers attention.

This causes the eye to vibrate when focusing on the image.

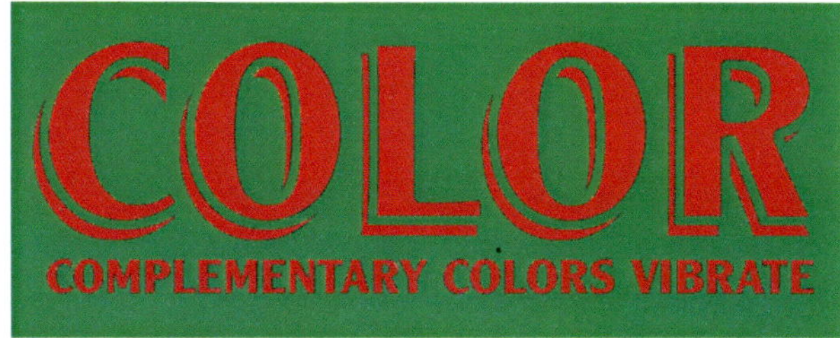

One way to fix this issue is to keep one of the colors at full strength and tone down the others. An easy way to tone down a color is to halftone it, or tint it back to around 50% of it's full strength. The following image is a toned down version of green. I tinted the green back to 50%.

Triadic Color Scheme

A Triadic color scheme contains colors that are equally spaced around the color wheel. If you form a triangle (or triadic) and then rotate that triangle around the wheel, you will find colors to use for this scheme.

The Triadic color scheme offers strong visual contrast while retaining balance and harmony. These colors work well together, but one color should be chosen as the main color. The other colors should be used for balance and support. If all three colors are used at the same value and intensity, it likely would push the image into disharmony. It would then be necessary tone down a color or two

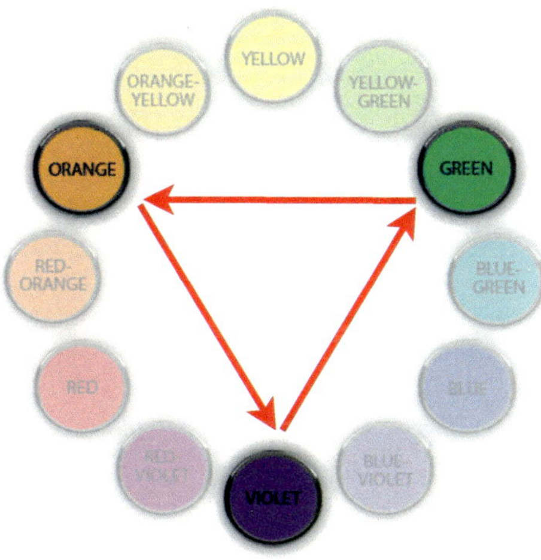

Above is an example of a Triadic design.

These are the three schemes you'll use most.

Spot Color

Spot color is probably the most common type of job for a screen printer. It's usually a simple image, one that contains few colors. Generally the colors it contains are simple fills. Sometimes you will find simple spot colored designs that may have halftones or tints, and shades of some of the colors in the image. However, the most popular form of spot color is solid fills.

Spot color designs have been around since t-shirt decoration began. It is the most commonly known process due simply to its longevity. Here's an example of a Spot Color design using two colors. On a white shirt, a screen printer, will need two screens. (one for the blue in the image, the other for the red)

Those who own a direct to garment printer should try to avoid this type of image if possible. Don't get me wrong, the printer can print it. However, when printing digitally, if any of the nozzles in the print head are clogged, streaking in the print will be the result. Because the image consists of smooth solid colors, there is nothing to camouflage the streaking nozzle. If the image contains some shadows and highlights, the imperfections will not be nearly as noticeable.

Process Color

Process color is used when you want to reproduce photorealistic prints. This would include a photograph or full color painting for instance. Because four colors are required to create it, it is sometimes referred to as Four Color. (Cyan, Magenta,Yellow, Black) This is the process that is used by the direct to garment digital printers.

A screen printer will need four screens. You will need to be in CMYK mode in Photoshop in order to be·able to print your separations. The separations for process printing usually require four different angles for the screens. There is much evidence that says only one or two angles can be used with just as good, if not better results. The problem with multiple angles on halftones is that it raises the possibility of moiré on the press. This is unwanted patterns or lines created by a row of dots being printed at an angle that fights the horizontal and vertical angles of the threads in our mesh.

It is very hard to get consistent quality results printing this way. Lets say you screen print an image today, and it looks good. A few months go by, and you want to reprint the same image. More times than not, you will have difficulty trying to duplicate the same results. There is a reason for this. It is a very volatile technique that requires transparent inks. These are very thin in viscosity. Very high mesh counts have to be used to control the thin inks. The higher the mesh counts, the more expensive the mesh. If you vary the pressure as you pull the squeegee, you will change the color that's printed.

Often times in order to get a good print, it will be necessary to add extra spot color or "bump" screens. A Red screen may be needed in order to produce a very red color. If you want to print a nice, rich, bright green, add that as a spot color "bump" screen also. This is really difficult to screen print, and not very many shops can do a good job with it. Besides, with the other techniques such as "simulated process color", why bother.

Simulated Process Color

This technique is designed to do exactly what it's called... Simulate Process Color... or give the illusion of printing full photographic color while using spot colors. The nice thing about this process and the reason that it is so much better to print, is due to its use of opaque plastisol ink. This ink will be much more vibrant and last a lot longer on the shirt than transparent ink.

This ink is very viscous; therefore, they can be printed using lower mesh counts. This, of course, will save money. Simply pick a spot colored plastisol ink, put it in the screen and print. Since colors are chosen this way, it's much easier to reproduce the job if you have to reprint it later.

This technique also uses halftones to reproduce a job. Halftones are all the same angle which simplifies things

quite a bit. Here are my recommended halftone details: 45 or 55 lpi or frequency (in the computer) and a 61° angle for all screens! You'll find more information on Halftones in Chapter 7.

RGB Color

RGB Color (red, green, and blue) are the primary colors of the additive color model. It is the type of color we see on our computer screens. It is created by firing red, green, and blue pixels at various strengths. These individual lights mix to create the secondary and tertiary colors.

The RGB color spectrum is much larger than that of CMYK. This is the color mode where we want to create and adjust our images. Although we don't actually print RGB colors using those three colors, we have to attempt to capture as much of the spectrum as possible using inks on a substrate. Once we do this, it becomes reflective light. The colors we see are reflected back to our eyes from the ink's surface.

I like to recreate all of my full color images using Simulated Spot Colors. Since bright spot colors can be mixed when screen printing, we can achieve more and brighter colors than we can using CMYK.

Some RIP software for the Direct To Garment digital printers require the image to be in RGB mode. The RIP reads this color information and translates it to the printer. It will then be printed either in CMYK or CMYK with other various additional colors.

Some Direct To Garment RIPs and printers require sending CMYK information to the printer. Since every printer is different, follow the recommendation of your machine's manufacturer for the best results.

Pantone Color

Pantone® Matching System also known as PMS Color is the graphics industries standard color chart. You will find these charts in the swatches palettes of most graphic software applications. Every art department should also have a Pantone Color book. These books are expensive about 75.00, but necessary. There is a reason for the expense. They are printed with spot colors! Each color is a special ink color. They are not printed using process color. Each color is identified by an individual unique number. These numbers are universally used throughout the world. The following example illustrates this benefit.

Lets say, for example, that your company prints all the shirts for Billy Bob's Grass Cutting and Landscaping. These shirts use a "special" green color that you mixed when first starting to print the shirts. You mixed a whole "butter dish" full. You labeled this butter dish by writing the name Billy-Bobs green right on the container. Normally, you print about a dozen shirts for his three employees once or twice a year. Then, good fortune strikes for Billy Bob, and he lands the city's largest landscaping contract. He now needs 2000 shirts for all his new employees. At that point it becomes necessary for you to outsource to a local printer that has an automatic press.

You can't tell them "Just use Billy-Bob's green". They need to know the exact color. You will be able to say that the shirts need to be printed with PMS 354 green, and any print shop worldwide will know the exact color needed.

Always remember, looking at colors on your computer monitor is different than looking at printed colors. Also keep in mind, the color of the shirt can alter the way the color looks when printed. A white underbase may need to be printed in order to get the correct color to print on top.

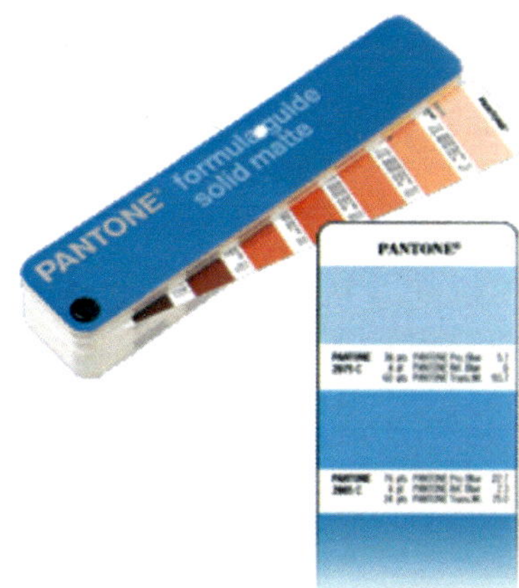

Various File Formats

There are far too many file formats out there to cover in this book. Just look at the list available when going to File Menu > Save As in any application. The file formats covered here are the ones needed on a daily basis or those that a customer may present to you. These are listed in no particular order.

.AI

This is Adobe Illustrator's native file format. It is a vector file format which means it is small in size and can be scaled up or down without limit or loss of detail. This is a very versatile file format, which can be opened with Photoshop and Corel Draw. It is an industry recognized format that is used with cutting plotters and embroidery digitizing software as well as many others.

.PSD

This is Adobe Photoshop's native file format. It contains both layers (transparency) and alpha channels, both of which became mainstream due to Photoshop. With this format multi layered files can be saved along with alpha channel information. I usually use this file format to create my artwork, and keep the original in layers. I usually save

my final production file in a different format depending on its use.

Some of the RIP software packages out there can't accept a .psd file; therefore, I might choose to save the file as a .tif or .eps.

.JPG or JPEG

This stands for Joint Photographic Experts Group. This is arguably the most used file format in the world today, and again arguably the worst file format we could use. I'm not sure why it is such a widely used file format, or who decided it would be this way. I sure would like to have a talk with that guy!

Here's the skinny on this file format. It's been around since digital cameras first surfaced. It has become the favorite format for displaying photographic images on the internet. Digital cameras use it because the file size reduces nicely, and more photos can be stored on memory cards. The problem with a JPG is it's a "lossy" compression format, (meaning losses to the quality of the image occur). Each time a file is closed, it is compressed, and data is thrown away in order to make the file size smaller. The image is degraded every time it is opened and closed! Once the "loss" occurs to the image, there is no going back, and the data cannot be recovered.

As the image is compressed over time there will be visual corruption in the image. Square chunks of color will start to form. If you plan to separate the image using Spot Process for screen printing, corruption on the separations will be evident because the file is damaged beyond repair.

My recommendation is not to use this format very often. Never would be best. If your digital camera only takes .jpg images, save them as something else the first time you open the files in Photoshop. Try saving them as a Photoshop .PSD or a TIF file

.TIF or TIFF

This stands for Tagged Image File Format. This file format is a widely recognized format and is loss-less; therefore, there is no worry about corrupting images. It also has compression that can be used while saving. This compression won't degrade the image. I find that I never use this compression. I'm never in such dire need of hard drive space, that I need to compress my images.

This format also allows you to save multiple layers, but will require the file to be much larger than it otherwise would be. I find this feature very convenient, and use it quite often.

.DCS 2.0

This stands for Desktop Color Separation. If you are a screen printer, it is important to know this file format. It will soon become your best friend. It is a "fancy" eps file that allows us to retain our separations in the form of alpha channels inside it. It gives a full color preview that can be used to place the image into a drawing program (such as Illustrator) and then work with it.
If using Adobe Illustrator, use this format! It will make life much easier while printing separations. If placed properly, the colors used in separations will automatically populate into the swatches palette. It is then possible to colorize the text and logos added with those colors, and both will print out on films.

You will learn how to save and work with this file format later in chapter 7.

.PDF

This is an Adobe file format and stands for "Portable Document Format." This document retains certain page layout and other document information. It is platform independent; therefore, it can be used by Mac and PC users alike. It is designed to bring or send electronically to a printer. All the printer has to do is simply open the file and print. All the document's information is there, so it will look like it was intended when designed. It is possible to save a PDF file from almost any standard graphics or page layout application.

.CDR

This stands for Corel Draw. This is a very common file format in our industry. It is not, however, a very friendly format to use with anything but Corel products. Most other applications will not recognize a .cdr file. It is often used by RIP software that run plotters and cutters. If using Illustrator, and someone sends you a .cdr file, ask them to re-save it as an .ai or .eps file in order for you to view and work with it.

.ZIP

This file format is referred to as a "zipped" file. It is a compression method that is commonly used by both Mac and PC. If several files are needed for a job, and are all put into one folder, each file will be compressed separately and contained in one "zipped" icon. Windows users can create a zip file by using a separate program such as WinZip. Mac users can simply right click on the file they want to compress and select "Create Archive". It is a feature built directly into the operating system.

Choosing Fonts

Every good art department should invest in a variety of fonts. This doesn't mean investing a lot of money, Invest some time on the internet. Download free fonts. The amount of free material is amazing. Be careful about the font sites you choose. Be sure they are a reputable company. It is easy for someone to hide harmful software inside a zipped font file. My favorite free font site is called Da Font, www.dafont.com. The site is very well organized and easy to navigate. It has fonts for Mac and PC.

Try searching for fonts by subject. For instance, use words like summer, fun, pirate, etc. depending on the type of design. Searching on Google will get you tons of sites with really cool creative fonts. It really works!

Using fonts that emulate the look and feel of your design, make it appear that it was all planned from the beginning. Often times using a unique font (one that most people are not familiar with), will lead the customer to think that you created it especially for their design. And there's nothing wrong with that.

Be careful to choose the correct fonts. Just because the font may look like it could be part of the "theme" of the design, doesn't mean it's necessarily the right one to use. Some creative type fonts are hard to read. Some of them are designed to be used in upper and lower case letters. Some might use either upper only or lower only. Play with, and try out a few different ones before settling on one.

Once you've decided on a particular font, don't leave it as a single color. If working in Photoshop, apply a Layer Style to it. Colorize it. Stroke it. Warp it. Look at the samples on this page to see some interesting techniques that will hopefully inspire you to have fun!

If working in Photoshop and choosing fonts, look at the font in it's own typeface right there in the font's drop down menu. This makes it really easy to see what the font will look like if selected.

Illustrator does the same thing, but it's not quite as easy to find. It's not in the main text drop down menu. You have to pull up the Character palette in order to see it. Because of that, I thought I'd show how to pull up that palette. It's really easy to do once you know where to find it. We'll do it here on the next page.

Above & Left: Samples of font treatments that work well.

Below: I see this type of treatment all too often, it just doesn't work. Too hard to read.

Choosing Fonts in Illustrator

In order to "see" what a font's name looks like in it's own typeface, do a couple of quick steps in Illustrator first.

It only takes a second or so to bring it up.

Here's how to do it!

These lessons display CS3 palettes. However the steps throughout the book have been updated to CS5.

CHOOSING FONTS IN ILLUSTRATOR

Step 1: Illustrator CS3 - CS5

Choose the Type Tool, the "T" in the toolbox.

In the Options bar along the top of the screen, Click on the underlined Character link to bring up the Character palette.

Step 2:

In the Character palette, Click on the font name to view the list.

A fly-out font list will appear and allow you to see the font in it's own type face. Once you see something you like, simply select it and let go of the mouse.

Before Starting Your Artwork

Before starting your artwork, there are questions that must be addressed. What am I designing for? If it's a t-shirt, am I going to screen print or digitally print it? Am I going to print it with my dye-sublimation equipment? Will I be outsourcing it to a sign shop or some other printer? If so, what file format and sizing do they need?

This will help determine the proper document size and resolution. For instance, if you have a design that will be a t-shirt as well as a large format banner, then create the artwork with the banner in mind first. This will insure that there is more than enough resolution for the t-shirt.

Take the time to gather the following information. What the maximum print area is for the printer you will be using. What's the largest size you can print on your direct to garment printer? What size are the palettes on your screen printing press? If you print dye-sublimation, what is the largest print size your printer is capable of printing?

The type of equipment you own will be a factor in this decision as well. Is it capable of printing thick substrates such as zippered hooded sweatshirts?

Once this information has been attained, tack it up on the wall as a cheat sheet next to the computer. It will always be available. This information can be invaluable. For instance, knowing that the registration marks will fit on the palette when screen printing. Also, for a large order for Sublimated mugs, knowing how many can fit on one piece of paper, will help figure out profitability. The more that fit, the cheaper the per-unit cost will be.

Create templates for the goods most commonly printed. That allows you to simply load the template for a t-shirt, mouse pad, mug, tote bag, hooded sweatshirt etc. Your art file will already be set to size and ready to go. Just open it and start creating.

ART ROOM EQUIPMENT

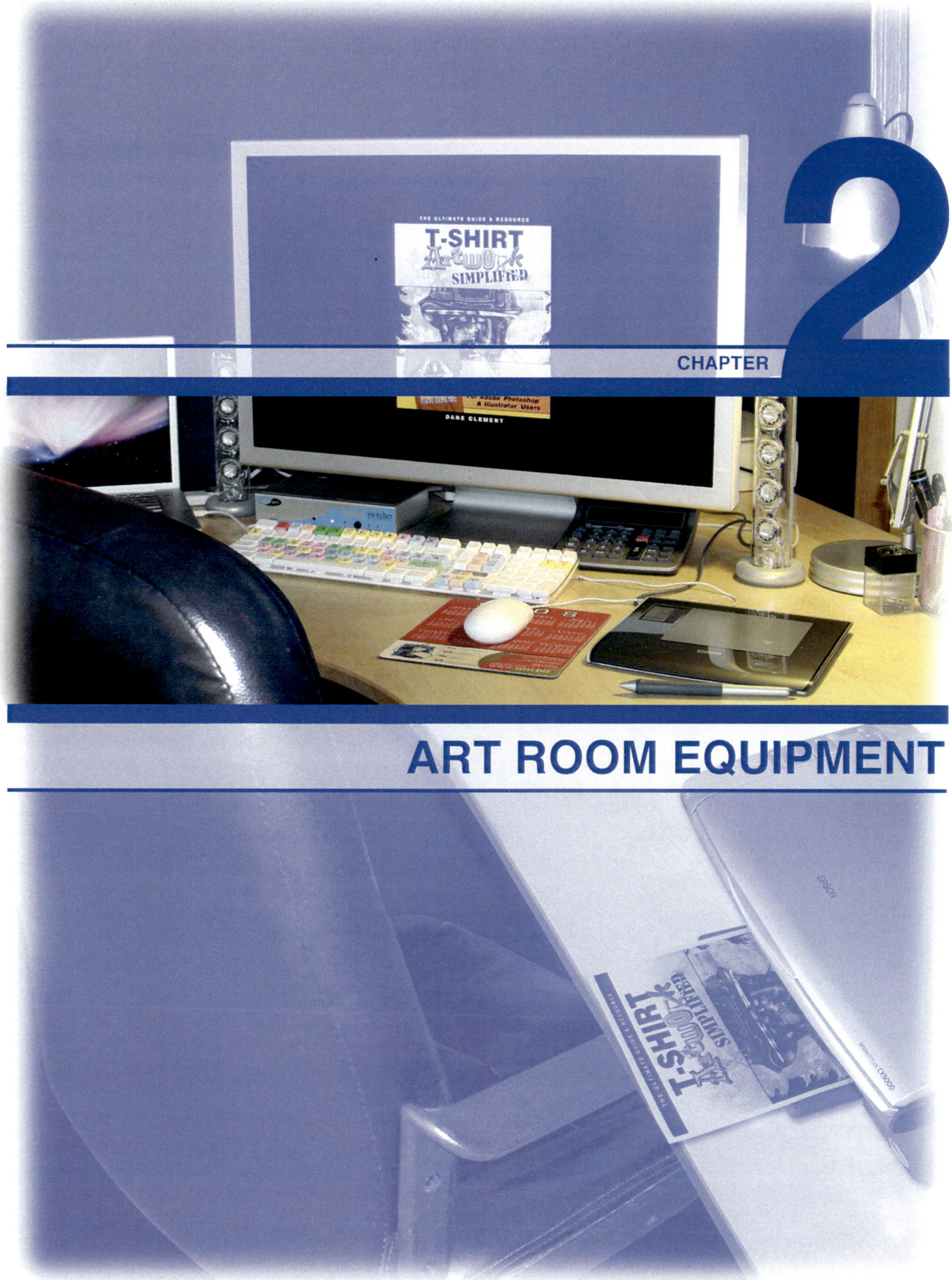

Art Room Equipment

Before beginning any artwork, make sure you have the right equipment. This book will not address creating artwork traditionally. There are enough other books out there for that. The focus will be on computerized artwork with an emphasis on producing finished garments and goods for our industry.

Whether you own a computer already and are looking to upgrade, or new to the business and looking toward starting up and purchasing your first one, there are a few things you will have to consider.

Upgrading can be done inexpensively many ways. Swapping out a small hard drive for a larger one and adding more RAM are the only upgrades I feel comfortable recommending. These are usually done fairly easily. Changing out the processor, adding a processor booster of some sort, or installing a graphics card are a little more risky. I've tried several times over the years to upgrade processors or processor boosters and have never been happy with the results. Generally, there are several different component manufacturers involved, and parts sometimes don't work well together. It's just too much of a hassle.

As reasonably priced as computers (with muscle) have become, I would recommend opting for a new one. An inexpensive computer performs well in our industry . Almost anything at your local electronics store can do everything needed on a daily basis. It is not necessary to spend a huge amount of money on a computer.

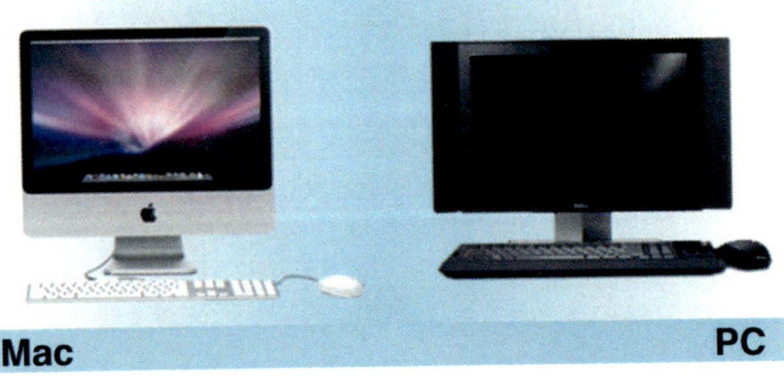

The first decision to make when considering computer equipment is the platform. Should it be a Macintosh or a PC? It doesn't matter whether you use a Mac or a Windows PC these days. The software required to get your job done comes cross platform and can be viewed and edited on each.

Setting up an art department requires more than just buying a computer and a clip art CD. The following is a list of all of the other components required to complete the computer system for your art department.

Computer

Once you've made the decision Mac vs. PC, here are some of the very next decisions to make. Processor speed, Hard Drive size, and the amount of Ram you will need must be decided. The easiest answer to all of the above is to get as much as you can afford. The faster the processor, the quicker the work will get done. You WILL use that whole 60 GB hard drive, believe me. As a minimum of Ram, I recommend 1GB. I definitely suggest more if you can afford it. The more Ram, the faster the machine will run, allowing you to get the job done more efficiently. This will ultimately save you money.

If the computer is for the art department only, I would recommend removing any software that is not needed in that department. Keep virus detection software current. Perform daily, weekly and monthly system checks and performance improvements religiously. There is no room for being lazy in this area. There are too many people on the internet that like to spread computer viruses. Stay on top of these things, and you should be able to run event free for the most part.

Monitor

Most software packages today are very diverse in their capabilities, and with that comes the need for many individual palettes or one huge bloated palette. Either way, you will be fighting monitor clutter. Having the  palettes open and at your disposal, will require a great amount of monitor real estate. Therefore, the larger the monitor, the better. I recommend a 30" high resolution flat screen monitor. A 17" is an absolute minimum.

Although I have a Cinema 30" display, I still use the extended desktop feature from my Mac. The same thing can be done on a PC. This allows me to use two monitors, the one on my laptop for tool palettes, and the other just for my artwork. This is a very efficient way to work. It will save time through the course of the day by just not having to return to the menu and come down to open a palette repeatedly.

Calibration

One question I hear a lot is "Do I need to calibrate my monitor? The easy answer is YES, absolutely. However, my response may surprise you. If you are a photographer, then YES. If you are in the T-shirt business, then YES again, but only the software type, no hardware purchase necessary.

If you are are a photographer and plan to print and sell the photos from your printer, spend the money ($250 or so) for an X-Rite, Eye-One Display 2 hardware unit. This unit does a great job and has terrific printer profiles for a typical Epson photo printer, for example.

If looking to manage color for a T-shirt business, then save your money and calibrate your monitors using the software calibration from Adobe. If on a PC, you will want to use Adobe Gamma found on Windows XP machines under the Start menu > Control Panel > Adobe Gamma. Just follow the steps.

On a Mac, go to the Apple menu > System Preferences > Displays. When the dialog box appears, click on the Color tab, then click the Calibrate button and follow the steps.

I don't believe hardware calibration is necessary for T-shirt printers, because we print on T-shirts, not photo paper. There is just no way to hold the detail and control the color on a shirt like that on paper. Besides, plastisol inks need to be mixed together. Most shops are still mixing ink by "eye-balling" the color, even though a mixing system and scale should be used. Printers still have to print films, emulsion and burn screens, and then print. There are too many steps from the monitor stage to have complete control.

 At least do the software calibration, and you should be fine.

Scanner

When buying a scanner, the most important things to consider are the optical resolution, the bit depth or color depth, and last but certainly not least in my book,

the scanning bed size. The optical resolution of your scanner will determine how crisp your scans are. The bit depth or color depth will determine how much detail is held, especially in the shadow areas of your scan. The larger the scanning bed the higher the price of the scanner.

While you can purchase an excellent quality scanner for $100.00 to $200.00, I suggest a legal size scan bed as a minimum requirement. This will increase the cost to around $475.00. The reason for the larger scan bed is that most artists still draw freehand on paper and then scan the drawing. The larger scanner allows for the capture of more of the drawing in one piece. All too often a letter size bed will require multiple scans. They will then have to be manually pieced together in Photoshop. This requires more unnecessary, non-productive work. This is exactly the reason I recommend a tabloid size scanner, if your budget allows. This will increase the price to somewhere between $1200.00 and $2500.00.

Software

You will need many different types of software packages to round out your library. The three main types are a vector based drawing program, a continuous tone pixel based image editor, and a separation software. All three are necessary to be a viable shop.

The three I just mentioned are the beginning of your software library. One small piece of software that every art department needs is a time tracking software. It is necessary for the artist to have something to help keep track of time. If it takes 3 hours to create a piece, be sure to get paid for it! I use DesignSoft's Stop Watch and Time Sheet Manager. Do an internet search and find one that works for you.

Vector Drawing Program

Since you've purchased this book, the Adobe® Products book, I'm assuming you are using Illustrator for your vector artwork. Using simple line art graphics such as clip art, adding type to your design, creating logos, etc. are just a few things to do using a vector program. Basically, anything you would want to print with smooth, clean, crisp edges will be produced from a vector based program.

Vector artwork can be scaled up to any size without the loss of detail.

Raster Software or Image Editor

Your image editor is Adobe Photoshop®. It is the industry standard. More user groups, magazines, and educational material are made for this image editor than any other. Most of the separation software available today comes in the form of a Photoshop Plug-In. Photoshop allows the ability to create and edit full color continuous tone images such as photographs or paintings. It also allows the ability to work with grayscale images and the cleaning of black & white line art. I'll address this in chapter Four.

Separation Software

I do recommend getting a separation software package. These packages will generate high end separations in a fraction of the time that it takes to do them manually in Photoshop. Some separation software is better than others; therefore, download a trial version of the most popular and give it a try. If a software application doesn't allow you to actually try it out, I'd be cautious. Would you buy a car without driving it first?

Some software applications to try out would be Spot Process/Separation Studio, T-Seps, Quick Seps, and Screenprint Separator.

I use Spot Process/Separation Studio in my studio.

Tracing Software

There was a time when tracing software was it's own application, such as Adobe's Streamline®. This now has basically been included inside of Illustrator and called Live Trace.

There are a couple of stand alone tracing software out there, one does a really good job for our industry called Imagaro-Z. I own this and use it quite a bit.

Tracing software allows us to quickly turn bitmap scans into vector based artwork. An example of this would be scanning in a client's logo as a grayscale image, cleaning it up in Photoshop, then converting it to vector art by tracing it automatically using tracing software. This is a valuable time saver, and something you will find yourself doing quite a bit.

Tracing Services

There seems to be a growing movement out there to have someone else do the tracing for you. If you look around the internet, you'll find several services that will take your original file and convert it to a vector file. Most are hosted and serviced by companies overseas in China or India. You might find a few out there still in the states. In fact, you can find a service that I like and would recommend on my web site. They do a good job and actually do the work right here in the states.

RIP Software

If you are not aware of what a RIP is, or that you may be using it, you are not alone. A RIP may be one of the

most misunderstood tools in the screen printing industry. What you may or may not know is that every time you send an art file to a printer, a RIP acts as an intermediary. It essentially makes sure the job gets translated in proper computer language from image file to output. If you're one of the many decorators who is totally in the dark about RIP, the following will help you better understand.

Defining RIP

A RIP, or raster image processor, is a software application that resides on your hard drive. It comes into play when you've finished creating separations and you're ready to print. At that point, the artwork file is sent to the printer via the RIP. For instance, in Adobe Illustrator, when you go to File/Print, the dialog box gives you the option to choose a RIP.

Why the extra step? Why not just go directly to the printer? In most instances, you're taking a printing device designed to print full-color continuous tone photographs, and forcing it to print black and white halftones and little rows of dots. The RIP acts as a translator, ensuring that the printer "understands" the art file. Without it, halftones could not be printed on an ink jet device. Moreover, if you can't control and print halftones, you can't do separations for true process, simulated, or index jobs in which you're combining colors.

Even if doing direct-to-garment printing, not traditional screen printing, you still need a RIP to tell the printer what to do. That's true even if you're not printing halftones with DTG. The need to translate and convey information to the output device is still the same. The exceptions are the Brother device, which is one of the few that uses a printer driver rather than a RIP; and some PostScript laser printers, which can actually print halftones without a RIP. Most digital direct-to-garment users find RIPs very helpful for creating the white underbase layer when printing on dark garments.

Don't let all these acronyms confuse you. It comes down to this. If doing screen printing, you need a RIP, unless you have a PostScript printer that can handle halftones. If doing direct-to-garment printing, you need a RIP; but check with your supplier, as some output devices don't require one.

Even when a RIP isn't required for direct-to-garment printing, you're generally much better off using one if there is one available to drive the printer. A RIP will manage the job better and give you more accurate, clean colors, including brighter reds and greens. In addition, a RIP will give you better control over the amount of ink is used. A printer driver can handle it, but you'll appreciate the greater control the RIP provides.

Set It and Forget It
RIP installation is as simple as installing any other piece of software on your computer. For the most part, a RIP operates effortlessly, but it is necessary to know how to set its parameters. There is a small learning curve of perhaps an hour or so. Wasatch RIP can handle up to four printers; therefore, it would be possible to set one or two full color printing and one or two for film output to an Epson. Some RIPs allow you to create preset printer queues or hot folders that have specific settings locked in for easier printing.

Do some test prints and check the density of the dots. If the black isn't dense enough, make some adjustments to the RIP for it to put down more ink by adjusting the density curves or changing the droplet size. Once you've made these types of adjustments, just set it and forget it. Let the RIP do its thing.

Because you essentially just set it and forget it, there is generally not much troubleshooting involved with a RIP. Occasionally you may need to adjust your settings — if ink is running on the film or if blacks aren't dark enough, for instance. If you should have trouble getting your printers, computer, and RIP to communicate, the problem may be your wireless connection. In theory, a wirelessly connected printer should work as well as one plugged directly into the network, but that is not always the case. Oftentimes, simply losing the wireless connection in favor of Ethernet cables will solve the problem.

RIP Compatibility
A single RIP can talk to more than one printer. You can choose from a variety of RIPs from different suppliers for a single printer. (Still, only select a single RIP for a job; in other words, you can't send one art file to two or more RIPs.) For instance, if you own an Epson 4880, you could choose from AccuRIP, Wasatch, MultiRip and numerous other options, regardless of what may have come bundled with the unit.

Certain RIPs can only drive certain printers, It is critical to talk to your supplier about compatibility before making a purchase, especially if you're shopping for a package deal. Most vendors for output devices have a relationship with the supplier of a RIP that works with the company's device and specific media.

Some machine manufacturers will tell you that you can only use their RIP with their machine. Be mindful of this. They want to sell their RIP to you, and there may be a far better option out there. Do your homework before you buy!

Speaking of compatibility, also talk to the supplier about your computer platform. Some RIPs are designed for Macs, some for PCs, and some for both.

Shopping for a RIP
Essentially, all RIPs do the same thing. They take information and manage it on its way to the printer. That definitely doesn't mean, however, that one RIP is as good as the next. Some packages come with many more features and options. These include greater control over ink density, for instance. In addition, some RIPs allow you to create a hybrid printer that enables more than one type of ink to be installed in the printer at once. For example, MultiRIP allows the user to print dye sublimation transfers and film positives from the same printer. Other key features to look for in RIPs are the ability to import/export printer files and build in density curves or profiles to coordinate with different types of media.

Again, printer compatibility comes into play, especially if you have more than one type of output device. For instance, if you own an Epson 4880 and a Mimaki, it would be helpful to have a single RIP that could drive both printers.

Expect to spend around $500 to $700 for a RIP for smaller desktop units, and up to around $4,000 for one designed to work with a large format printer. Clearly, the larger your printer, the more you'll spend on the RIP.

When shopping for a RIP, ask the supplier about platform compatibility (Mac and/or PC), training, and the type of technical support available. Also ask if a demo version is available, and make sure the version you purchase is the most up-to-date one. Some RIPs require the use of a dongle to allow the software to properly work on a computer, while others use a validation system. If you need to install the RIP on multiple computers, then ask the supplier how many licenses or dongles come with the purchase of one RIP. You may be able to buy additional licenses or dongles if necessary. Some RIPs such as AccuRIP allow sharing your printer over a network for the convenience of printing to it from multiple computers.

The bottom line, a RIP will allow you more control over how a printer handles the information sent to it and will provide better results.

Painting Software
Even though this book is dedicated for the Adobe® products, I would be remiss in my duties if I didn't mention my favorite program of them all, Corel Painter. Painter is a program that simulates the look of natural art media such as pastels, water color, oil paints, etc., allowing the creation of an unimaginable amount of

looks within your designs. The combination of this program, a digitizing tablet, and a good artist is something to behold.

Be sure to do yourself or your artists a favor and visit the web site: www.corel.com/painter . See what this great software can do. Also, visit my web site and read the article I wrote for Impressions Magazine on Painter X. It really is a fun and powerful program that, in my opinion, belongs in every serious art department.

Printers

I'm always asked, 'What's the best printer for me?"." What should I have in my art department?" There's just no easy answer to that question. An art department should have several printers.. Each printer should be doing specific things. You will need a regular laser printer for everyday office and task work. A desktop inkjet printer is useful for doing the same thing only in color. A color laser printer is helpful for reports and presentations. Then comes the printer that will be the backbone of the art department. This is the one for printing out your separations to everyday, all day long. The type you choose could make or break your production workflow.

The types of work you do (or want to do) and your budget are the first things to consider when looking for printers. The following will be information on Laser printers, Inkjet printers, Thermal, and Imagesetters.

Laser printers were among the very first types of printers used in our industry. Almost everyone had one, and some still use them. They were a relatively inexpensive solution to printing separations. You can purchase one that prints tabloid or 13"x19" for about $1600.

If printing any separations using halftone dots, you must have a PostScript laser printer. Most, but not all, of the larger format laser printers will have PostScript.

Can your business make it on a laser printer? It's possible, but I wouldn't recommend it unless all your company prints are one color designs.
Laser printers use tremendous amounts of heat in order to "fuse" the toner to the paper, or vellum (the milky looking paper). Because of that heat and the variable moisture content that the vellum may contain, you will notice the vellum will shrink, and you will fight with registration of multiple colors.

Some vellum manufacturers have come out with a frosted acetate or plastic based mylar paper. They did this to try to have a more stable substrate. While this was an improvement, it's still far from a perfect solution.

For instance, if you have a four color job to print, the first two colors may print out just fine, and then you'll notice that the third color is a little short. The fourth color might be a little long, thus not registering on press. These can be very costly in terms of time in the art room or setting up on press.
There are a lot of interesting fixes for this. Running your vellum through your conveyor dryer first to get the moisture out, or running blank paper through the printer to heat it up can work.. However, this is just not the best way to run a business. Too many steps will just bog down the production process.

If you do decide to use a laser printer, be sure to have some artist's fixative or Caseys' Page Mill's Ultra Black handy to spray over the vellum to darken the toner for better exposures.

Using vellum or frosted acetate will require slightly longer exposure

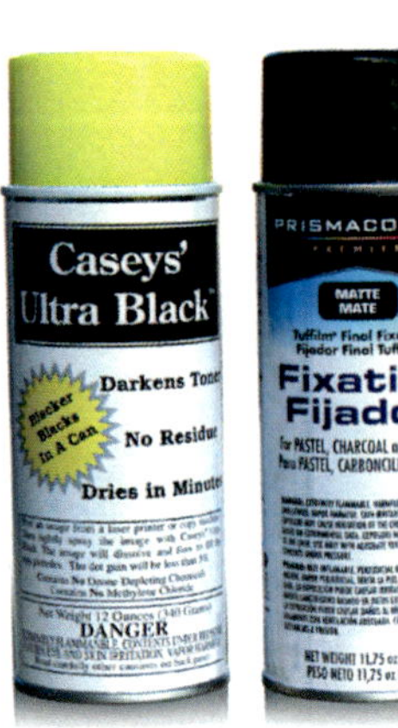

times than one of the other types of printers printing to clear film.

Inkjet printers are fast becoming the printer of choice for screen printers. They print on special coated clear film. There is no heat introduced into the process; therefore, no worry about shrinkage as with laser printers. They do require a RIP software to print separations and halftone dots.

I would recommend buying one from an industry supplier instead of just going to your local computer store. They usually have package deals that come with a RIP specific for our industry.
Another advantage is the size available for printing. It can range anywhere from 8 1/2" wide up to 44". Some go to 64", but those usually aren't used in a textile shop.

They're a lot of package deals in the marketplace, so it should be easy enough to find a package that fits your budget. An entry level inkjet printer such as an Epson R1400 with a RIP software can be found for about $1100. The next level up might be an Epson R1900, with a RIP for $1500. After that, an Epson 4880 with RIP is about $3100. They go up in price from there to a 7880 and larger. Obviously, the price keeps climbing. Any of the afore mentioned printers will get the job done, the 4880 and 7880 are more of a production print engine and will out perform the lower end units in both speed and longevity.

One of the things I like about the Epson 4880 and 7880 printers is that they print on roll media, This is cheaper to use. I also like the fact that I can swap the film out, put in a roll of paper, and print full color posters. It takes about 30 seconds to do!

Can you imagine, you've just finished printing a nice large job for a customer. You want to do something nice for him/her without spending too much time or money. Why not just print out a full color poster sized image of

the design you just printed onto the shirts? I assure you they will be thrilled. They'll hang it up and be reminded of "you" every time they see it.

Thermal devices are very nice. They probably give the densest blacks next to true image setters. The print resolution is only 600x600, but works perfectly well for the halftone sizes we need to print.
Thermal printers, unlike image setters, require no chemistry to develop the film. This is a huge plus. They do use heat to develop the films, but the film is much thicker and more stable; therefore, there are not the registration problems that occur with laser printers.

Although a little expensive, entry level desktop units start at about $10,000 dollars. If there is budget for it, you will be happy with quality of your films.

Image Setters have been around for years and were used mainly in the offset industry. These units can cost upwards of $25,000 dollars. This makes it cost prohibitive for most shops. Only a few of the very largest shops still use these.

The resolution can range from 1200 dpi to 2400 or more. While that sounds great, it tends to be overkill for what is needed to print on T-shirts. The blacks are really dense, and that's a plus, but an Image setter requires chemistry for processing films. This chemistry requires cleaning, maintenance and disposal. This results in more time and added costs. Most people, including me, do not find it worth the effort. Stay away from these.

Digitizing Tablets
This is probably the most under utilized tool available for an art department. I don't know why that is. In my opinion, it's the first tool you should get! These are input devices. They are tablets that allow the artist to draw more naturally on the computer. It uses a cordless stylus pen that simulates a real pencil or brush. They are pressure sensitive. This means the harder you press, the darker or wider the stroke, much like the real thing.

They can be purchased from your local computer store for about $69. The more expensive of these tablets sell from $999 to $1999. These allow drawing and painting right on the screen!

The tablets allow you to do tasks with a cordless pen that would normally require a computer mouse. This saves time, because it is a much more natural experience. When beginning to use a tablet, you will save 5 to 10 minutes per job. That will quickly add up over the course of a day or week, and they are fun to use.

In almost all of my travels visiting shops around the world, I rarely see them used. Yet, in my consulting visits, I show and use one of my own tablets. I have a Wacom Intous 3 (the one pictured here), it travels everywhere I go. I also have an Intous 4 (the latest model). By the time I'm finished with a consultation, every artist in the place will usually have one. It is easy to see the value in time saving alone. You should consider getting one!

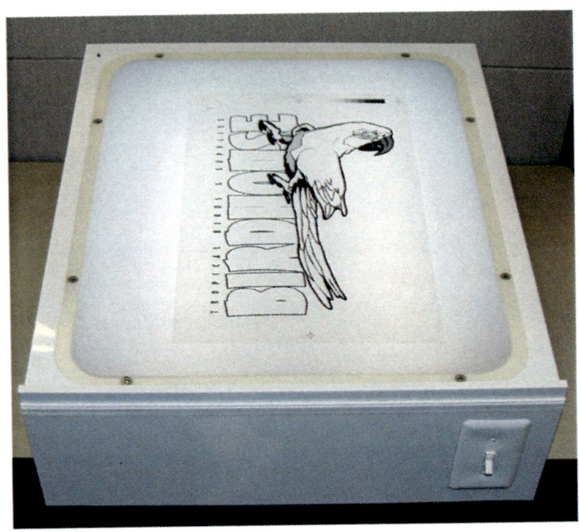

Light Table

One of the last things but definitely not the least is a light table. A light table is useful in the art department to check printed films for registration and content. This same light table will come in handy for tracing images in order to scan them in. It doesn't really matter whether you have large table or just a small table top one. As long it's large enough to hold your films, you should be fine.

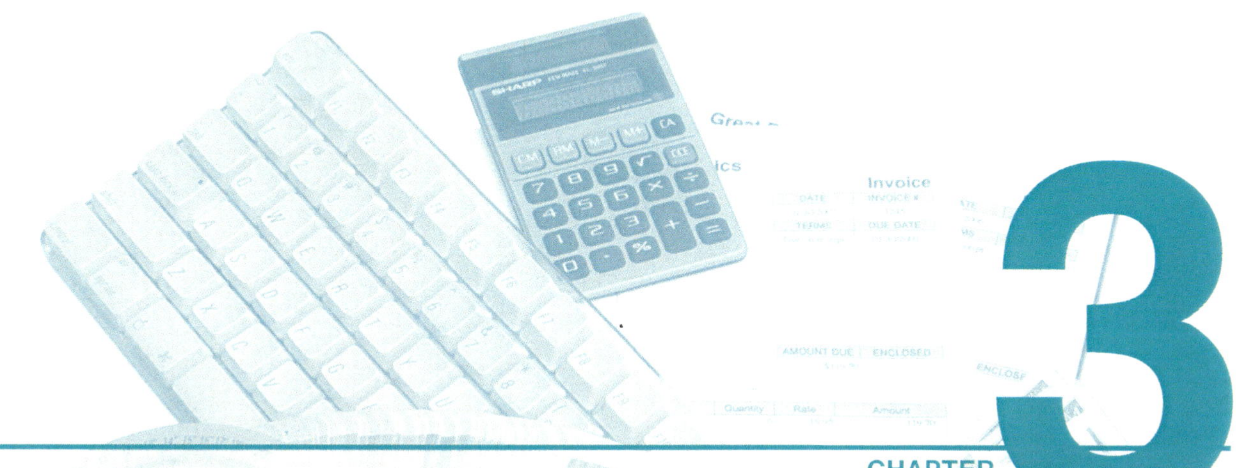

MANAGING THE ART PROCESS

Managing The Art Process

This chapter is designed for people just setting up their printing businesses. This group would include managers / owners who are managing the art process, or people that are neither artists or printers who intend to contract out the art and or the printing. In other words, this is for those new to working with the other side of the brain.

Vector Art, Raster Art, What's the Difference?

Drawing programs such as Adobe Illustrator create vector graphics. Vector graphics are made of lines and curves defined by mathematical objects called vectors. Vectors describe graphics according to their geometric characteristics. For example, a baseball in a vector graphic is made up of the mathematical definition of a circle drawn with a certain radius, set at a specific location, and filled with a specific color. It can be moved, resized, or the color changed without losing the quality of the graphic.

A vector graphic is resolution-independent. It can be scaled to any size and printed on any output device at any resolution without losing detail or clarity. That makes vector graphics the best choice for text, especially small type and bold graphics that must retain crisp lines when scaled to various sizes. An example of this would be a logo.

Bitmap images — technically called raster images — are made up of a grid of dots known as pixels. When working with bitmap images, pixels are edited rather than objects or shapes. Bitmap images are the most common electronic medium for continuous-tone images such as photographs or digital paintings. The fact that they can represent subtle gradations of shades and color makes this so.

Bitmap images can lose detail when scaled on-screen because they are resolution-dependent. They contain a fixed number of pixels, and each pixel is assigned a specific location and color value. Bitmapped images can look jagged if printed at too low a resolution, because the size of each pixel is increased.

The image to the right shows what happens when each type of art is scaled up at a larger magnification. This is why it is very important to create raster artwork at the proper resolution before starting. Be sure to create it at the actual size it will be printed.

There really isn't a" which is better" scenario. Each is perfectly fine in it's own right. The questions to ask

yourself when creating the artwork are as follows. "What kind of design do I want to create?". " Is it a photographic or full color painting type of image?" If so, create it using Photoshop as a Raster image. If it is a corporate logo, one that will be cut on vinyl for instance, then be sure to create it in Illustrator as a vector design.

Working with Artists (creative people)

Working with artists is unlike working with any other group of people. There really is something to be said for the whole right brain, left brain issue. Left brains and right brains that work well together in this business have bigger bank accounts. Artists or creative types normally work on their own wave length, in their own world. They tend to be free spirits that don't conform well to rules and time schedules.

If working on something late at night, for instance, an artist would likely stay up till dawn and get a job done, and then sleep most of the next day. The last thing an artist wants to do is quit working on a project when in a "groove". The concept of stopping work just because the clock says it is time doesn't sit well with this type of personality.

Some artist are able to conform better than others. It's all about what motivates them and keeps them going. If it is at all possible to be flexible with their schedule, then it would probably be beneficial to bend a little. If on the other hand, it is not an option to be flexible and work must start at 8:00 and end at 5:00, be firm and stick to it. If everyone has to live by the clock in order for the business to function, be sure to find an artist that is capable of doing so. Otherwise, the morale of other employees may suffer, if they believe the art guy is getting preferential treatment. It is important that all employees are aware of the long hours an artist may be working, if that is the case.

Staffing Your Art Department

Before buying a computer, scanner or printer, consider your most important art department asset … your artists. Any shop is capable of purchasing computer equipment. BUT, the shop that succeeds, the shop that wins awards, the shop that really makes money is the shop that is investing in true artists.

All too often people think they have what it takes to run an art department simply by purchasing computer equipment and a few clip art CD's. If you want to WOW your clients and win business, the proper personnel must be hired. These people must be capable of conceptualizing what your clients' needs are, and have the necessary skills to bring those needs to completion.

First and foremost, your business needs someone with the ability to draw. Although this may sound a little crazy,

most art departments in our industry are staffed with people that cannot draw! If you want your business to stand out above the competition, then staff up with an artist that can draw. There are other qualities to look for in artists. These include an eye for color, being proficient in operating the graphics programs in your shop, and understanding the separation process for screen printing. If you find someone with all of these abilities, consider yourself lucky, and hire that person immediately.

Most likely you will find someone with a few of these abilities. It will then be necessary to train them in the other areas. It is my opinion, finding someone who has artistic abilities, can draw well, has a flair for design, and an eye for color is paramount. If they are willing to learn, the computer skills and screen printing separation techniques can be taught. With all of the magazine articles, training DVDs, seminars, and workshops available today, any true artist will be able to learn enough to be up and running in a relatively short amount of time.

Over the years I have come to know and employ some of the best artists available. More than a few of them have had little or no computer skills. I've even had a couple who didn't know how to turn a computer on! But, these guys could draw and paint like no one else. That's why I hired them. I put a Wacom tablet in their hands, showed them some basic tools in Corel Painter and Photoshop, and off they went. If they have talent, the computer skills will come.

Having your artists spend some time with your pressmen on the shop floor, burning screens, setting up on press, and pulling the squeegee on a couple of their own creations is an invaluable and enlightening experience. The knowledge they will gain from this one thing is unparalleled and can be incorporated back into their design work. I consider this a "must-do" for every shop. If you take the extra time and go this extra mile, your staff will quickly gain the knowledge necessary to win the quality accounts your business deserves. This should also help develop strong bonds between the art department and the production floor.

Do I outsource my art?

If you are just starting out in business and aren't sure you can hire an artist immediately, there are a few things that will buy some time and help get your business off the ground.

First, find help and advice buying stock art and clip art. Even when an artist is hired, these will be a valuable asset. Why pay an artist to re-draw a tiger, if you can simply buy one already done. All the artist will have to do is put type around it, and in no time the design is done. Quality stock art is a tremendous help.

Second, locate a freelance artist. Ask other shop owners or call the colleges in town to find a student just out of school looking for a little extra money. Check with industry magazines. Most of them will do features yearly that may help locate one. Check with associations like the SGIA. They have an area on their web site that will help as well.

Working with Contract Artists

Working with contract artists on a freelance basis can save your company a lot of money, especially in the early stages of business. Salary becomes a non issue. It is just a matter of paying the cost of each job as it comes in. You should be able to pass that cost on to the customer; thereby, having it cost you and your business nothing.

When working with freelance artists some decisions and ground rules need to be made up front to avoid surprises later on.

As with most things in life, you generally get what you pay for. If you find several freelancers with which to work, you can be sure that their fees will vary. Factors such as years in the business, skill level etc. will affect rates. Keep this in mind, and use them accordingly. If the job you have today is somewhat easy and non complicated, then use one of the less expensive artists. If you get a rather large job, one that is crucial in terms of skill level and time frame for delivery, be sure to use one of the better, and sometimes more expensive artists.

Fees will vary. Depending on the artists you work with regularly. It may be possible to negotiate lower than normal prices if you send them steady work. I know I would always consider that when pricing our jobs. If you provide and artist with steady work, he should be happy to give you a discount for the patronage, and you should be able to count on on time delivery of the finished art.

One very important thing to have when working with freelance artists is a "Work For Hire" agreement. This is a document that needs to be negotiated between the employer and the artist. It states the name of the job, the price to be paid, and transfers all the rights to you. It also protects you and your business from liability in case the artist gets lazy and uses something someone else created. This would be copyright infringement, and those are headaches no employer wants. Be sure to have the artists sign a Work For Hire agreement for each job they do. If this is not done, The artist owns the rights and can sell the same artwork to someone else. You can be found liable if they did steal someone else's art.

One thing I personally avoid is working on royalties per print. There are many companies out there that do set up some sort of royalty for the artist on a per piece basis. It is just not for me. I never liked the idea of having to keep track of all the details. Besides, if the prints don't sell, and there is nothing to give to the artist, it just doesn't seem right. I am aware that it is a risk both sides have to make, but I have never felt comfortable having someone do work and not get paid for it.

Setting up a Drawing Station

Aside from all the computer hardware and software, some basic art materials in your art department are necessary. Even though most of the art these days is done on computer equipment, a large portion of the initial stages of design will take place with traditional media. I would suggest you have one drawing station setup with all the appropriate tools needed. Unless you have an abnormally large amount of artists, one station should work just fine.

There should be a board that can be adjusted to a comfortable position for each artist. There should be a comfortable chair and a light box or tracing table at this station. It should also include all the necessary art supplies. (pencils, tracing paper, sketch pads, brushes, drawing pens, etc.) A big advantage in having a drawing area set up is that all the necessary tools for that particular task are out and readily available for use. One of the biggest wastes of time is having to stop and locate appropriate tools and supplies before starting to sketch. Having one area devoted to this task will greatly enhance productivity.

This area should be well lit with natural light or florescent and incandescent lighting to simulate natural light. A typical scenario for an artist working on a job is first to sketch an idea, then revise it to finished pencil on tracing paper, take it to the scan station, scan it into the computer, transfer the scan to his/her computer, and finally work it up to a finished piece. Once that artist has completed work at the drawing station, other artists are free to begin their work there.

Scanning Station

If your art department has more than one person, a drawing station and a separate scan station make the most sense. A scan station need be nothing more than the oldest or slowest computer with a scanner attached. It is not necessary for each artists to have a scanner at individual workstations. They can scan whatever they need at the station, then transfer the file to their workstation via an ethernet network.

Ideal Environment For the Art Staff

In my opinion, aside from the drawing station and scan station, each artist should have an individual work space. This will typically include a computer, and their own personal "things". Creative people often surround themselves with a wide array of toys, icons, slogans etc. Many people may consider these things junk, but for the creative mind they are often forms of inspiration and expression. It is generally a good idea to locate the art department a good distance away from the lobby where your clients will normally visit. Most creative people listen to music, and depending on the mood for the day, it may be loud. As long as it is not disruptive to other departments, you will find that giving creative people room to create without much more than the job specifics and a deadline will bear greater results. The noise can be controlled through the use of iPods and headphones. I say let them have fun and listen openly, and this will help to unite them as a team.

Another thing that impacts the work flow in your art department is the layout of the art room itself. I believe an art department should be one room if possible. However, each artist should have an area divided by a counter or wall. The wall should be a height which allows each artist to see over it from a sitting position. This will encourage the artists to bounce ideas off of each other without having to leave their station. One can offer suggestions to another by simply looking at the other's monitor. A design will always benefit from the input of more than one person. This setup will allow for just this.

The art room, with the exception of the drawing station should be a low light space. Avoiding strong lighting from above will help reduce glare and eye strain. Each station should have its own desk lamp to provide workable light.

There should also be a common work table. This should be a place free of clutter to lay out reference materials or mount color comps to art board for presentations. It is also a good idea to have an empty wall that can be used to tack up design layouts for observation and critiquing from the entire staff.

Last but not least is the visual reference required to produce quality work. Your art department should be stocked with reference books. These books should be filled with lots of pictures covering a broad range of subject matter. A glance through my reference library will produce books on planes, trains and automobiles. There are books on trees, shrubs, underwater marine life, and just about any kind of animal imaginable. These books need not be purchased new. Look in used bookstores, or garage sales to add to your library.

Another valuable, yet inexpensive visual reference asset would be a morgue file or "scrap" file. This is a set of files used to store pictures of things, such as cats, dogs, birds, etc. Each of these categories can be broken down into sub categories. For instance, "Category Birds" - sub categories- parakeet, eagles, parrots, etc. These photos, magazine clippings, etc. should be stored alphabetically for easy retrieval. This file over time can become very extensive.

Clippings are used as reference only. I do not recommend copying or scanning any of this material due to copyright laws. I do, however, recommend having this material on hand for your artists. A visual reference of subject matter will allow your artist to create a design which will be much more convincing. Drawing something with many photos from various angles will help your artist embellish and develop his own interpretation of the design at hand. I recommend you have your artist set aside one hour a week to work on the scrap file. The more your file grows, the greater the benefit to your artists.

Unfortunately, in 2005, hurricane Katrina destroyed my studio in New Orleans. When it did, I lost lots of things including one of my prized possessions, over 20 years of morgue files! Looking back now, that name truly describes what happened. It was a morgue file. It drowned under six feet of water, where it stayed for more than a month.

The Creative Process

The creative workflow in my studio works like this. We have a creative meeting on Monday morning to discuss the jobs that need to be done that week. This meeting has all of the appropriate players involved. All of the creative staff including the art director, illustrators, and account executives are in attendance. Spend no more than ten minutes discussing a job and the information that needs to be contained in it, ie: dates, times, event names etc. Then move on the next job on the list.

We use a white board to write down a list of the things for each job. Using this information, we start to write down words that are associated with that job. This starts the process of developing ideas or "themes" for the design. During this time, the illustrators sketch gestural thumbnails as we go. Often times we have several good ideas sketched out to get us started. Once the initial concept is done, one of the illustrators will flesh out the idea with a tighter sketch to present to the customer.

Backup, Backup, Backup!

I don't think I can stress enough to you about how important it is to backup the work you do on your computer. It's not really all that difficult to do, and there are many different ways to do it. It took a hard lesson and losing 8 GB worth of artwork for me to fully understand the importance. The hard drive in one of my computers crashed, and I couldn't recover any of the art.

It is a difficult and awkward situation when a good customer comes to you and says, "The design you did for our event last year was such a big success, we want to use it again". You then have to tell him you no longer have the job that you did for him last year, because you neglected to back up our computers! Do you then charge him full price to re-create the design he already paid you once to create? There's no easy answer, but it is a hard lesson to learn.

One very simple and inexpensive way to backup is to copy everything to a CD or DVD disk. I started backing up this way years ago.

This is how you do it. Create your client or jobs folder. Inside that folder have individual folders for each customer you're working on at the time. Keep an eye out for the size of this folder. If, for instance, you decide to backup to a CD, be sure when the size of the folder gets to around 650 MB, you burn the contents of this folder to a CD. When you burn the disk, be sure to burn a second copy. I labeled my CDs, 1-A, and 1-B. I put all the A disks in a binder with CD sleeves. These can be purchased at any office supply store. I took all the B copies home and placed them in a similar binder. Now, I had my artwork backed up to two separate disks in two separate locations. The only problem with this is that it takes up a LOT of room on the shelves. I stopped using CDs when I reached CD number 400!

I then began using DVDs. I backed up the exact same way. This proved much better than CDs. A DVD can hold about 4 GB to while a CD has a 650 MB capacity. Much more art will fit on a DVD. The problem I had with DVDs was the time it took to locate certain files we needed. We used software called DiskTracker to keep track and catalog the contents of each disk, but it still took too long to find things. At this point I began using large capacity external hard drives on my network. I used the same concept of having a backup at work and one at home. I bought two hard drives. Once we were finished copying the backup files to one drive, we would copy them to a second drive. Each night I would bring the second drive home.

I can tell you from experience, it comes in extremely handy when disaster strikes. Computers do crash. A backup allows you to live to fight another day.

It is a different thing entirely when "everything" is lost as when a hurricane strikes. I would normally say insurance would replace the lost items, but for me that wasn't the case. I was just one of the unfortunate people that was treated unfairly by my insurance company. It still makes me angry every time I think about it. But, I didn't lose a single piece of art. I had one set of backup disks and drives with me. I packed these up with my

family and left town. My art director took the second set with her. Both of our backups survived!
Now, I back up my business via the internet. I have a four bay Raided hard drive box containing 2 TBs of capacity. When I copy files to one drive it is automatically raided to a second drive. I can now back up my artwork from anywhere in the world at any time. With employees in different states this makes it very easy to keep track of the" life blood" of my business, my artwork.

Do I Charge for Artwork?

Absolutely! If there's one thing that really gets to me it is the devaluation of artwork by some idiots! Some shops give art away for free. That just simply means they overcharge their customers somewhere else. The art guy still must be paid. The money needs to come from somewhere.

It has been my experience that the shops that give art away do so because no one would want to pay for it. The artwork is inferior... plain and simple. You charge for screens or setup don't you? This involves employee time and, therefore, employee pay. Artwork is no different.

Look at it like this. Does a person really need a BMW? What is it's purpose? It gets the driver from point A to point B. Well, a Dodge Neon can do the same thing! Why do people pay four to five times more money for the BMW? They like it and think it's better. If they think "your" artwork is better, and they like it, they'll pay for it.

How many t-shirts do you think you would sell if they had no images on them? Even an inferior image would sell more than the blank ones.. Now imagine how many more you'd sell if the artwork was outstanding and everyone wanted to wear it! Spend a little time creating quality art, because the guy down the street isn't likely to. Go the extra mile, you'll win every time.

It is not necessary to spend tons of time or a lot of money on art. Quality Stock Art and Clip Art are available to the industry. Each image of Stock Art on my web site takes days to paint and create. Once you own one, customize it in minutes by adding your own text to it. You'll have a quality design and be printing shirts in no time.

What clip art should I use?

Be sure to use clip art designed for the screen printing industry. This goes for non screen printers, the digital, and sublimation printers also. The box of Art Implosion that you can get from an office supply store for $49. might not be the best money spent. Most of the clip art you find in those places is created for the offset printing industry. There are no completed shapes that you can simply click on and change the color. Most are built with lines and shapes literally stacked on top of one another. This causes all sorts of problems when trying to print out separations. It leaves no way for you to trap an element if needed. It causes overprint and stroke outline problems. It's just more trouble than necessary.

Good quality artwork for our industry is available. Look at these art giants in the industry. Great Dane Graphics, known for the best full color raster artwork out there, Digital Art Solutions, known for some of the best vector art and Smart Designer software and Action Illustrated, also known for quality clip art.

These companies teamed up to create some of the coolest and most unique art packages out there to date. Digital Graphics Collections,1&2 contain full color images from GDG that are placed into templates by DAS. Simply choose a template you like, choose a main colored image, and change the school or team name. It's that quick and easy. Check them out at their respective web sites.

The Necessity of Documentation

Documentation is a must! If you want any chance to be sure the art was done right, the job was printed correctly, and you can reproduce it exactly the same later on, then you need to document everything.

Before getting started, let me remind you of how right brainers work. They don't work with forms! They are not good at keeping track and using them. But, if it is made 100% clear that in order to be paid, forms must be used. They will use them.

The art department really doesn't have to do too much form management. That is mostly left to the account rep or office person. The art department should have a Job Order form, some sort of time sheet, and a work for hire agreement.

The Job Order Form is the first thing filled out when a new job comes through door. This should be filled out by the account rep or office person taking the job. It should contain all pertinent information. This information should include all of the details of the job including the sizes of the garments or goods, the position they will be imprinted, when the order is due, if there are any text or dates that need to be included, if the customer included any artwork to use, and if the job consists of new artwork only.

The Time Sheet may not be a "sheet" at all. You may use a software application that tracks time, like I do. The total time spent on the job can be collected upon completion. You might want to record this total time on the job order to keep all the important info in one place.

The Work-For-Hire Agreement only comes into play if you hire a freelancer to do the art for a particular job. There should be one WFH Agreement for every job paid. It is also possible to set up an all inclusive agreement which states that every time you and the freelance artist work together, the rights are relinquished for each job once he is paid in full. Help solidify such an agreement by placing a memo on the check that reads something to this effect. Cashing this check releases all rights of the artwork to (YOU) the one writing the check. This will eliminate the need for you to have a new agreement with every job.

What kind of files should I accept?

I If you are going to be in business for yourself as a printer, or you plan to contract out the services; you need to know what types of artwork to accept and what file types to use. You should set up an "Artwork Spec Sheet".

It should state, "We can accept these file types:"

Adobe Illustrator files. (.ai files)
Adobe Photoshop Layered files. (.psd files)
PDF files.
EPS files.

Be sure to request that Photoshop files be layered. Whether you are a screen printer or a digital printer, you will need the artwork on a transparent layer. Receiving them this way will save you a lot of time. Be sure to tell the customer this in the beginning, so he is more likely to give you what you need. The file should be set up at the actual size it will print with the resolution set at least to 150 to 300 pixels per inch.

You won't actually need this much resolution to print properly. But, depending on the size of the elements in the image, the more you have, the better control you have over the finished print. If they provide an image at 300 ppi, there is enough resolution to enlarge that element in the design without damage.

If your customer uses Corel Draw® and wants to give you a file, be sure that the customer saves it as an .ai file or as an .eps file. Illustrator does not recognize Draw files.

Do not accept and work with low resolution .jpg files. These simply will not work well, and you will lose money in the long run trying to make them work.

Fixing Bad Art

What is bad art?

Bad art can be many things. Many businesses are very diversified these days. Screen printers offering digital garment, dye-sublimation, and large format printing is one example. Because of this, bad art can be a multitude of things. It could simply be a bad design. One in which the layout has no continuity and balance, or the colors used don't work well together.

It could be a really bad photo. If the colors are really muddy, dull and contaminated, the final execution of the print will be terrible. Not to mention, proper resolution is needed for the type of printing to be done.

Maybe someone wants a photo of something on a shirt, banner, or mug. The photo they give you may be very dark or too light to work. If put it on a shirt it would look even worse. It must be fixed in order for the final product to look as good as possible. *(for a full explanation, refer to Optimizing your photos in chapter 6).*

Some things go far beyond bad "art". But, as you will see later this could work in your favor, and become a way to help you capture a new customer.

How do we get bad art?

Usually we get bad art from our customers. They know what they want (sometimes) but don't know what we need from them in order for us to achieve it. Often times they bring us a small .jpg file they found on the internet. This scenario is almost always a disaster. It is usually too small with not enough resolution to print properly. Please do not forget the copyright laws involved with something like this.

If you get art like this, it is best to reject it outright. Chances are it will take forever to fix, if it can be fixed at all. How small and how low the resolution will determine if it's fixable. How much do you need to enlarge the image to get it to the size needed? Is it possible to enlarge it only slightly and use other elements to finish out the image? Can you use text or logos as the "main" focal point and use the smaller .jpg image as a secondary element? This way you may be able to keep it smaller and have better success.

Sometimes bad art is our fault. If we are too busy for instance, and don't spend enough time on a piece, bad art is the result. It is usually not that we are not spending enough time working on the piece, but rather we don't spend enough time "thinking" about the piece

before we start. There is much can be gained by spending a few minutes thinking about what needs to be created. Determine what will or will not work with the design at the start of the process, before wasting time and later realizing something is wrong once well into the project. Determine color scheme's to use, images to use, all the text and elements needed in the image. Spending three minutes doing simple thumbnail sketches will help determine the balance, proportion, and layout of a composition that works. Once the basic "plan" of the design is acquired, we can execute it in much less time.

The biggest waste of time occurs by opening a file in the computer, looking at a big white page, and pushing elements and pixels around without a plan. Plan ahead and save time in the end.

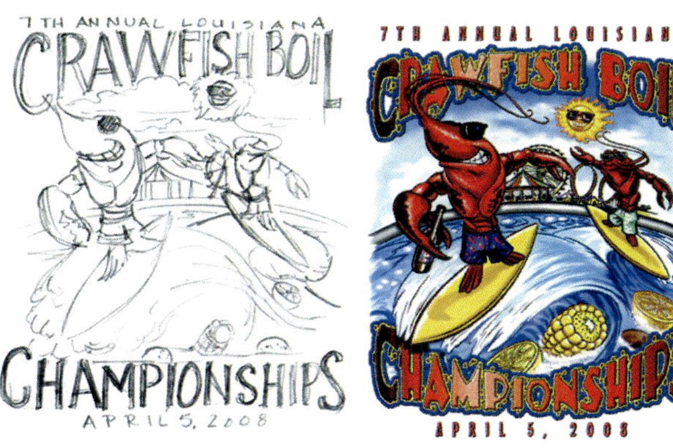

The images above illustrate the "thinking" process I'm talking about. Very quickly sketch a rough idea for the layout using all the info that needs to be included. Try a few different layouts. Your sketches don't even have to be this detailed. Rough gesture drawings will work.

Once you decide on your favorite, develop that one completely.

How do we fix bad Art?

In order to fix bad art we need to determine what is making it "bad art" in the first place. We need to study and analyze the image. Is it a bad layout? Does the composition work? Is it in balance? Are the colors used working well together? What kind of art is it? Is it vector art or photographic art? How will we be printing the final image? Will it be screen printed, direct to garment, sublimated? The answers to these questions will determine what our next step toward fixing will be.

The above left Fire Dept. art is an example of a bad layout. It has no design to it whatsoever. The layout to the right, on the other hand, looks much better. The elements look as if they belong together.
Not all clip art is created equal. Some clip art packages are designed for the offset industry, and aren't built in a way that works best for our industry. Below are examples of a bad piece of clip art and a good one.

As you can see, the first football helmet artwork is just one color. There is no dimension or detail to it, and it makes for the start of a very boring design. The image to the right, on the other hand, has dimension and detail. It has shadows and highlights. This image will be a great start to a much more interesting design.

Is there a way to gain new business with bad art?

As long as you aren't the one creating the bad art, you can sure benefit from others that do. One way to try to grow your business is to look at various image and prints your competition is creating. Find a customer that is using a design that you consider bad art. Study what they have and create something better. Go present your design to the potential customer. Go the extra mile and actually print a shirt. Don't just show them a comp of the design. When I had my shop in New Orleans, every time I tried this, I left the meeting with new business.
Do something that the guy that has the job right now can't do. Upgrade the design, and try a couple of more colors or a simulated process type of look. WOW the customer! Show them why you are the better choice. Chances are your competition's only recourse will be to try to go cheaper with his price. A really strong, quality design often times will win out.

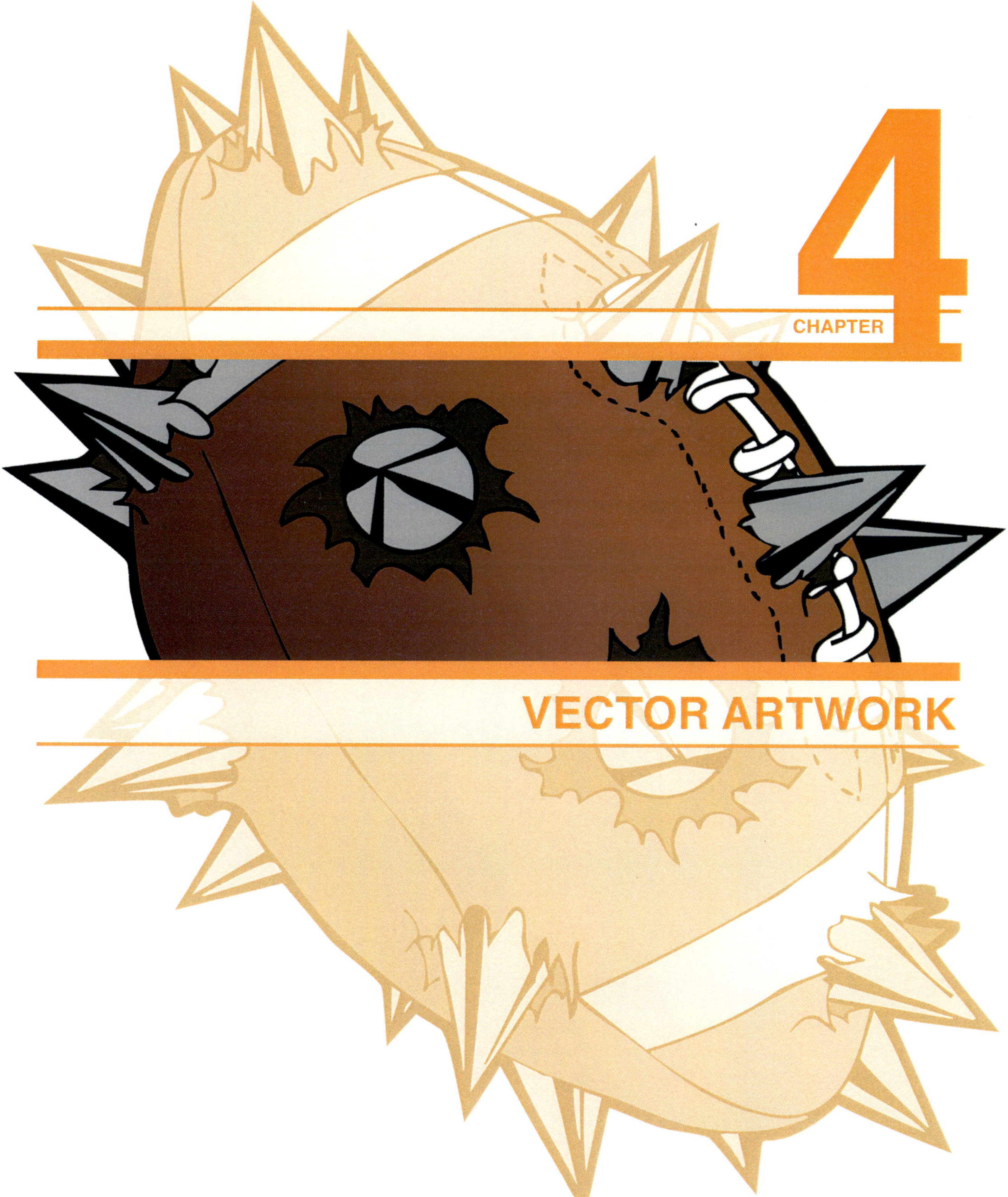

CHAPTER 4

VECTOR ARTWORK

Vector Artwork

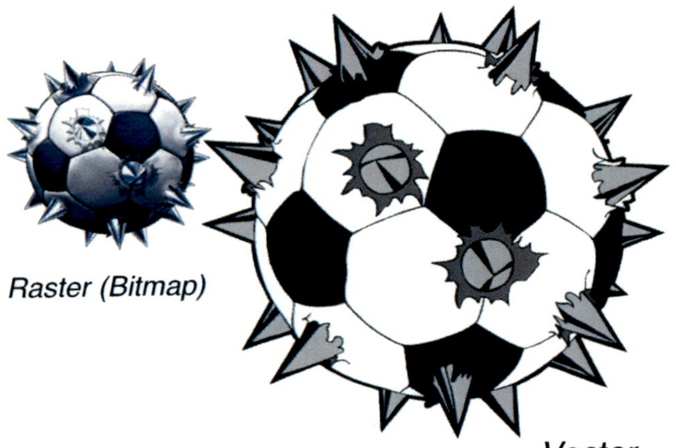

Raster (Bitmap)

Vector

Vector artwork is created by using a series of closed paths or shapes filled with color. These closed paths work together to produce an image. Each individual element of the design can be selected and manipulated.

Vector artwork is the most popular form of artwork in our industry. This is the case for a couple of reasons. It is easy to create. It is possible to create a nice, simple vector image in a couple of hours, as opposed to a full-color raster image which could take a couple of days. Artwork is developed in the computer by creating paths or scanning in black line images that use an auto trace program which converts the image to outlines in a matter of seconds.

There is another reason vector art is very popular. It is most commonly printed using only a few colors, making it easier for screen printers with smaller presses to use. The simple click and select method makes it easy to add, change, or remove colors to suit any need.

This type of artwork is recognizable in clip art form. Most of the companies in our industry that offer clip art, offer it in the form of vector graphics. It is fairly easy to create these graphics. The file sizes are very small which makes it possible to fit many on a CD.

Notice the two images here. One is a vector graphic, while the other is a raster graphic. The vector graphic is much simpler and less involved, composed of simple outlines and simple fills. While it is possible for vector artwork to be more involved and more detailed using halftones and gradients; in general, vector artwork, especially clip art, is simple and basic. Generally, it takes much more time to create a single piece of Raster art than it takes to create Vector art. Looking at the images, it is easy to see the Raster graphic is a painted image with a realistic look. It uses a continuous tonal range of color to create the image.

Throughout this book, I use both styles. They each have their uses. Vector artwork is very useful for digitizing, and vinyl sign cutting. Since the the artwork is already created using outlines of color, this saves embroiderers and sign cutters the time of having to trace and draw the outlines for the artwork. In the case of raster artwork, it would have to be recreate it in a vector format in order to sew or cut out the design properly.

I would not recommend printing Vector graphics on a Direct to Garment digital printer. The very nature of vectors can cause any print head imperfections to really stand out. If printing vector graphics, try using some graduations and blends to help break up the art, so the print head issues will not be as noticeable.

Below: A Vector graphic shown as a solid fill, and outlines with Bezier handles.

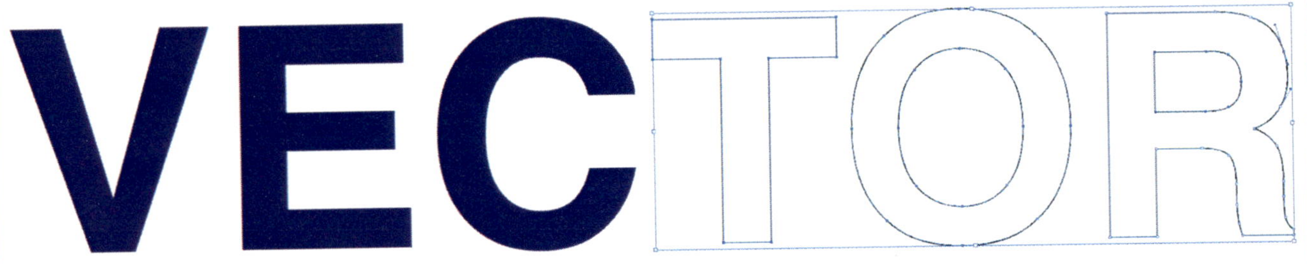

Simple One Color Design

There is very little setup for creating a one color design. It is easy to do.

Even though registration marks are not necessary in order to register a one color job, I still recommend printing the artwork on a template. The two center registration marks will help the press operator center the job on press quickly.

I'll show how to set up a template file later on in Chapter 7.

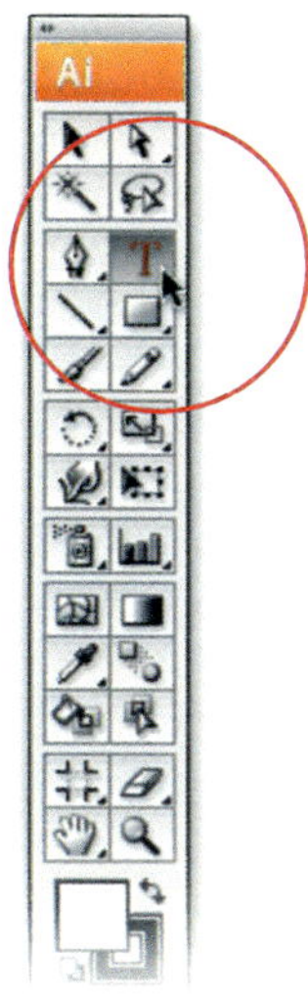

Step 1: Illustrator CS3 - CS5
Go to FILE > NEW.

In the New Document window, make the document the size you want. In this case I made mine 13"x16".

Click OK.

Step 2:
Select the Type Tool from the Tool Box.

Click in the center of the page.

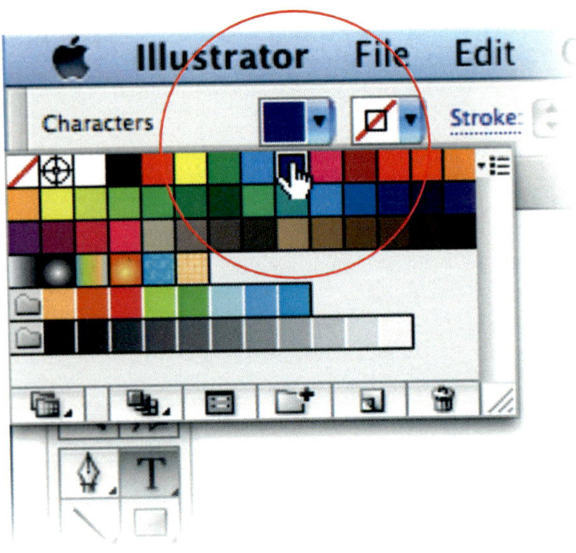

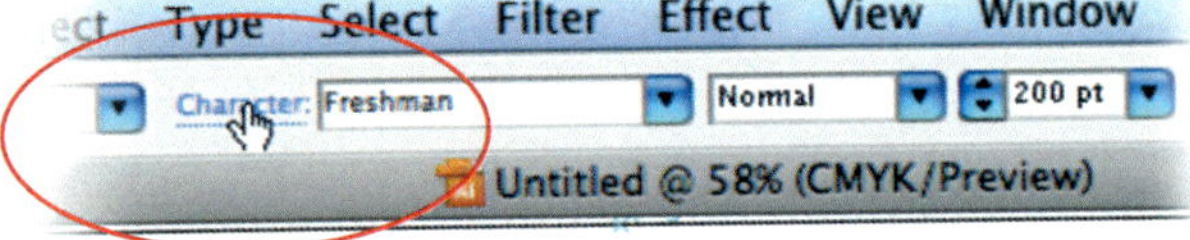

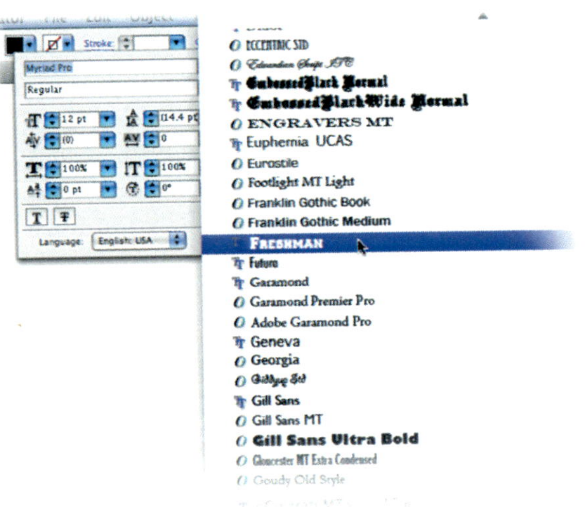

Step 3:

Change the color of the type by clicking on the Fill box at the top left of the screen.

Click on the color swatch you want.

Step 4:

In order to be able to choose the font by looking at it in it's actual face, click on the "Character" word link at the top of the screen.

Step 5:

Click on the font drop down arrow. The fonts will be there in their actual type faces. It's much easier to pick a font when you can see what it actually looks like.

Select the font you want to use.

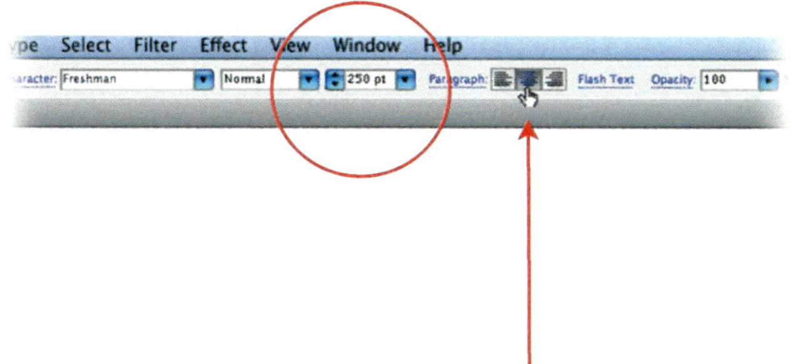

Step 6:

At the top of your screen, set the size you want the font to be. In this case I chose 250 pt.

Click on the Center Paragraph Alignment icon.

Step 7:

Type your text. If it is too big, click onto a corner, hold the shift key, and drag it to the size needed.

With your text selected. Click on the "Make Envelope" button at the top of the screen.

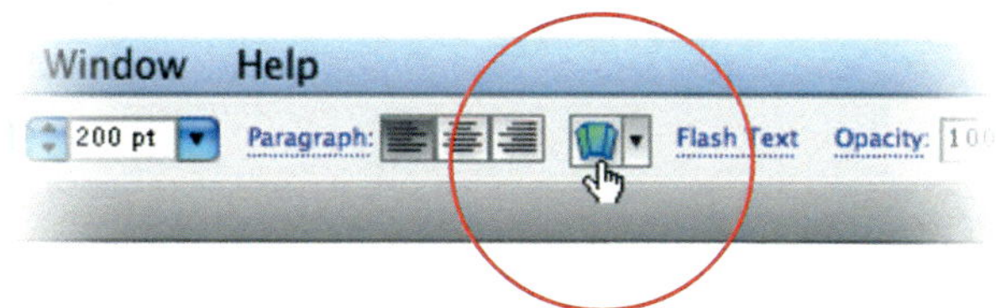

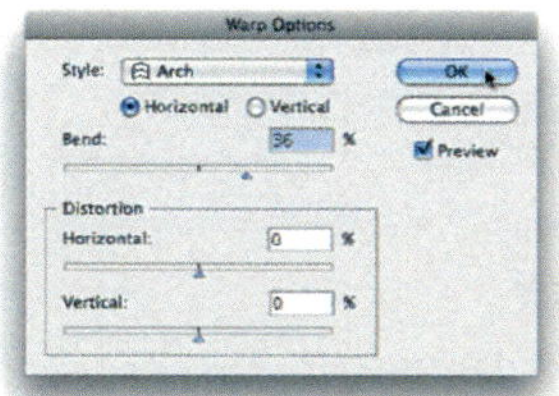

Step 8:

In the Warp Options dialog box, choose the style of envelope to use.

In this case, I chose Arch. Be sure the Preview check box is checked. This is necessary in order to be able to see the effect on screen before clicking OK.

Move the "Bend" slider to the right for more of an upward turn, move it to the left for a downward turn.

The design is complete, but it is still necessary to do something else before we can print.

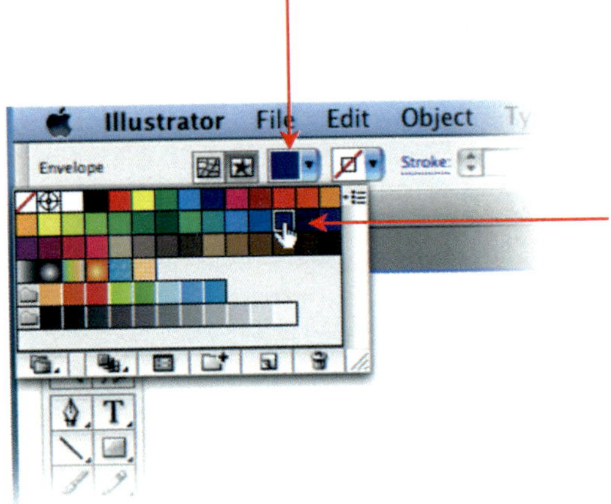

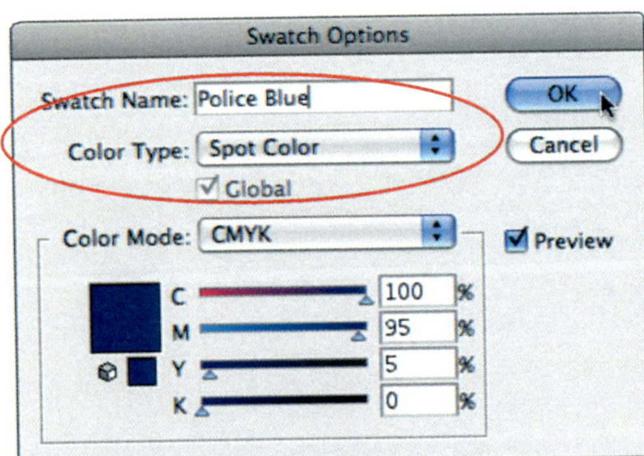

SIMPLE ONE COLOR DESIGN continued

Step 9:

Double click on the word. This will select the text. Notice the text is straight across. This indicates the text is still "live", and can still be edited.

Step 10:

Since the text is selected, it's color can be seen by looking at the Fill Box at the top left of the screen.

Double click the colored square to open up the Swatch Options window.

Step 11:

In the Swatch Options window, change the "Color Type" to Spot Color.

Give the color a name.

Click OK.

Look again at the Fill Box at the top of the screen. The color box now should have a small white corner with a black dot in the middle. This indicates it is now a Spot Color.

Now when printing separations, we will print only one piece of film.

(More to come on printing separations in Chapter 7)

Starting With Clip Art

We're going to create a new design using a standard Clip Art image. This lesson will show you how to get the file off of your disk.

You can use any Clip Art company's disk you want. I'm using one from our Great Dane Graphics book.

Put the Disk in the computer.

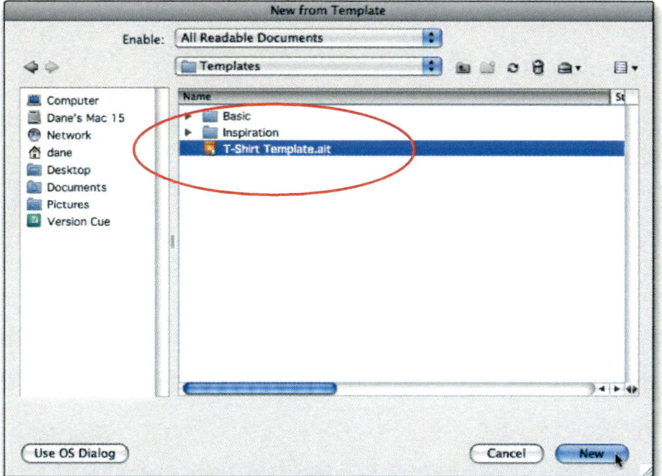

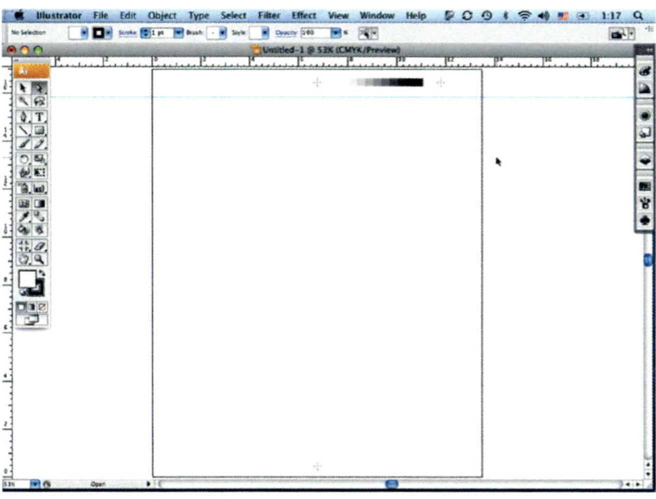

STARTING WITH CLIP ART

Step 1: Illustrator CS3 - CS5

I recommend opening your Artwork Template before working on any new design. I will show how to create one in Chapter 7. If you don't choose to create one now, just disregard the references to the template in this lesson.

Go to FILE MENU > NEW FROM TEMPLATE.

In the New From Template widow, choose the saved Template.

Click New.

Step 2:
You should see the Template with an empty page.

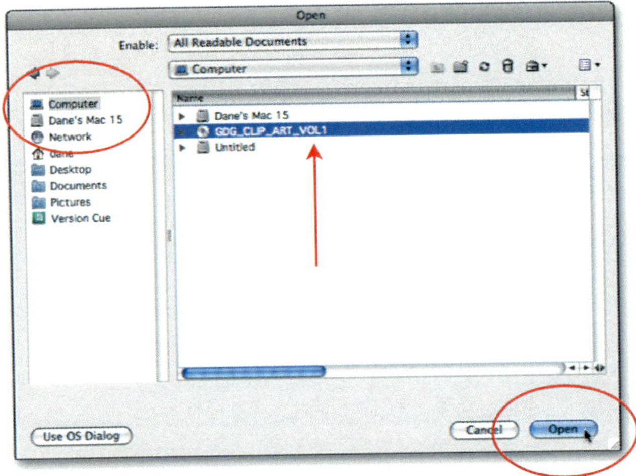

Step 3:
Go to FILE MENU > OPEN.

Choose "computer" in the list. Select the Clip Art Disk.

Click Open

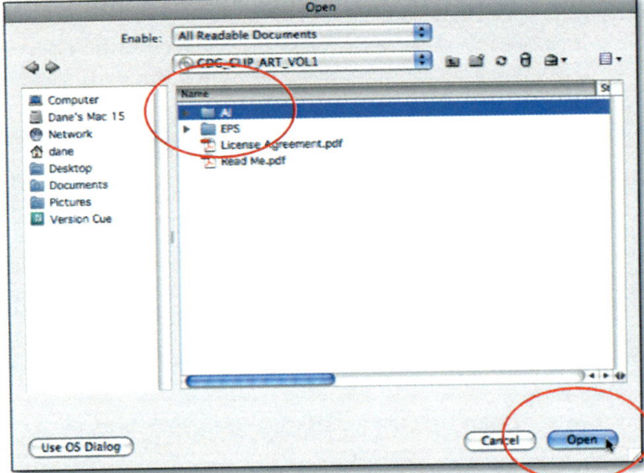

Step 4:
Assuming an image has already been chosen, select the AI folder.

Click Open

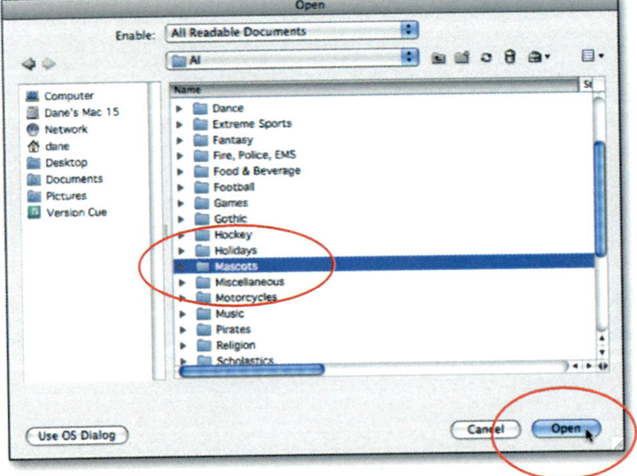

Step 5:
Select the folder/category the image is in.

Click Open.

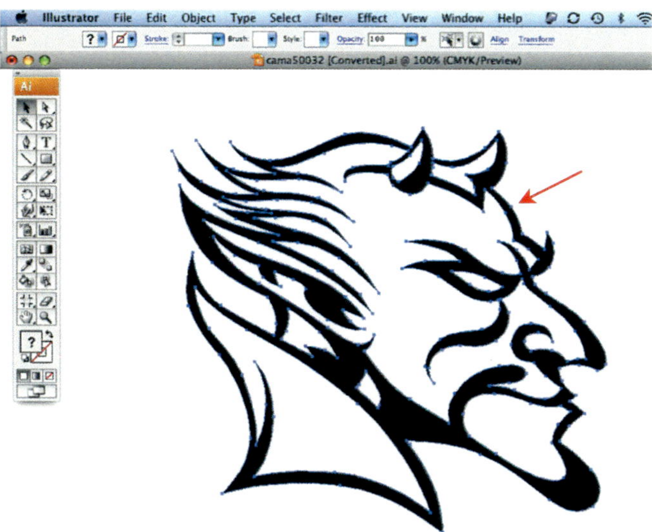

STARTING WITH CLIP ART continued

Step 6:

Select the image you want to use by finding the correct file name in your book.

Click Open

The image should open on screen.

Drag select the entire image. It should look selected with little blue lines and anchor points as shown.

Go to EDIT MENU > COPY.

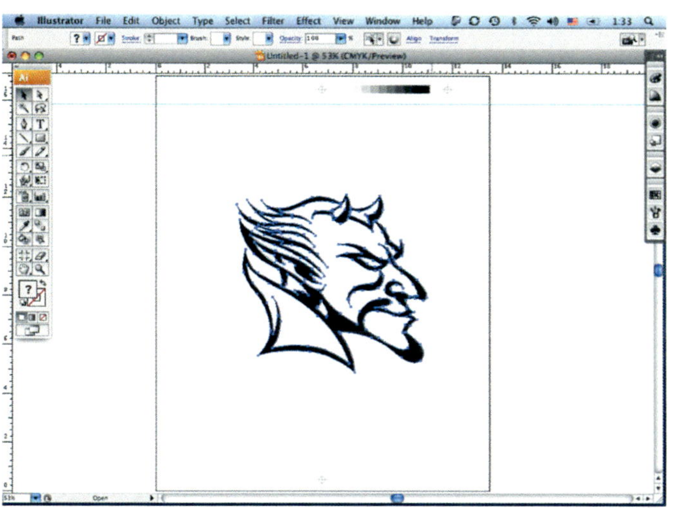

Step 7:

Close this window by "X-ing" out of the window.

When prompted to save, click Don't Save.

Step 8:

You should now be back in the Template window.

Go to EDIT MENU > PASTE.

The image should now be placed on the page of the Template.

Now the design is ready for work.

Creating a Design With Underbase

When printing an image on a dark garment, an Underbase (usually white ink) is necessary under all of the colors in the image except Black. Always print Black ink directly on the shirt.

This lesson will teach how to create an Underbase properly in order for it to print correctly.

I will use this image later in Chapter 7 to demonstrate how to print the separations.

This lesson picks up exactly where the previous lesson ended. Lets get started!

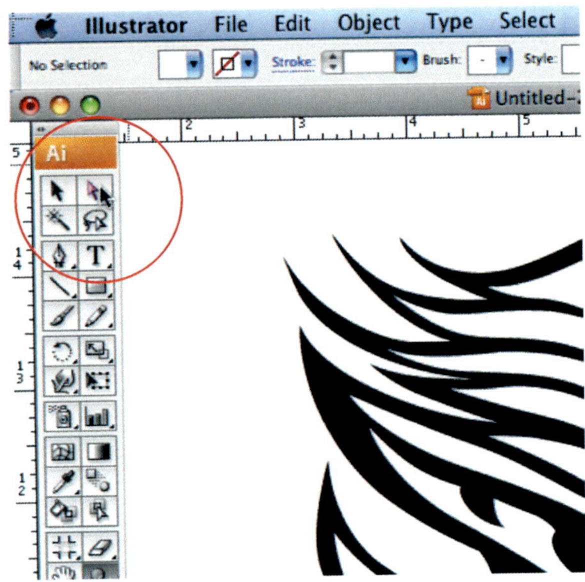

DESIGN WITH UNDERBASE

Step 1: Illustrator CS3 - CS5

Zoom in on the image using the Zoom Tool from the Tool Box.

Select the Direct Selection Tool from the Tool Box. It is the White Arrow tool in the upper right of the Tool Box.

Step 2:

Using the Direct Selection Tool, click the white areas of the image that you want to colorize.

Hold down the Shift Key to select multiple areas.

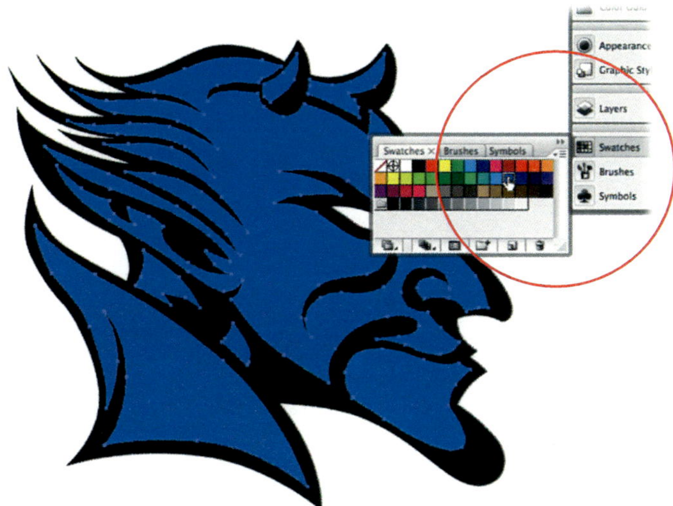

Step 3:

Click on the Swatches Palette. If it is not visible, go to WINDOW MENU > SWATCHES to bring it up.

Click on the swatch of color you want to use. Don't click off of the image yet.

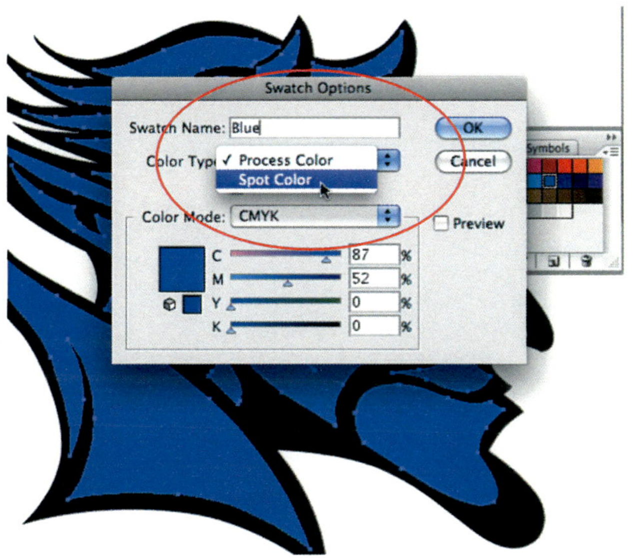

Step 4:

With the color still selected, double click the Swatch of color you used.

In the Swatch Options window, give the color a name and change the Color Type to Spot Color.

Click OK.

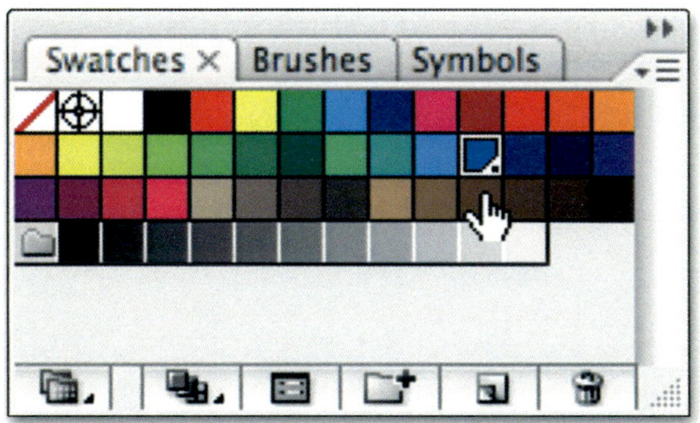

Step 5:

The swatch should have changed. It should now have a white triangle in the lower right corner of the swatch that has a black dot in the middle.

This is the icon for a Spot Color. If screen printing, this should be the type of color almost always used.

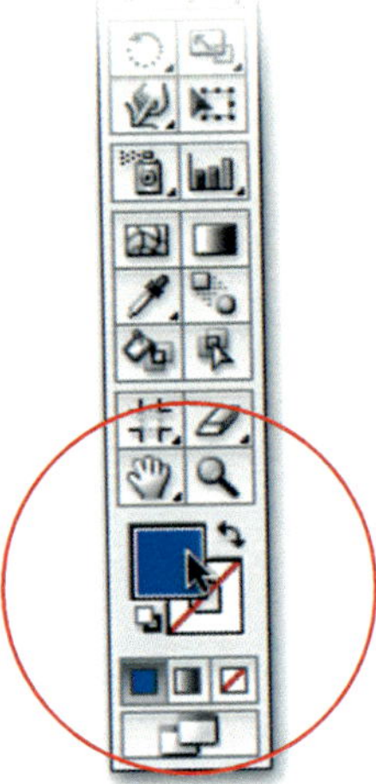

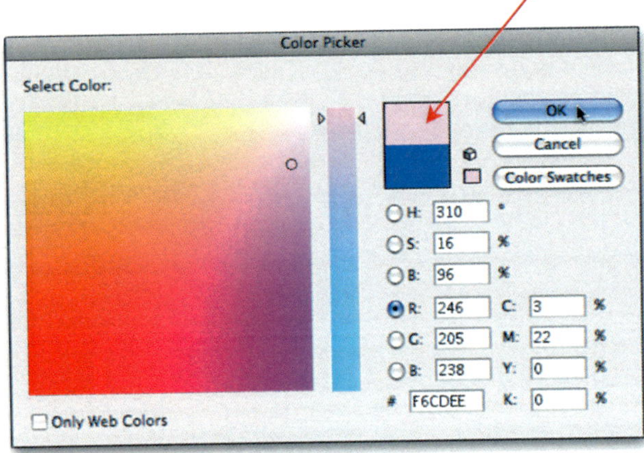

Step 6:

I is now necessary to make a color for the Underbase. The regular White swatch cannot be used, because the computer sees it as a "lack" of color. I normally create a light Pink color for my underbase. This way it has some numeric value, and the computer will recognize it.

Since it is Pink, I can "see" what is colorized in Underbase color on screen.

Double click the Fill color box in the Tool Box.

Step 7:

In the Color Picker window, select the color to use as the White Underbase.

In this case, I chose a light Pink.

Click OK.

Step 8:

With the Swatches Palette open, click and drag the Pink color square to the Swatches Palette.

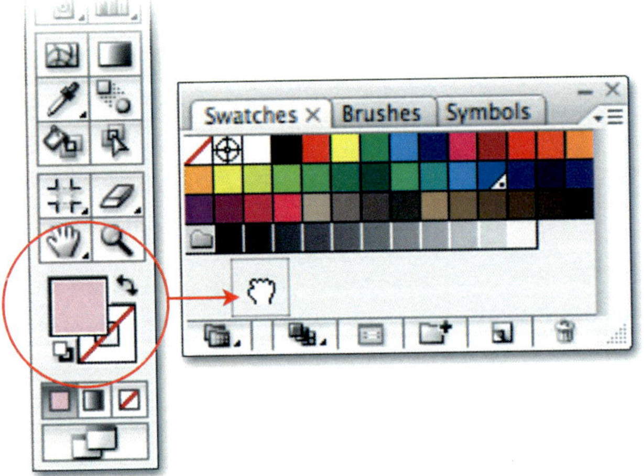

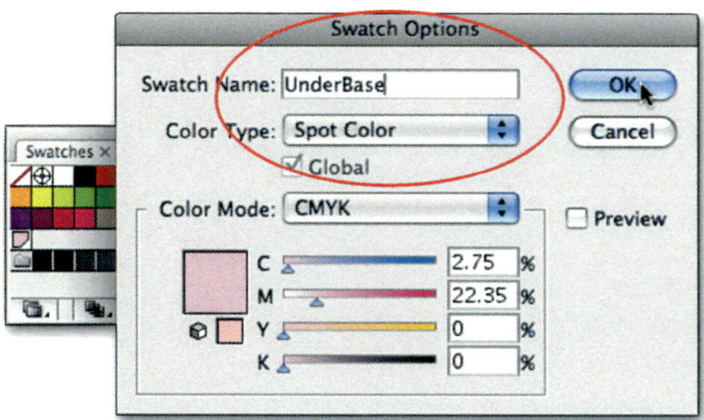

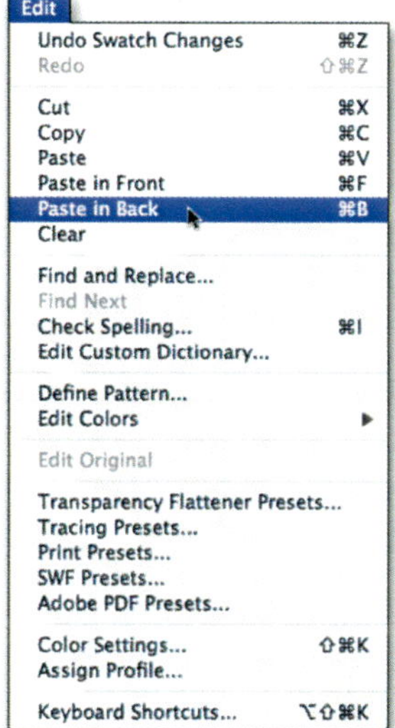

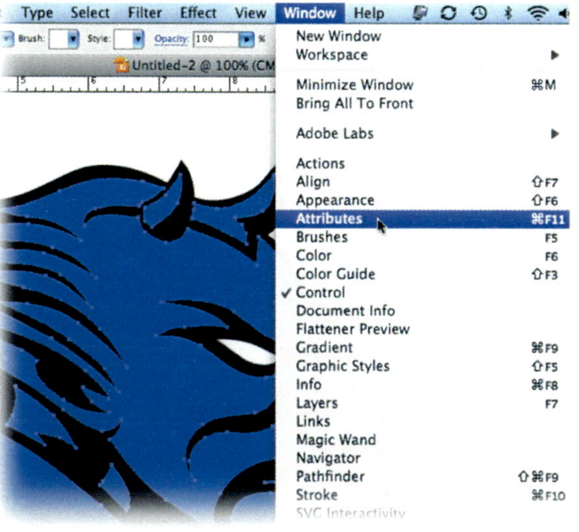

DESIGN WITH UNDERBASE continued

Step 9:

Double click the Pink Swatch. In the Swatch Options window, give it a Name and change the Color Type to Spot Color.

Click OK.

Now this color is a Spot Color also.

Step 10:

Now using the Direct Selection Tool, hold down the Shift Key and select all of the Blue areas.

With all of the areas selected, go to EDIT MENU > COPY.

And EDIT MENU > PASTE IN BACK.

Don't click off of the image yet.

It won't look like anything has changed, but the blue areas were copied and placed in the back of the ones you see now.

While everything is still selected, click on the Pink "Underbase" swatch you made.

You've just colorized the stuff in the back! That's what's actually still selected. Click off of the image now.

Step 11:

Now select all of the Blue areas one more time by using the Direct Selection Tool. Hold down the Shift Key and click on all of the Blue areas.

Once it's all selected, go to WINDOW MENU > ATTRIBUTES.

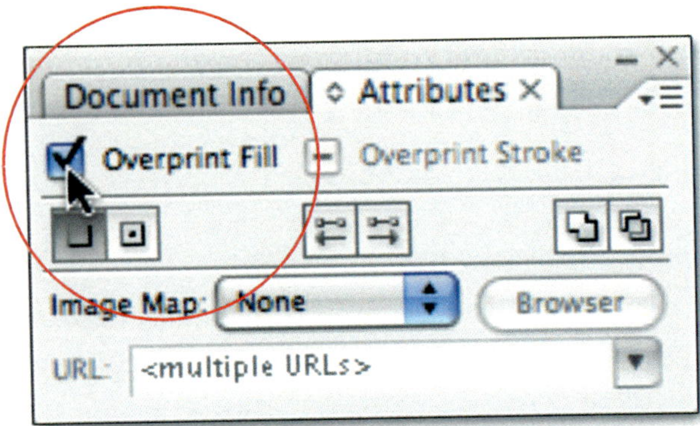

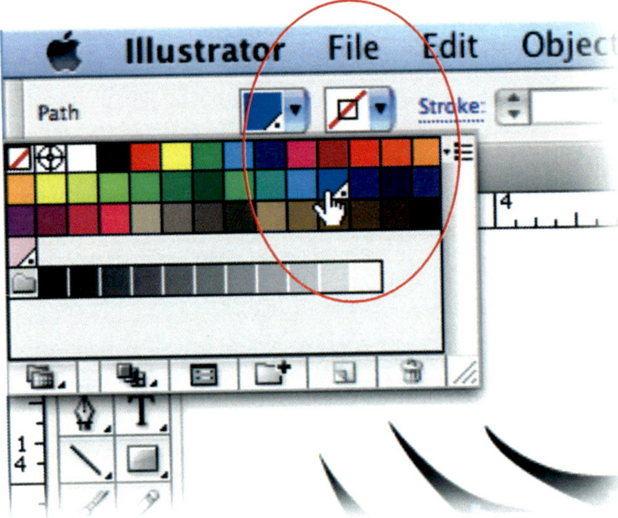

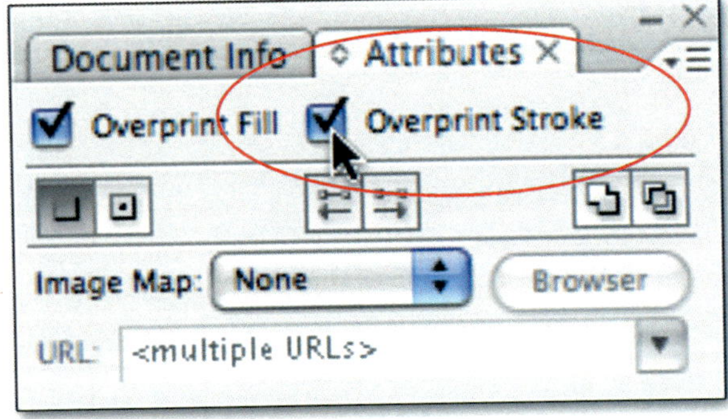

Step 12:

With all of the Blue still selected, in the Attributes window select "Overprint Fill".

Step 13:

Now put a small stroke around all the Blue areas. At the top of the screen, click on the Stroke button and choose the same Blue color.

Step 14:

Now that there is a stroke around everything, go to the Attributes Palette and check the "Overprint Stroke" box.

Our Stroke weight is 1 pt. That means that half of that point is going to overprint over the black of the image. This will stop the shirt color from "peeking" out around the edges.

This is called TRAP Registration. You will learn more about that later in Chapter 7.

Step 15:

If I want his eye to "print" in White ink, I need to colorize it.

Using the Direct Selection Tool, click on the eye. While it's selected, click on the Underbase swatch in the Swatches Palette.

This will colorize the eye "Pink" and it will print White.

Step 16:

Now I need to make the Black in the image a Spot Color.

Double click the Black swatch in the Swatches Palette. Give it a different Name and change the Color Type to Spot Color.

Click OK.

Now the black will print correctly.

Step 17:

Add some text to complete the design. Be sure to colorize the text using the Spot Black just created.

Using Gradients

Using gradients is a quick way to add interest to almost any design. I use it on text a lot. It just seems to give the design that finished touch.

When creating gradients, blend Spot Color to Spot Color. Illustrator does a great job of this.

When separations are printed printing, they will be printed as halftone screens. I recommend 45 or 50 lpi at a 61° angle for all colors.

Lets get started!

USING GRADIENTS

Step 1: Illustrator CS3 - CS5

This image was put together and colored like the last lesson, only this one will not have an Underbase since it is a white shirt only.

The text was converted to artwork by going to the TYPE MENU > CREATE OUTLINES.

Step 2:

Click on the Selection Tool in the upper left of the Tool Box.

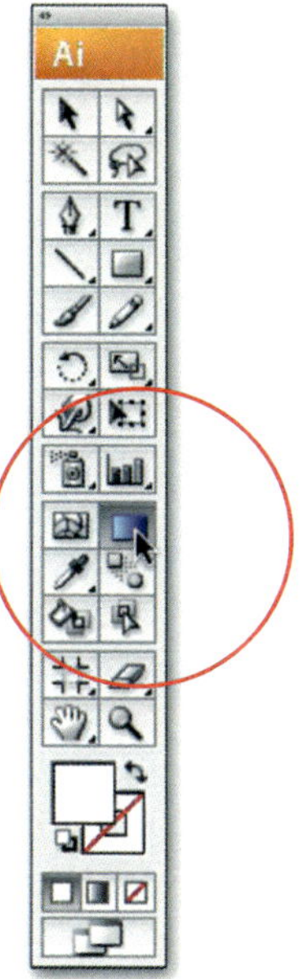

Step 3:

Click on the word Birdhouse to select it.

Step 4:

Open the Swatches Palette. Go to WINDOW MENU > SWATCHES to bring it up.

Step 5:

Double click on the Gradient Tool in the Tool Box.

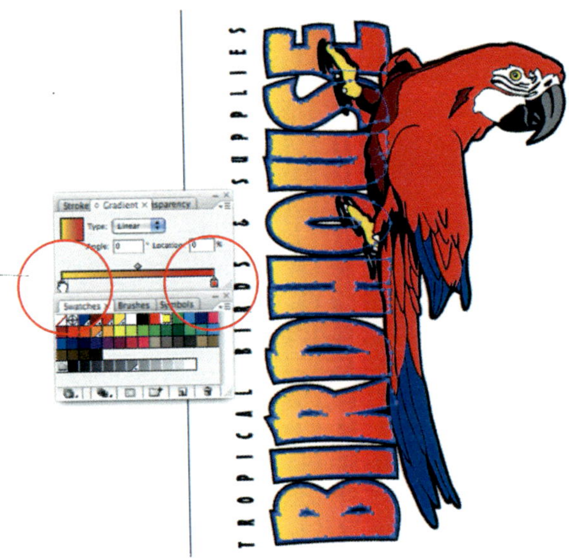

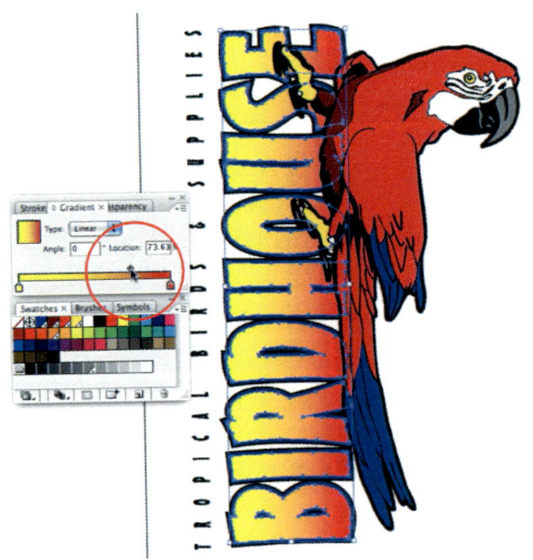

Step 6:

In the Gradient Window, select the "Type" of gradient to use. In this case I chose Linear.

Step 7:

Drag and drop the square of the color chosen on top of the little "houses" in the gradient slider.

Step 8:

The look of the gradient can be controlled by moving the small diamond on the gradient slider.

Slide it each way to see how it adjusts the blend.

Putting Type on a Path

One really simple thing to do with your type when creating T-shirt art is to wrap the type around your image.
I'll start with a simple piece of clip art and put some type above and below the image.

I will be putting the type on the top and bottom of a circle.

Here's how!

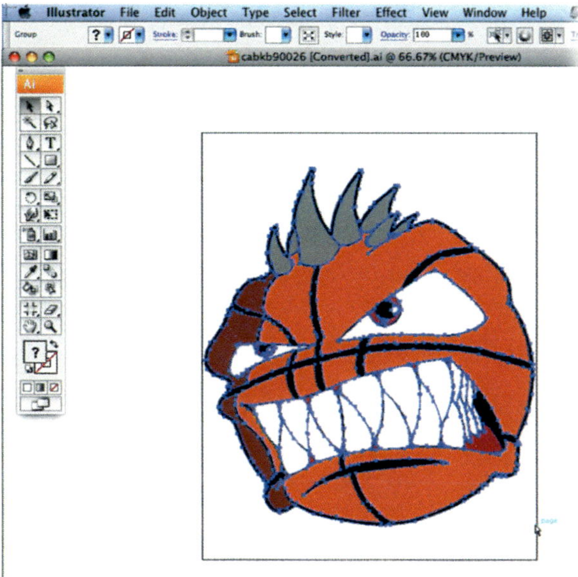

PUTTING TYPE ON A PATH

Step 1: Illustrator CS3 - CS5
Open the T-shirt Template by going to FILE MENU > NEW FROM TEMPLATE.

In the New From Template window choose the T-shirt Template and click New.

If you don't have a T-shirt template yet, I'll show you how to make one in Chapter 7.

Step 2:
You should now have your template opened on the screen. Now go to FILE MENU > OPEN and find the clip art image to use.

Drag select the entire image using the Black Arrow Selection Tool.

Go to the EDIT MENU > COPY.

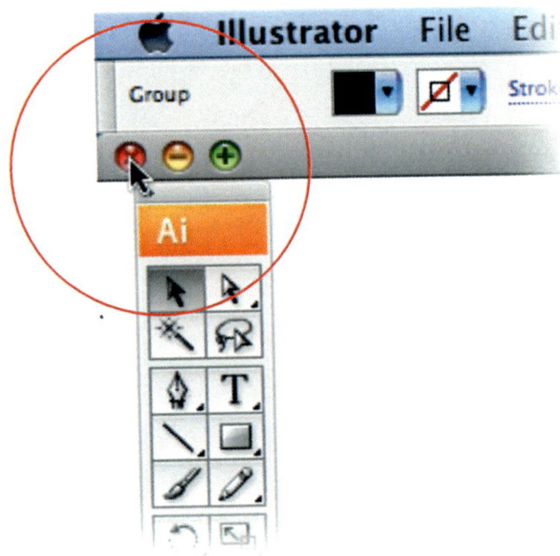

Step 3:

Close this window by "X-ing" out of it.

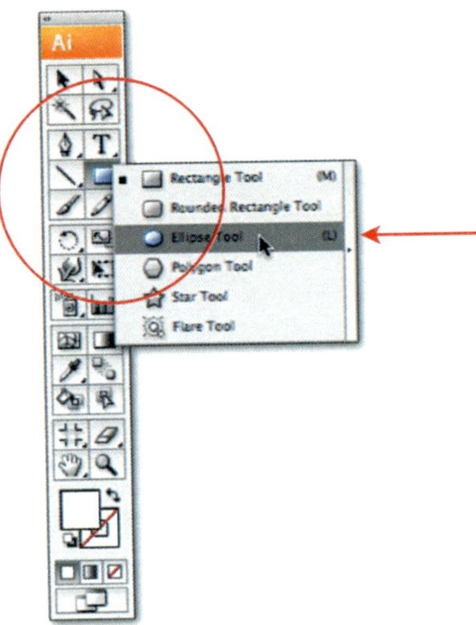

Step 4:

Go to EDIT MENU > PASTE. Now the image is in the template.

Select the Ellipse Tool by clicking and holding down the Rectangle Tool.

Step 5:

With the Ellipse Tool, drag select a circle by holding down the Shift Key to constrain it. Make the circle slightly larger than your image.

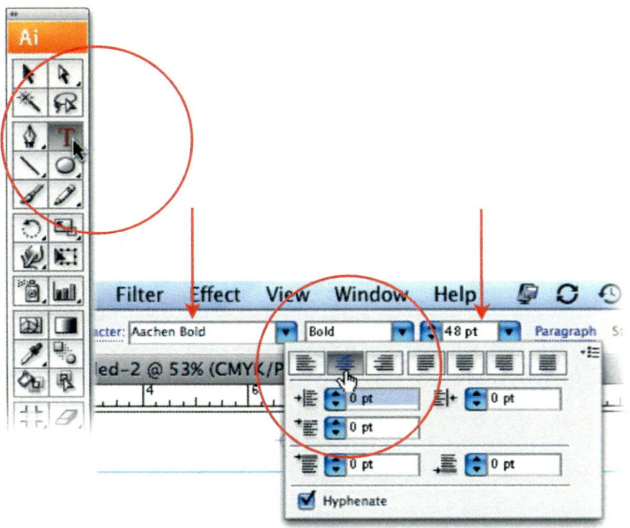

Step 6:

Select the Type Tool.

At the top of the screen, choose a font. Select the size of the font and click on the word "Paragraph" to bring up the Paragraph window.

Choose Align Center for your type.

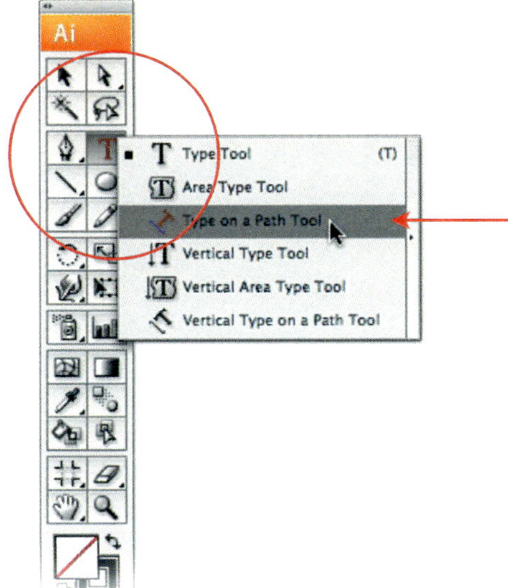

Step 7:

Now click and hold down the Type Tool, choose the Type on a Path Tool.

Step 8:

Click on the top of your circle. You will see a blinking insertion point at the bottom of the shape. This is OK. Simply type what you want.

This does this because the Align Center is chosen. Clicking puts a starting point. Since it's a closed path, Illustrator puts an ending point right next to it. Since we have Align Center chosen, the text goes in the middle.

No problem, I'll show you how to fix it next.

Step 9:

Click off of the text and select the Black Arrow Selection Tool. Grab the small blue center line and drag the type around to the top.

Step 10:

Your text should be at the top of the circle now.

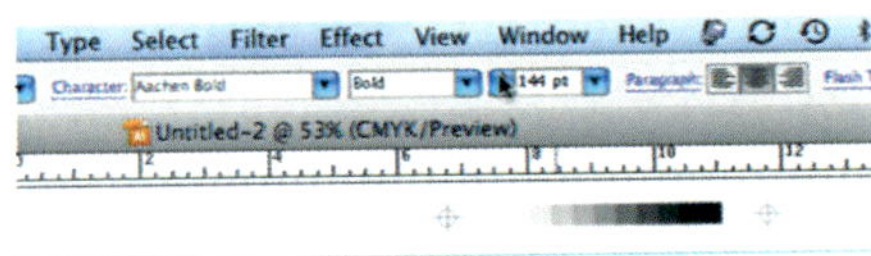

Step 11:

Use the same Type on a Path Tool and select the type.

I made mine my type much larger by changing it's size at the top of the screen.

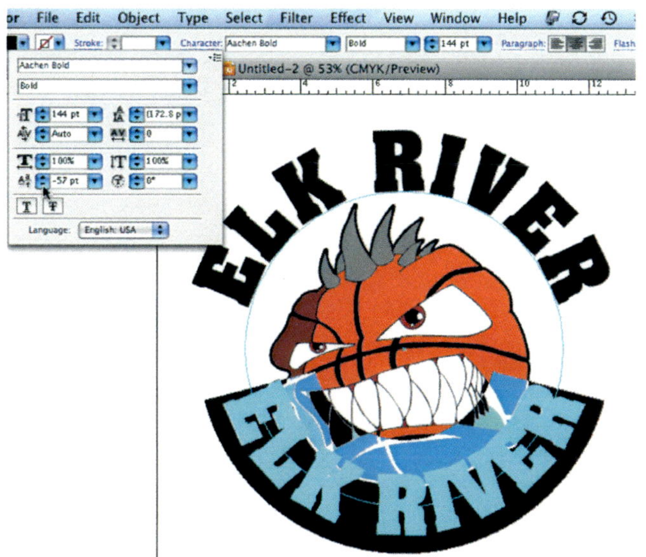

Step 12:

Using the Selection Tool. Drag select both the text and the circle.

Go to EDIT MENU > COPY.

EDIT MENU > PASTE IN FRONT.

Step 13:

Using the Type on a Path Tool, select the text. Drag the text around and down. While still holding the text, push up slightly. This will put the text on the inside of the line like you see here.

Step 14:

With the type tool, select the text.

Click on the Character word at the top of your screen to bring up the Character window.

Put a negative number in the Baseline Shift box, or just keep clicking the small down arrow. This will move the baseline of the type. Keep doing this until the text is pushed all the way out and lines up with the top row.

Change the words to whatever you like. I chose BASKETBALL.

Colorize the text anyway you choose.

Multiple Outline Effect

One of the most popular type treatments in T-shirt art today is the Multiple Outline Effect. It has been around for decades and is used in the sign and graphic industries as well.

This is a great way to utilize team colors and add interest to any design.

Printing out separations can get a little confusing; therefore, starting off with "a less is more" approach is best until you get the hang of it.

It's really easy to do. Here's how!

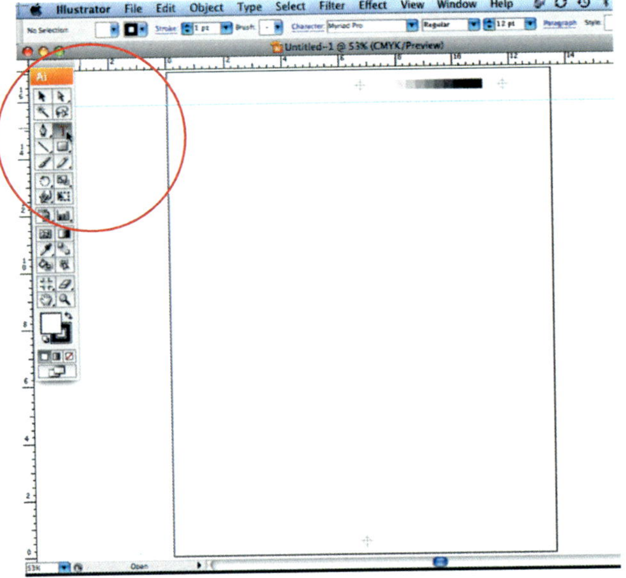

Step 1: Illustrator CS3 - CS5

Open Illustrator.

Go to FILE MENU > NEW FROM TEMPLATE.

Choose the T-Shirt template, click New.

If you don't have a Template made yet, I'll show how to create your own in Chapter 7. Mine can be found on the CD.

Step 2:

You should now have an empty Template.

Select the Type Tool in the Tool Box.

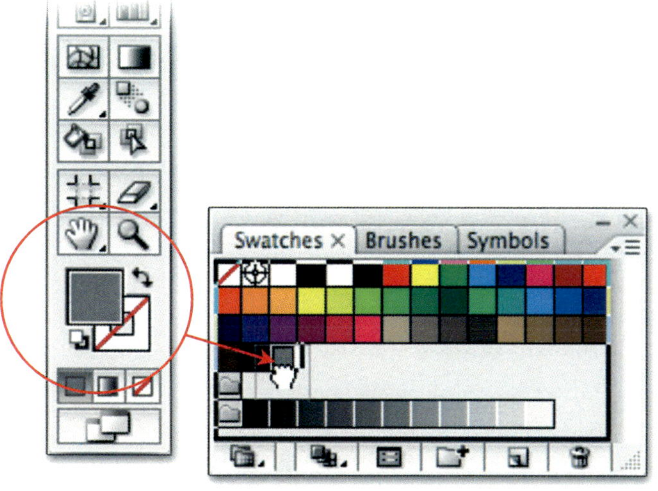

MULTIPLE OUTLINE EFFECT continued

Step 3:

At the top of your screen, choose a font, font size, and the color.

Click on the page and type your text.

Step 4:

Since the school's colors are Red, Gray and Black, I'm going to colorize the type with gray.

Open the Color Tab by clicking on the Color button to the right of your screen, or go to WINDOW MENU > COLOR.

In the Color Window, make the Black 50% color and the other colors 0%.

Step 5:

Open the Swatches Palette. WINDOW > SWATCHES.

Click and drag the gray swatch from your Foreground Color box to your Swatches Palette.

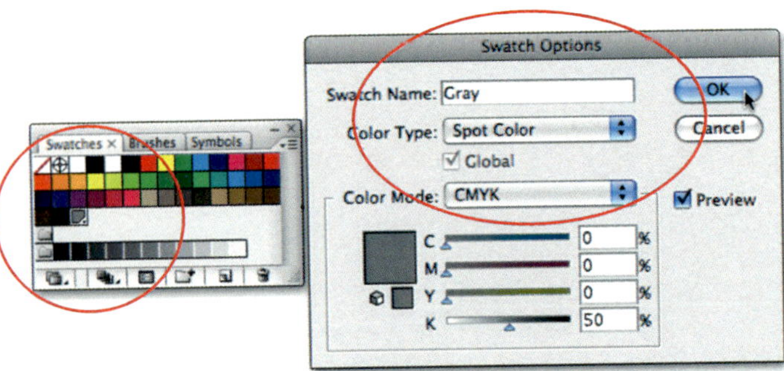

Step 6:

Double click the Gray Swatch to open the Swatch Options window.

Give it a Name.

Change the Color Type to Spot Color.

Click OK.

The swatch should have changed. It should now have a white triangle in the lower right corner that has a black dot in the middle.

This is the icon for a Spot Color. If screen printing, you should almost always be using this type of color.

Step 7:

Double click a Red Swatch and make it a Spot Color. Make a Spot Color Black as well. Now all three colors will be Spot Colors.

They can be identified as Spot Colors by the small White triangle with the Black Dot in the middle.

Step 8:

Select the type. At the top of the screen, colorize with gray. Stroke it with Black.

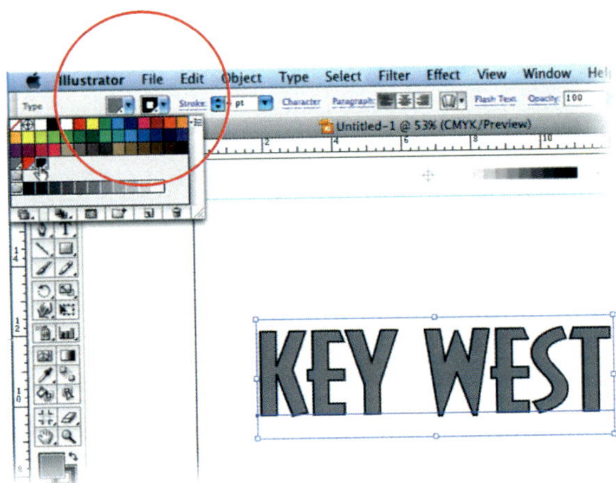

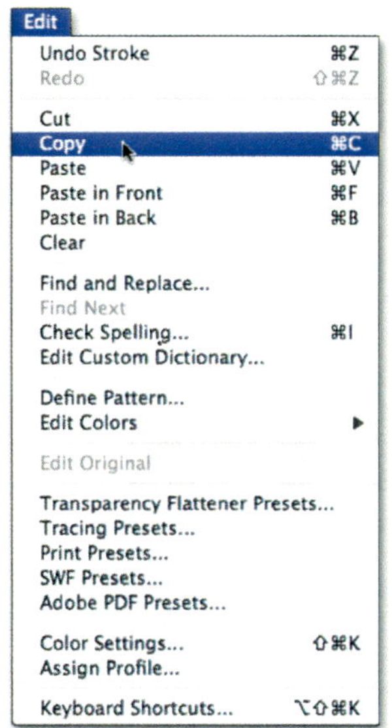
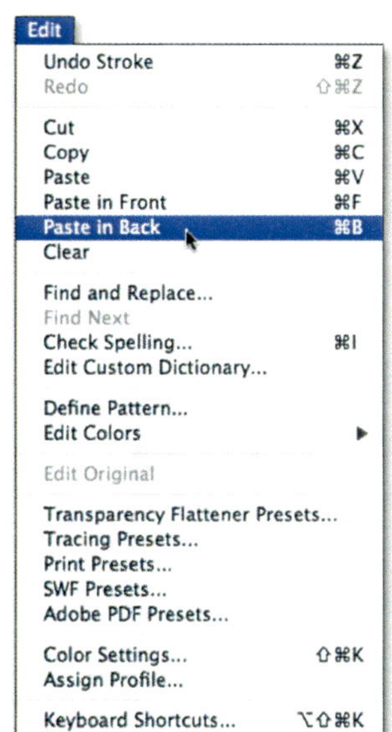

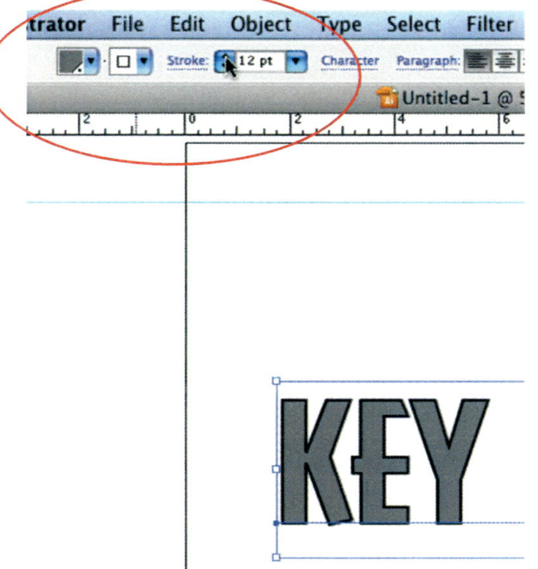

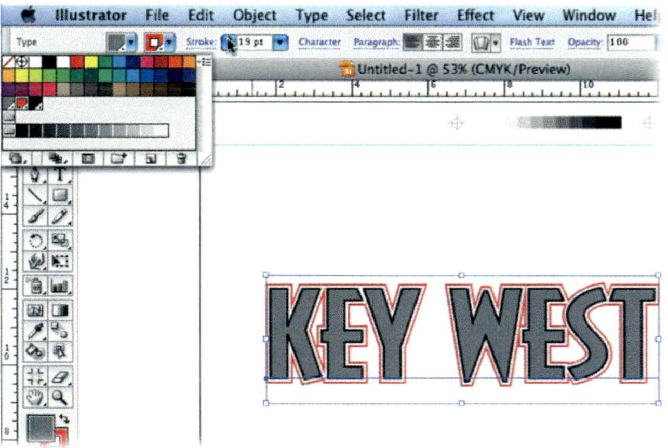

Step 9:

With the type still selected, go to EDIT MENU > COPY.

Then, EDIT > PASTE IN BACK.

Don't click off of the text yet.

Step 10:

With the text still selected, change the color of the Stroke and enlarge the size of the Stroke.

You won't see a change, because I chose White. But, you will see the next one.

Step 11:

Since I didn't click off of the type, it's still selected.

Go to EDIT MENU > COPY.

Then, EDIT > PASTE IN BACK again.

This time I changed the Stroke Color to Red and enlarged the Stroke weight to 19 points. Now the White outline can be seen.

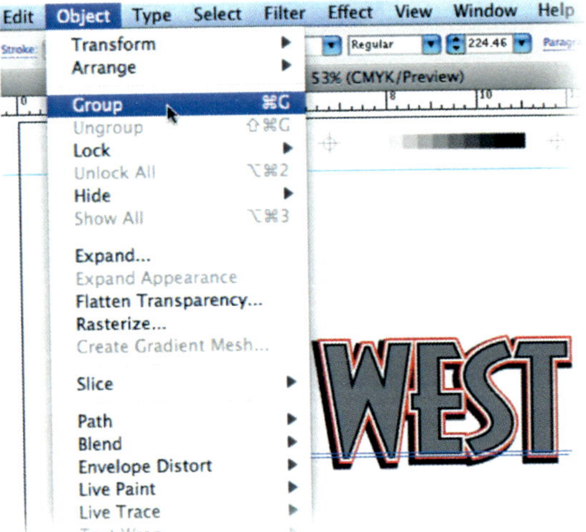

MULTIPLE OUTLINE EFFECT continued

Step 12:

I repeated the steps. While the type is still selected, go to the EDIT MENU > COPY. Then, EDIT MENU > PASTE IN BACK.

I changed the Fill color to Black and the Stroke color to Black.

With the text still selected, use the arrow keys on the keyboard to move the text in, back down, and to the left. This gives the effect of a solid drop shadow.

Step 13:

Drag select everything.

Step 14:

Go to OBJECT MENU > GROUP. This groups everything as one element, in order to be able to move things around much easier without fear of ruining the look.

I repeated the same steps for the word "Conchs", and finished the design by adding a clip art baseball.

All of the elements, both words and the baseball, are colored with three Spot Colors.

Recreating Existing Artwork

This will no doubt be one of the most important lessons learned. This will happen in your day to day business, and believe me, it will happen a lot!

A customer will come in with a business card and ask you to create a T-Shirt from it. You will have to scan the card in *(That lesson is in Chapter 6)* and recreate the logo.

Once you know how to do this, you can recreate almost anything this way.

From this

To this finished design.

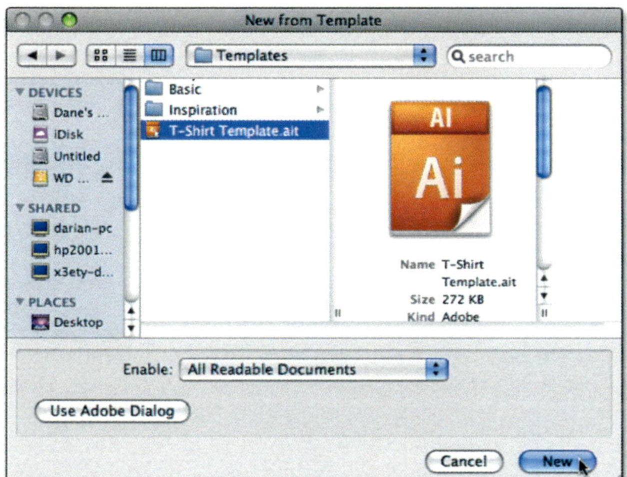

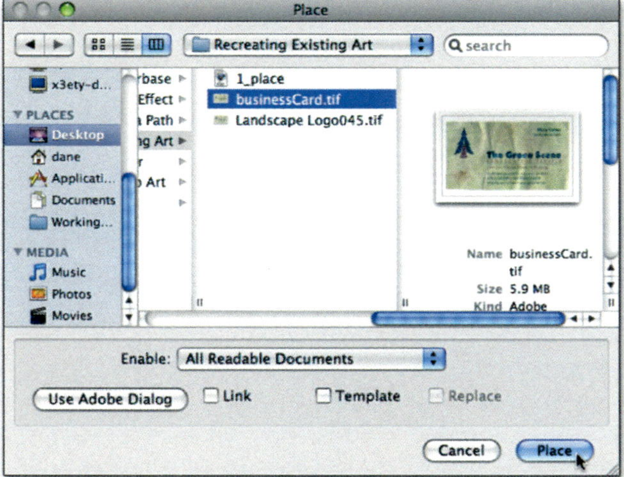

RECREATING EXISTING ARTWORK

Step 1: Illustrator CS3 - CS5
This lesson starts by using a scan of the business card. That lesson can be found in Chapter 6.

Open Illustrator, go to FILE MENU > NEW FROM TEMPLATE to get a starting Template.

Click New.

Step 2:
A template should now be open on your screen.

Go to the FILE MENU > PLACE. Find the scan of the business card that needs to be traced.

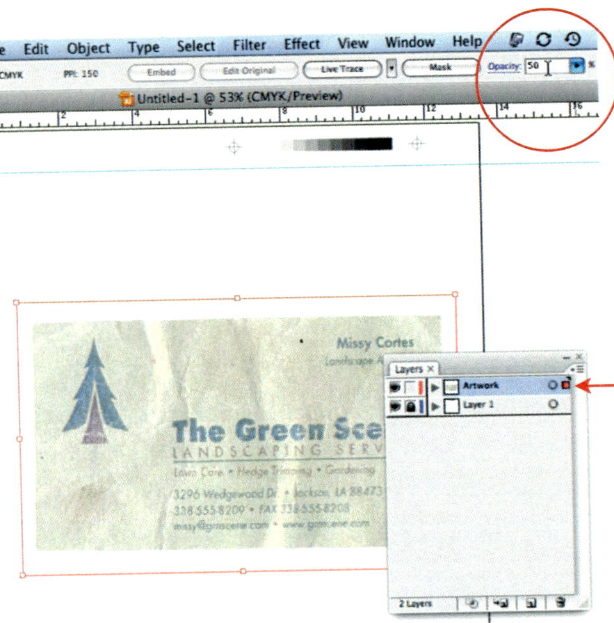

Step 3:

With the Layers Palette open, WINDOW MENU >LAYERS, select the Artwork Layer by clicking on it once.

At the top of the screen, change the Opacity to 50%. This reduces the opacity of that Layer.

We do this is in order to see the new lines as they are drawn. The layer must be Locked to insure that nothing accidently moves while tracing.

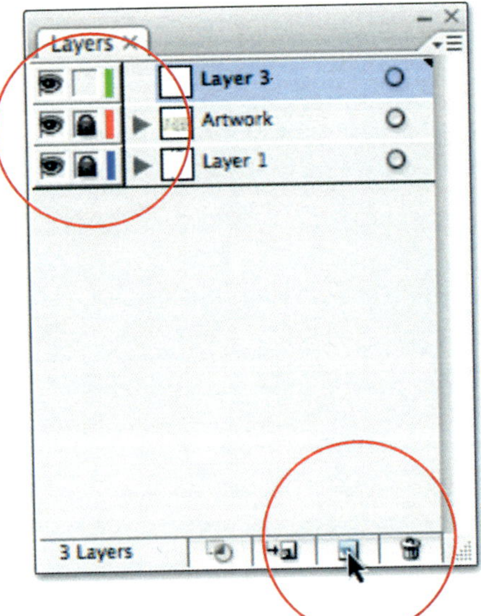

Step 4:

In the Layers Palette, click to lock the Artwork Layer.

Click on the Create New Layer icon at the bottom of the Layers Palette. This Layer will contain the artwork created.

Step 5:

Since this art is two colors, Green and Brown, we need to create two Spot Colors. Open the Swatches Palette. If it's not already open, go to the WINDOW MENU > SWATCHES.

Double click a Dark Green Swatch. In the Swatch Options window, give it a Name and change the Color Type to Spot Color.

Do the same for the Brown.

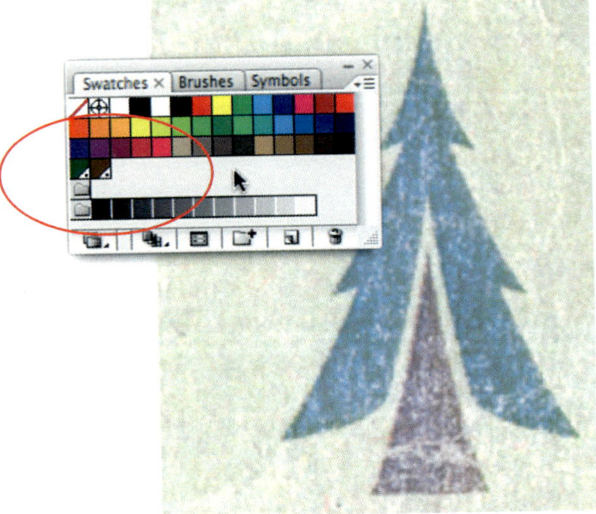

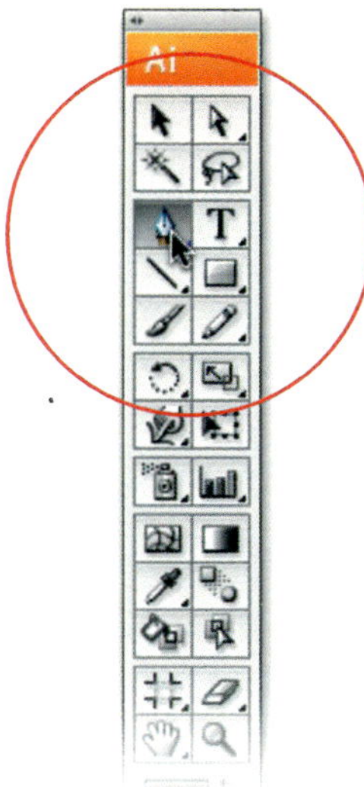

RECREATING EXISTING ARTWORK continued

Step 6:

Select the Pen Tool from the Tool Box.

Step 7:

Be sure to set the Fill Color to None and the Stroke Color to Dark Green.

Step 8:

Find a good starting point in the image and click to apply the first anchor point.

Click a second point. While still holding down the mouse, move the bezier handles and "Shape" the line to follow the logo.

Once you have it, hold down the Option / Alt key and click in the last anchor point to remove the bezier handle in order to be able to change directions as anchor points are added.

Step 9:

Keep adding points and changing directions by using the Option / Alt key and clicking on the last point.

Step 10:

Once the shape is complete, click on the Fill Box in the Tool Box and click on the Dark Green color swatch in the Swatches Palette.

Step 11:

Repeat these steps for the Brown Trunk.

Step 12:

Now we need to set the type. Sometimes you might know the font that was used. If you do, just reset the text. If not, you might be able to trace it as we just did with the logo.

This looks to be Futura Bold, so I'll set it.

Select the Type Tool.

Step 13:

Choose the font, and font size. Start typing. Use the Character Palette at the top of the screen to fine tune the text.

You can change the kerning, tracking, size etc. all from this palette.

Repeat the steps for the second line of text.

It appears as if there was a space added in between each letter.

Step 14:

The bottom row of type was set slightly different from the business card. I thought it would look better this way on a T-shirt. Be sure to get this kind of approval from the customer before printing.

I rearranged the image, drag selected the entire design, and grouped everything together.

Now it is time to print separations.

DISTRESSED OVERLAY EFFECT

This technique will require a scanned image of a distressed piece of paper. I'll show how to do this in detail in Chapter 6, "Creating a Distressed Texture".

This lesson will show how to apply the texture to a design inside of Illustrator. It is super easy to do.

Here's how!

Step 1: Illustrator CS3 - CS5
Open the image you want to distress.

Step 2:
Go to FILE MENU > PLACE.

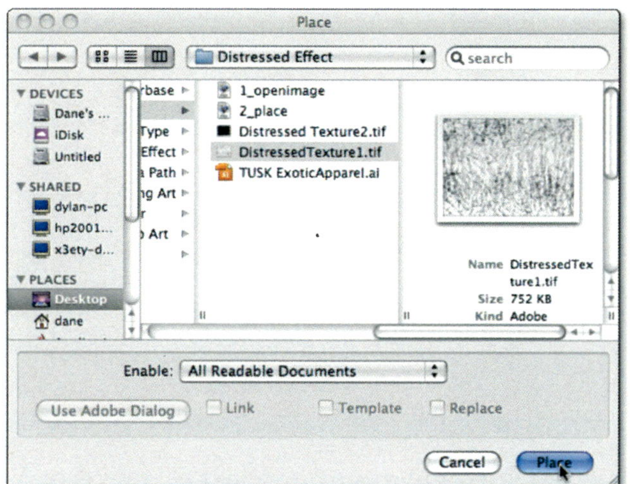

Step 3:
Find the Texture file you want to use, Click Place.

Step 4:
This is the TIF after it has been placed. Notice that Bitmap TIFs are transparent. That is exactly why this technique is so easy to do!

It automatically fills with Black.

It is evident that the file is too small for the image. It needs to be enlarged it in order for it to cover the entire image.

Step 5:
Grab a corner of the TIF file. Drag it out until it covers the entire image.

Step 6:

With the TIF still selected. Go to WINDOW MENU > SWATCHES to bring up the Swatches Palette.

Click on the White swatch in the Swatches Palette. You will see the Texture change colors. White is a non-printing color; therefore, it will knock out all the colors beneath it.

Step 7:

You can control the interaction between the image and the TIF by changing the TIF's size and position.

I've zoomed out, so you can see how the texture actually lays over the image. The blue box is the size of the TIF.

Step 8:

This image shows an extreme example of distressing. I've made the TIF much smaller and duplicated it to the right. Now I have two TIF's placed over the image. It is easy to see how much distressed the effect is this way.

Enhancing Your Type

In this lesson I'll show a simple way to add interest to your type. We'll create texture using irregular shapes, lines, and squiggles at different sizes and colors.

For this design, I will be adding Vector text to a Raster Image. The Raster image is a full color TIF file for Digital Printing. That is why I can have as many colors as I want!

This is one of my favorite kinds of images!

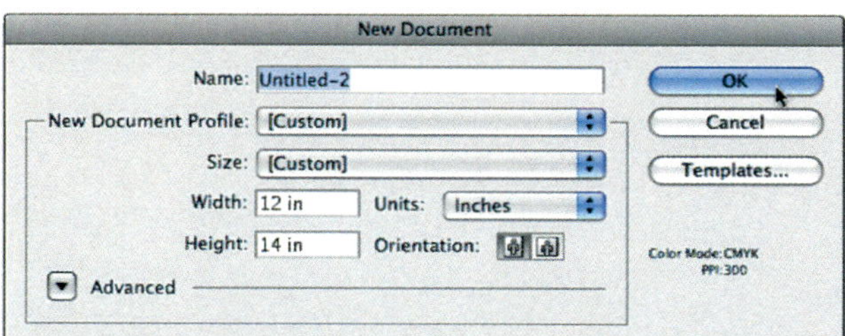

ENHANCING YOUR TYPE

Step 1: Illustrator CS3 - CS5
This job will be a digital print; therefore, we don't need to use our screen printing template.

I created and document and made the size 12" x 14".

Step 2:
Go to FILE MENU > PLACE to place the image.

Find the image you want to Place. This one is one of our Stock Art designs, and it is on a transparent layer.

Remember to ALWAYS use transparent backgrounds!

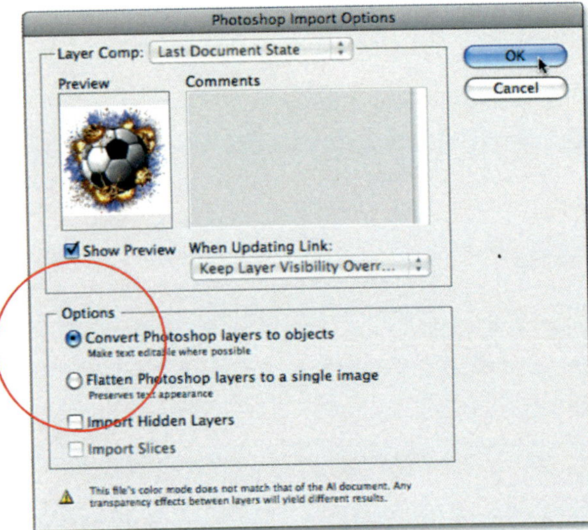

Step 3:
CS5- This step does not apply.

In the Photoshop Import Options box that comes up, choose "Convert Photoshop Layers to Objects".

We don't want to Flatten the artwork.

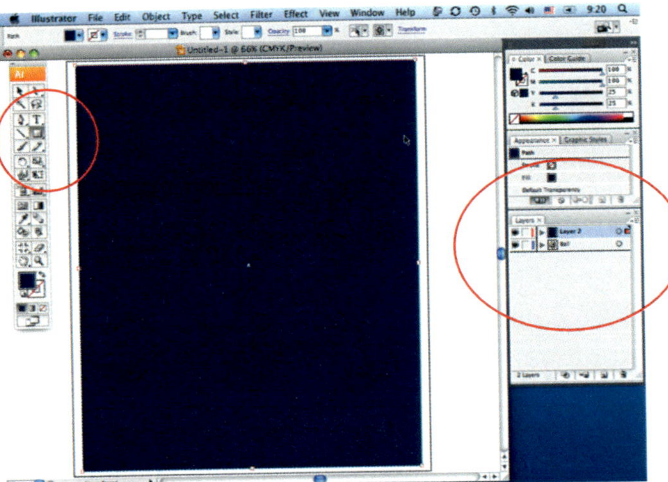

Step 4:
If your Layers Palette is not visible, go to WINDOW MENU > LAYERS to bring it up.

Double click Layer 1 to Rename it.

Click on the Create New Layer icon at the bottom of the Layers Palette. With the Layer 2 selected, draw a box for the shirt color. In this case, I'm going to use a Dark Blue.

Step 5:
Go to the Layers Palette, grab the Layer 2, and drag it below the "Ball" layer.

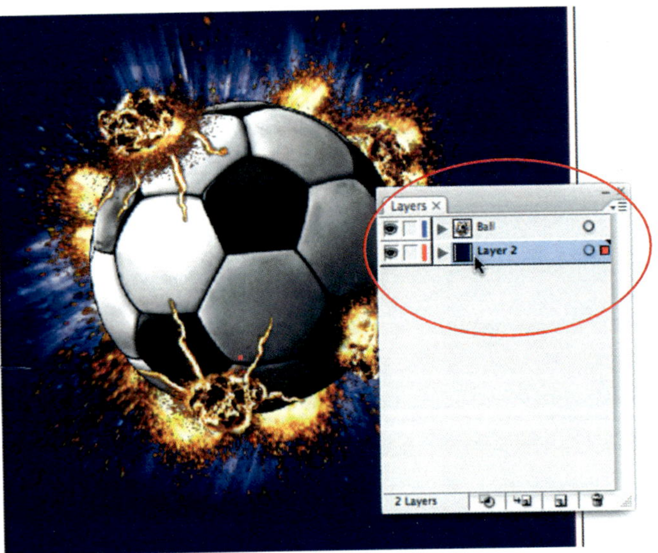

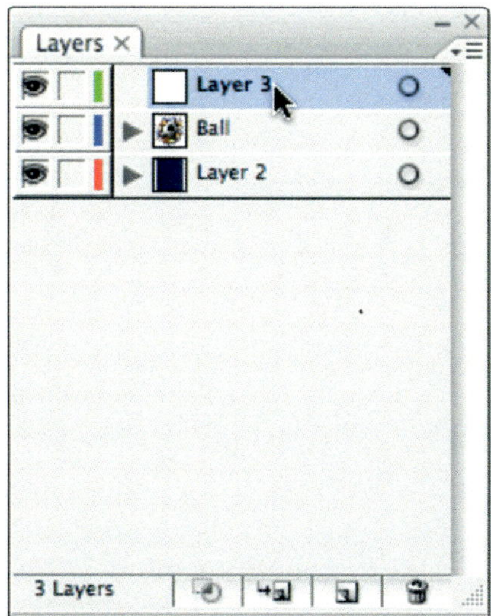

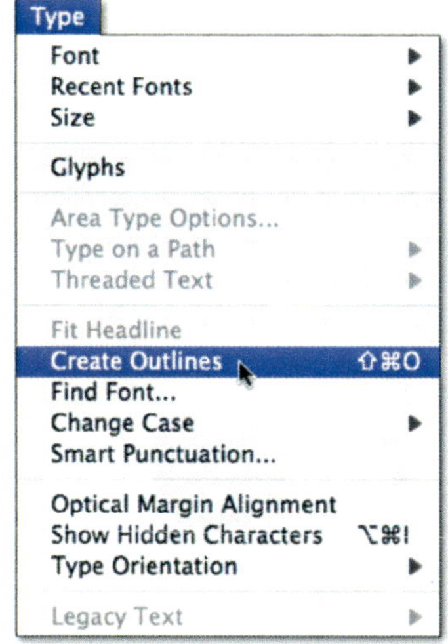

Step 6:

Create a New Layer by clicking on the New Layer icon. Drag this layer to the top of the list.

Step 7:

Select the Type Tool. Select your font and font size, and set your text.

Select the word and mouse over a corner. Once you see the small "bent" arrows, rotate the image a little.

Step 8:

With the word still selected, go to the TYPE MENU > CREATE OUTLINES.

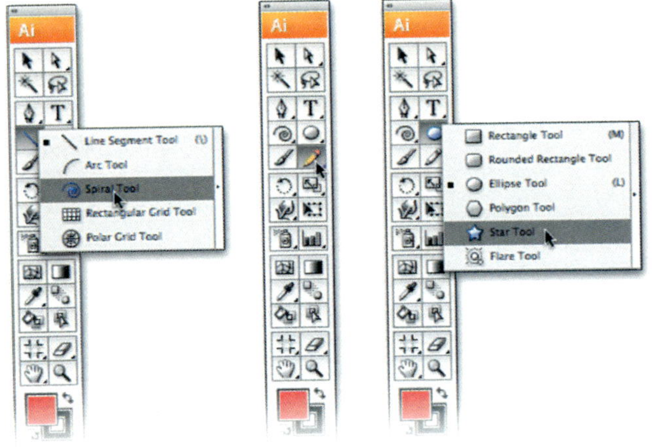

ENHANCING YOUR TYPE continued

Step 9:

Select the type. Go to EDIT MENU > COPY, then EDIT MENU > PASTE IN BACK.

While it's still selected, change the color of the fill and the stroke. Enlarge the size of the Stroke.

Step 10:

Repeat the same steps. Change to Yellow and add to the Stroke.

Step 11:

Scroll down in the window a bit to see the empty space beneath the page.

We're going to make a texture using all sorts of shapes, lines and squiggles. After all, a GOAL is a cause for celebration!

Use whatever tools you want to draw the shapes.

These are some of the Tools that I used for this one.

Step 12:

Draw shapes of various sizes and colors. Use object tools, pencil, and lines tools. Use anything you can imagine..

On my shapes I chose only Fill's, no strokes.

On my lines I chose only Strokes, no fills.

Step 13:

Drag select over all of the shapes and group them all together. Go to the OBJECT MENU > GROUP.

Now grab the word and move down over the texture. Hold down the Option / Alt key to duplicate it.

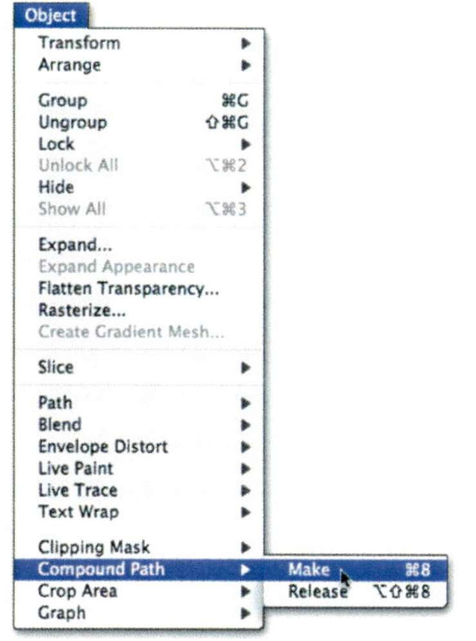

Step 14:

With the word GOAL still selected, go to the OBJECT MENU > COMPOUND PATH > MAKE.

This will make the word fill with none and stroke with none. While it's still selected, hold the Shift Key and click on the texture shapes to select both.

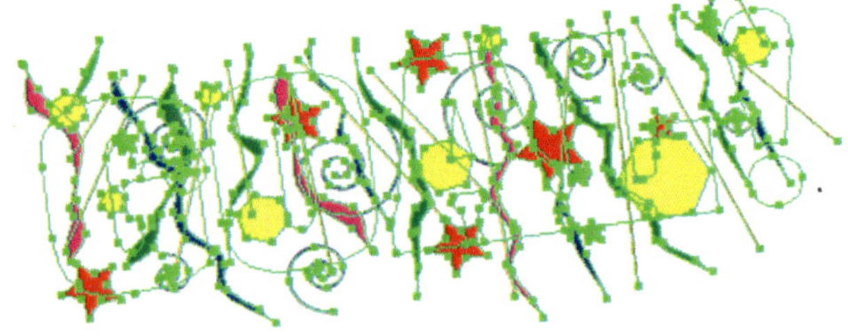

Step 15:

It should look like a jumbled mess similar to this one.

If you look closely, the word GOAL is still visible because it's still selected.

Step 16:

While everything is still selected. Go to the OBJECT MENU > CLIPPING MASK > MAKE.

Step 17:

Keep everything selected, drag the word back up on top of the word in the image.

Now it's ready to print!

RASTER ARTWORK

Raster Artwork

Vector

Raster (Bitmap)

Raster Artwork is created using pixels. It is used for photographic type of work. The examples above show a vector version and a raster version. Notice the raster version is a more realistic photographic painting. My studio made a name for itself with this type of work. We specialize in full color raster designs.

Raster art can be used for all types of printing, especially digital printing, direct to garment digital, dye-sublimation etc. Since those techniques use full color printing, this style of artwork fits perfectly. Screen printing these designs is also an option; however, it becomes necessary to create separations.

In any of Great Dane Graphics' Stock Art, the separations are already created in the channels palette of the Photoshop file.

Starting a Raster Design

When thinking of raster artwork, immediately think of Photoshop or Corel Painter. These are the graphics programs I use in my studio to create raster art. The images we create are full color paintings like the Fire Mask image above. If you are interested in creating artwork like this, you too should be using one of the two programs mentioned.

Artwork like this is created with a combination of both old school and new school techniques. By old school, I mean drawing the idea on tracing paper. This is the way artwork has been created forever. Simply sketch the idea, scan it into the computer, set up the file with layers, and begin to paint. This requires going back and forth from Photoshop to Painter pretty regularly.

If a design is to be printed on a t-shirt, either screen or digital printing will work. It makes no difference, I setup the file making sure the size of my file is set to the

actual print size. If a print needs to be 12" wide on a shirt, I start with a file at 12"w x 12"h and a resolution of 150 dpi. This is all the resolution needed to achieve quality prints however it is printed.

A Vector program will not produce the same look. Raster art uses continuous tone, pixel based imagery.

Although the work we create is usually full color, it is possible to also create artwork as a grayscale image with no color. It is possible to print a converted photograph or create a painting using different shades of gray either way. If screen printing, separations are still needed.

When creating raster artwork I like to work in RGB mode. This is a color space that contains the most color. It contains many more colors than CMYK. It is generated on screen by using red, green, and blue light.

Whenever an image is converted from RGB to CMYK, there will be a loss of color. This is simply because CMYK mode can't hold those extra colors. The best workflow is to begin with an RGB file. If a printer requires a conversion to CMYK, then there is no choice. Keep in mind, some RIP software that drives some direct to garment printers will do a better job if it is sent to the RIP as an RGB file. On the same note, some RIP software will only recognize CMYK files. Therefore, when finished with the artwork, be sure to know what the printing situation requires.

If creating a raster image that will be printed on a mouse pad, mug, or some other product using dye-sublimation, it is still necessary to have the file setup at actual size. I have found that 150 dpi will work well for these products; however, you may want to use 200 to 300 dpi. The fine detail will look slightly crisper.

Setting Up a Raster File

When setting up a Raster artwork file, the most important thing to do is be sure to have the proper resolution. Because these files are built with pixels, if the resolution is not correct, the printed piece may look jagged and pixelated. Also important is to be sure the artwork is on a transparent layer.

If printing a T-Shirt, the resolution should be from 150 ppi to 200 ppi. If printing a larger format poster, banner, or Dye-Sublimation piece use 300 ppi.

It's easy to do. In fact, it should be the first thing you do.

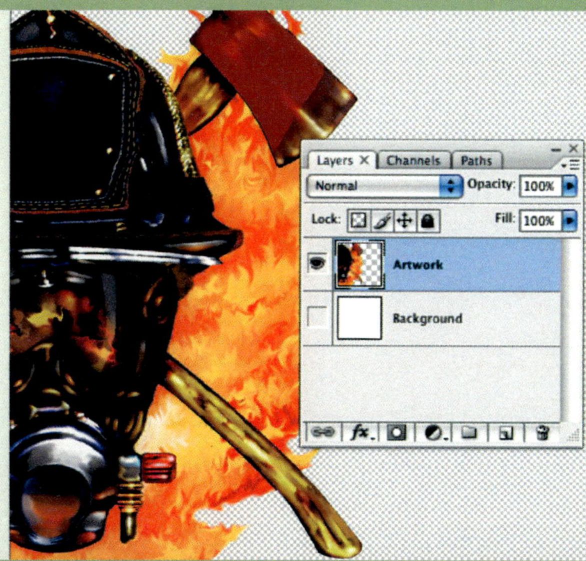

SETTING UP A RASTER FILE

Step 1: Photoshop CS3 - CS5
Go to FILE > NEW.

In the New dialog box, set the size of the image to be printed. In this case, I chose 12" x 14". Set the resolution to 150 ppi (if it's a T-Shirt). Make sure the Color Mode is set to RGB with a transparent background.

Click OK.

If starting from scratch, it's done. If setting up a file using a sketch or some other original, follow the steps below.

Step 2:
Open a pencil sketch or file in order to begin working. Be sure Photoshop is set to Window mode. This allows both documents to be seen in their own window. (The scanned sketch window and your New document.)

With the Move Tool selected, click and drag the Layer of the sketch to the New document.

If prompted that it will not move because the layer is locked, simply double click the small preview icon on the sketch layer. This will unlock the layer.

Create a new Layer above the sketch to use for the painting.

Resizing an Image

Let's say you have an image ready for a t-shirt. It is setup at the proper size and resolution, and the design is finished. But, you want to use this same file to create something else, perhaps a mug.

That's what I'll do here.

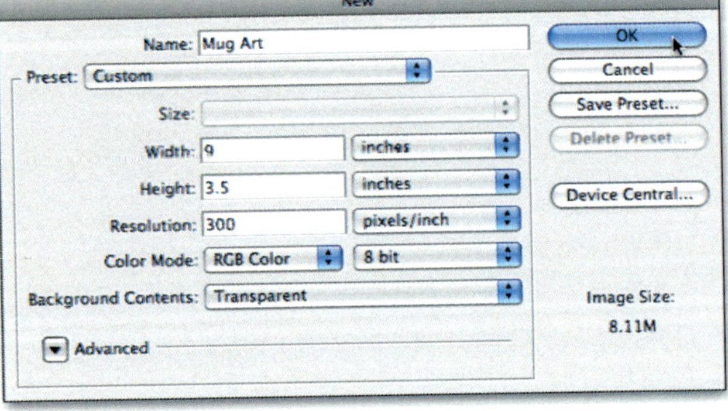

Step 1: Photoshop CS3 - CS5

I'll be going from a T-Shirt document to a Mug document in this lesson.

Open your existing artwork.

The one I have here is designed for a t-shirt. The size, resolution, and color mode are shown.

Step 2:

Go to FILE MENU > NEW.

In the New dialog box, set the size for the mug. In this case, I set the Width to 9 inches, the Height to 3.5 inches and the resolution to 300 ppi.

Color Mode is set to RGB, and the Background is ALWAYS set to Transparent.

Click OK.

RESIZING AN IMAGE continued

Step 3:

Be sure Photoshop is set to Window mode, in order to see both documents in their own window. (The scanned sketch window and the New document). To do this, drag the "name tab" of one of the windows you have open out to it's own space on your screen.

With the Move Tool and the Artwork Layer selected, click and drag the Artwork Layer to the New document.

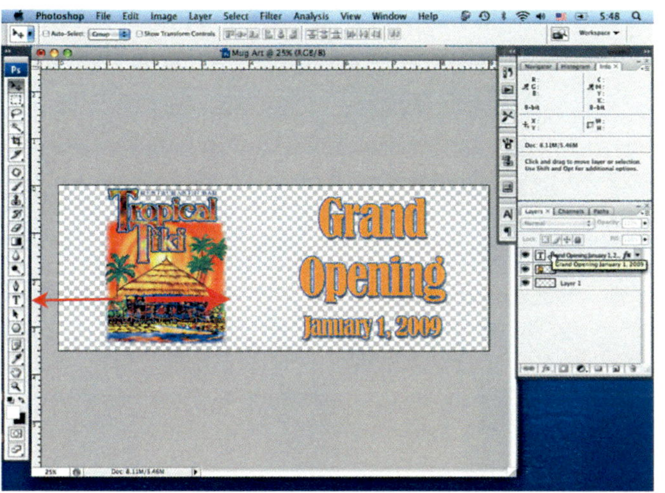

Step 4:

Since the T-Shirt document is much larger than the Mug size, only a portion of the art will be visible.

With the artwork Layer selected, Go to EDIT MENU > FREE TRANSFORM. This shows
a binding box around the rest of the hidden art.

While holding the Shift key to constrain the proportions, click and drag one of the corner anchor points to reduce the size of the art.

Once it is sized properly, Double Click inside the Free Transform box to accept it.

Step 5:

Select the Type Tool in the Tool Box.

Click in the open space to set type. Once printed this entire document will wrap around the mug. The Tropical Tiki artwork is on one side, and the Grand Opening type on the other.

I added a Layer Style to this text. I added a Stroke of 4 pixels, colored blue, and a Drop Shadow.

That's it! The transfer is ready to print.

Working with

Layer Styles were first introduced to Photoshop back in Version 6. Since then, it has been one of my favorite features of Photoshop. There is so much stuff to do with it.

Just look at the headline above. Simply by clicking on one button in the Styles palette, it can change from one of these looks to the next. If applying the Styles to text, it's possible to change the type instantly. It will update "live". For instance, if something is misspelled, simply click and select the letter or word that is misspelled and correct it. The Style effect will update itself to the new text. Layer Styles can be applied to any element; shapes, objects, photos, and text on any layer except the background layer.

Before the layer styles, several steps would be necessary just to give an element a drop shadow. Today, it only takes a matter of seconds, and the artist has much control.

Digital direct-to-garment printers provide many benefits for a print shop. One is the capability to print full color prints almost as easy as going to File > Print. Because of this, Layer Styles are perfect for digital printing. Really cool, colorful, and complex looks can be created very quickly.

If printing digitally, design for digital instead of designing for screen. Most screen printers would prefer printing one or two spot colors in order to make their job as easy as possible. With digital, full color printing is the norm. Skipping the messy screen-making stage is a big plus. However, because they use transparent inks, DTG printers don't provide quite the same rich, vibrant colors produced with screen.

Due to the nature of the technology, (ink being printed through small openings in the print heads), it is easy for one or more of the openings to become clogged which leads to streaking in the print. It is best to avoid plain, large fills or big areas of solid color. Instead, opt to use fill textures, bevels, drop shadows, wood grains and blends to add variety and interest.

In other words, fill textures help inks "jump out" rather than appear flat and lifeless. They also hide imperfections created by the print head. A clogged nozzle can create banding or streaking in a field of solid color.

Adding these textures is quick and easy. It is really just a matter of selecting a texture effect. For example, if working on a team sport's name, it is possible to put a texture or gradation inside of the letters. The resulting variations will keep the letters' insides from looking smooth and flat.

Once a suitable texture has been created, save it as a style, and begin creating a library of textures. It is quick and easy to swap out different textures and effects. This makes it a breeze to try a variety of looks on a particular piece of artwork.

From fur and rust, to metal and diamond plate, textures give artwork tons of effects and looks. So many, in fact, that it's impossible to list or describe them all.

The football texture in this design was created using one of our Great Dane Graphics Layer Styles. Download free styles at our website.

Here is a sample some of the Great Dane Graphics Layer Styles that are available for download. For another good reference web site, visit AdobeStudioExchange.com. This is an Adobe community site. Designers put up their own layer styles to download. Some are free to use, and others will cost only a few dollars. When visiting the site, look for Photoshop > Layer Styles to see some stellar textures created by an army of Photoshop users. Download stock textures. Use photos and artwork as pattern overlays. You may be inspired enough by what you see to create your own original textures.

No matter how textures are created or acquired, they are an ideal way to add interest to designs in no time.

Below: The Layer Style Dialog Box

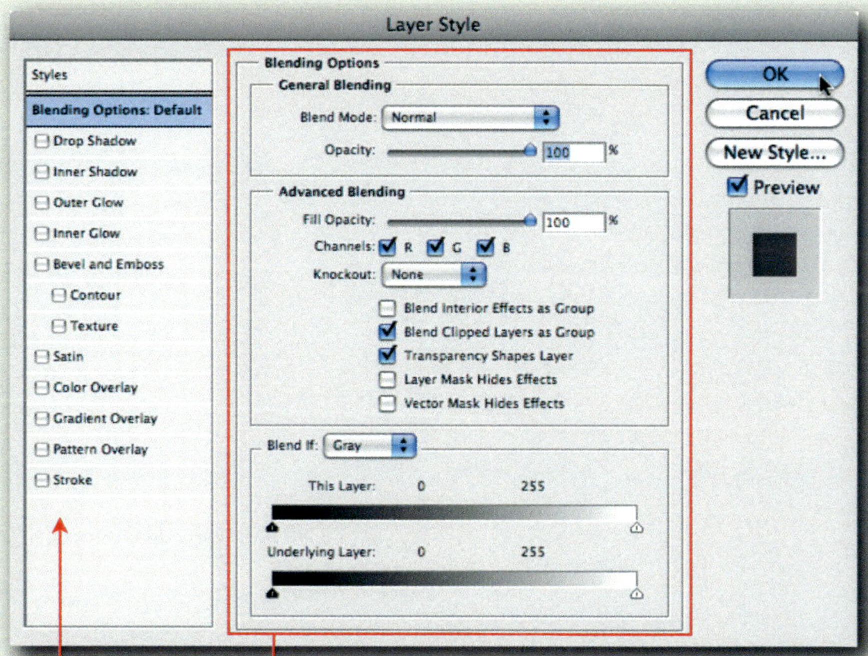

To hide the Layer Styles attribute list, toggle the small triangle.

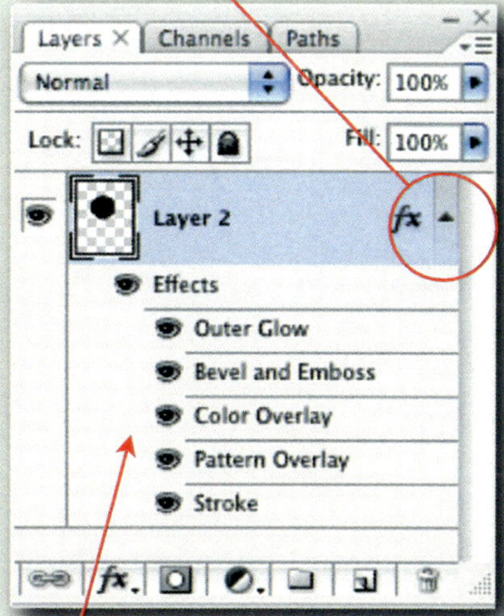

The Options area is where you can change attributes of the Layer Styles. The options will vary depending on the Style used.

Once a Layer Style is applied, you can see what attributes it contains from the Layers palette.

These are the types of Styles you can apply to any layer other than the background.

Adding a Drop Shadow

A drop shadow is probably the most widely used of all the Layer Styles. It is very easy to create. That is what I'll do here.

One thing to remember is that a document with a transparent layer must be used. Photoshop needs some place to add the shadow effect. It can't add the effect to the background layer.

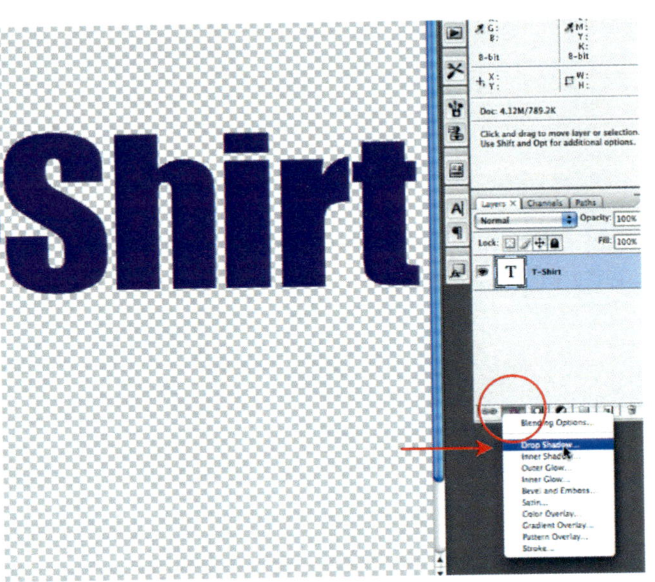

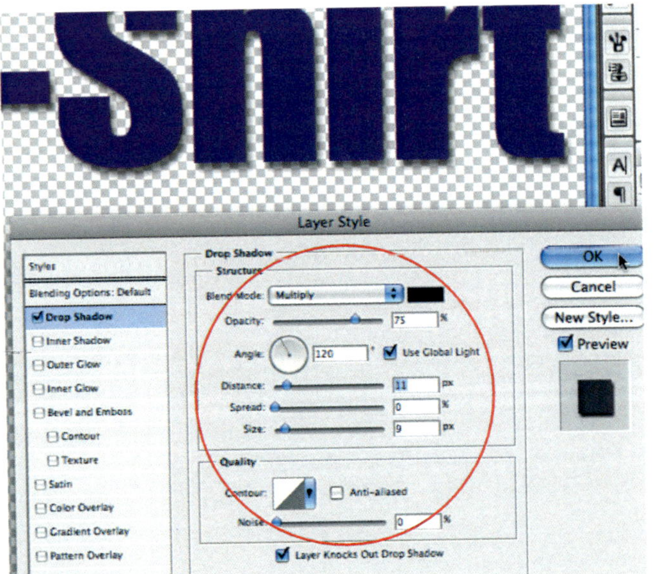

ADDING A DROP SHADOW

Step 1: Photoshop CS3 - CS5
Select the layer for the shadow in the Layers Palette.

Click the Add Layer Styles button at the bottom of the Layers Palette. It's the small "FX" icon second from the left.

Choose Drop Shadow.

Step 2:
In the Layer Styles dialog box, there should be the Drop Shadow options. Adjust the attributes until you find something suitable.

Most times you will want to change the:
Opacity
Distance
Spread
Size

Click OK.

That's it!

Adding Type to a Path

In this lesson I will set some type to follow a path. This technique can be used any time to set type in a non-traditional way.

I will use this image to show a few different lessons. Once I'm finished with all of them, you will have seen the complete workflow to finalize a great design!

Let's get started.

ADDING TYPE TO A PATH

Step 1: Photoshop CS3 - CS5

This particular image will have three words applied to the paths in order for it to fit inside the three banners.

Click on the Paths palette to select it. Now click on the Create New Path icon at the bottom of the palette. Give it the name of the word or words that will be on it.

In this case, Anoka.

Step 2:

Click on the Pen Tool in the Tool Box.

Draw a path to follow along the bottom of the banner. Be sure to stay just a little above the bottom of the shape.

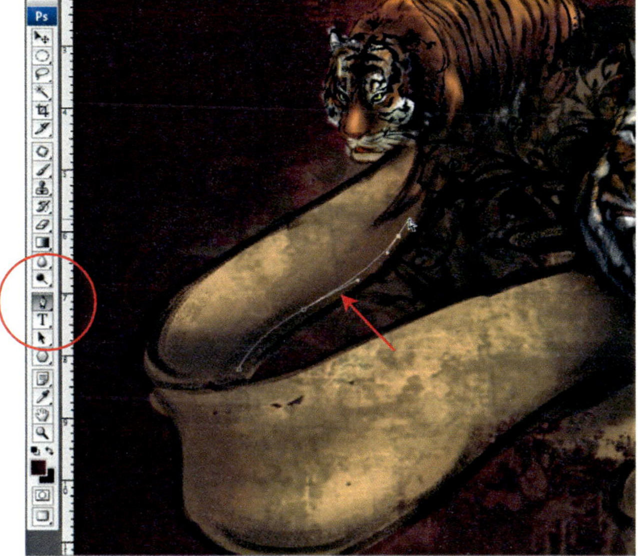

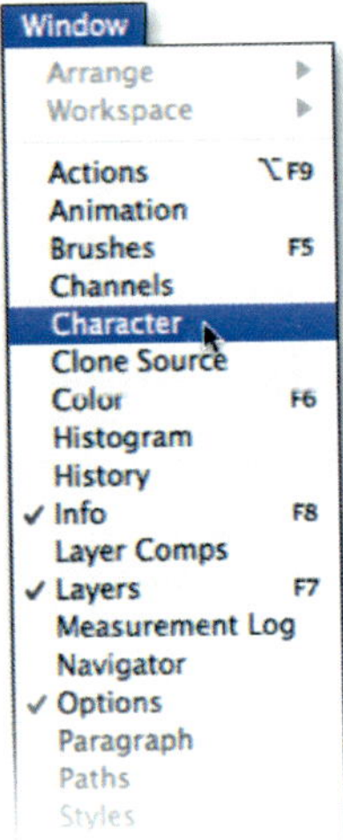

ADDING TYPE TO A PATH continued

Step 3:

Click on the Layers Palette to select it.

Click on the Type Tool in the Tool Box.

Select the Align Left button in the Options bar at the top of the screen.

Now move the mouse over the path. The icon will change when it is in place. When it does, click to set the starting point of the type.

Type the text you want.

Step 4:

It may be necessary to adjust some Spacing / Kerning between some letters.

In this case it is necessary to squeeze the "A" and "N" closer together.

Step 5:

Now, bring up the Character Palette. Go to WINDOW MENU > CHARACTER.

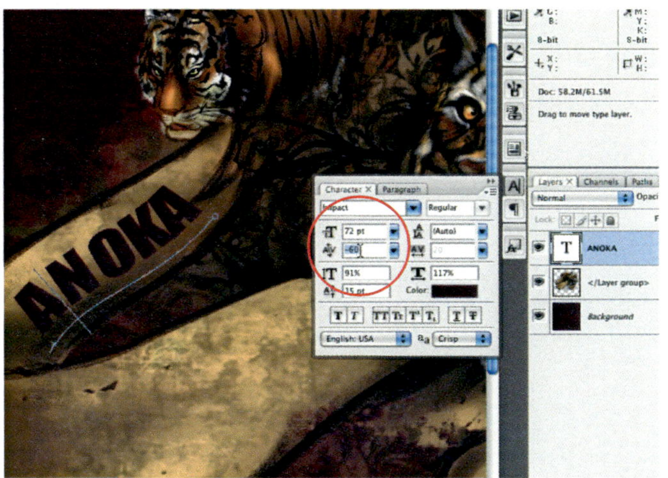

ADDING TYPE TO A PATH continued

Step 6:

In the Character Palette change the Kerning number to a negative number to squeeze the letters together.

Change to a positive number, if it is necessary to add space.

Step 7:

Repeat the same steps for each of the other banners.

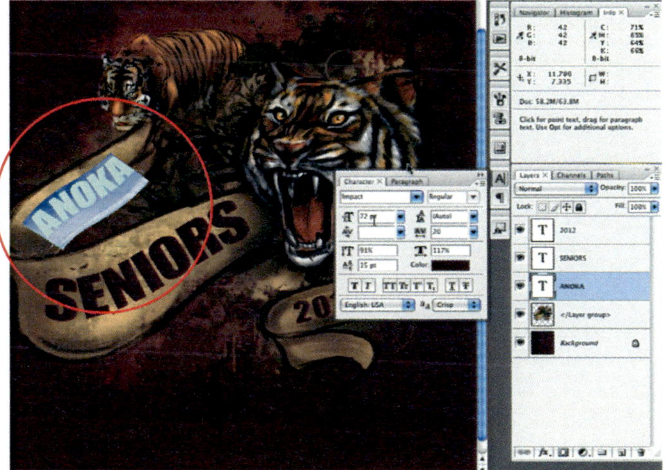

Step 8:

A good tip tip is to double click on the Text Layer icon to select the text as shown.

Now, when adjustments are made to any of the options in the palette, the change will happen "live" on screen.

Using the WARP Command

Sometimes it might be necessary to make alterations to the shape of the text in order to make the image more believable.

This technique can also be used to Warp or Map an image to an object. It is useful for placing artwork on a mug in Photoshop, for an image in a catalog, or simply as a proof for approval before a production run.

This is how to do it.

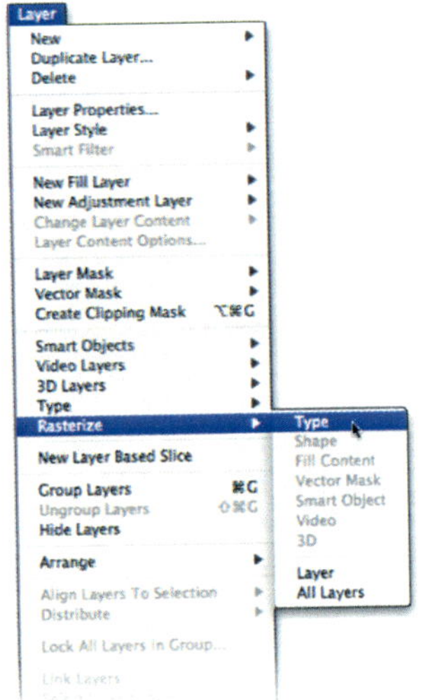

USING WARP

Step 1: Photoshop CS3 - CS5

First, duplicate the layer you are going to work on by dragging it to the new layer icon at the bottom of the Layers Palette.

This way it is always possible to go back to the way it was if you're not happy with you adjustments.

Step 2:

With the new Layer selected, go to LAYER > RASTERIZE > TYPE. This converts the text layer to pixels.

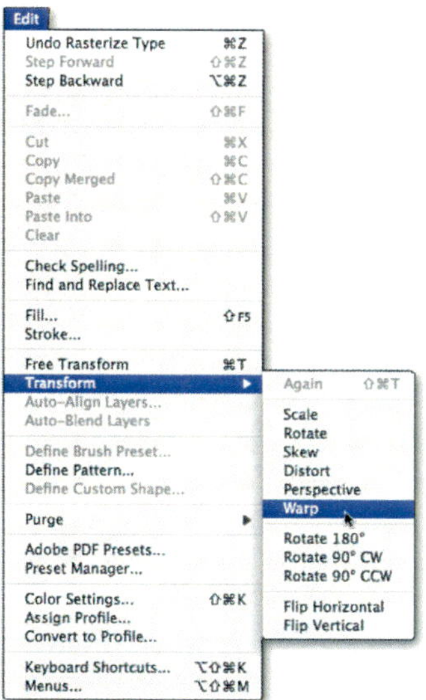

Step 3:

With the layer selected, go to EDIT > TRANSFORM > WARP.

Step 4:

The Warp Grid will pop up on screen.

Step 5:

Simply click inside the grid and drag the image around. You can either use the corner anchor points to move the image or click inside the grid and push or pull the image to get what you want.

When you like what you see, press the Return Key to accept.

Using Layer Styles

In this lesson I'll use some Layer Styles to put a little "Snap" in the text on this design. I want to make the text stand out a little better. It's a little boring as is.

I'm going to start with the largest word, "Seniors", first. We will have to make some minor changes in the effects for the smaller words in order for them to look the same.

Let's get to it!

USING LAYER STYLES

Step 1: Photoshop CS3 - CS5

Select the Layer to be worked with first by clicking once on it to select it.

Click on the "Add Layer Style" button at the bottom of the Layers Palette and go up to Stroke.

Slide the "Size" slider to a size preferred.

To change the color, click on the color box. I chose a silver gray for this image.

Step 2:

With the dialog box open, check the Inner Shadow box.

Click on the Inner Shadow word in order to be able to change the attributes of the Inner Shadow that is to be applied..

I changed the "Size" to 133 pixels.

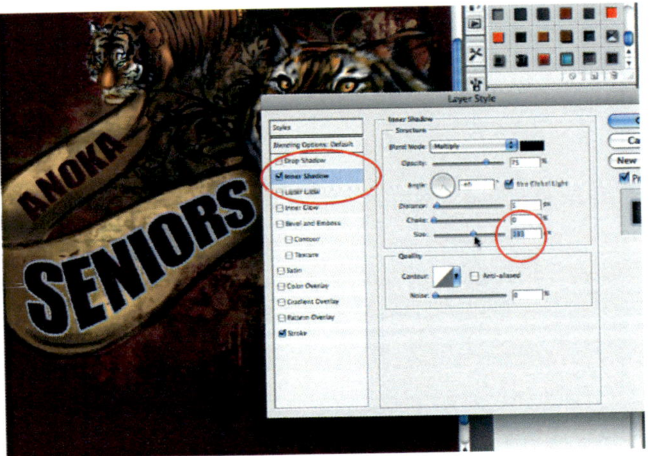

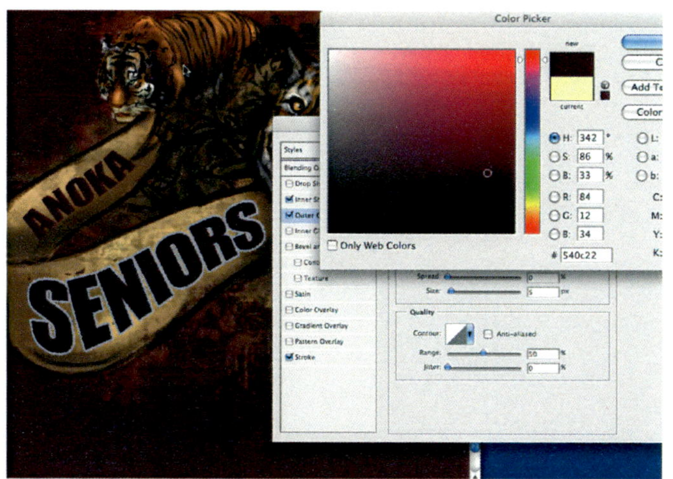

Step 3:

Now check the Outer Glow check box.

Click on the Outer Glow words in order to change it's attributes.

I'm going to change the color by clicking on the colored square. I'm going to choose a maroon color from the image.

Click OK.

Step 4:

Change the Blend Mode to Normal.

Change the Spread to 23% and the Size to 73 pixels.

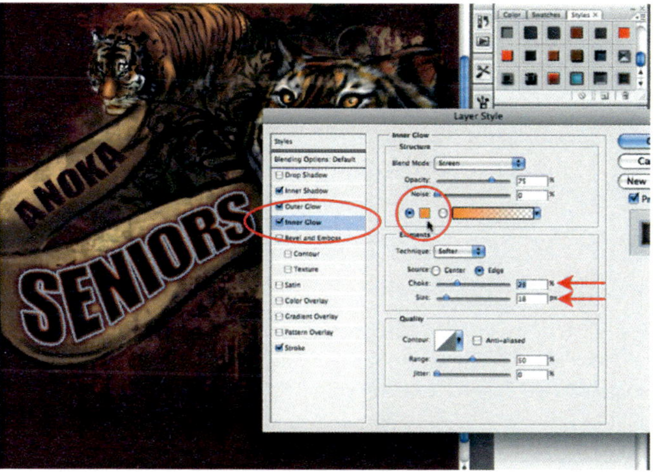

Step 5:

Now turn on the Inner Glow option by clicking on the Inner Glow check box. Click the Inner Glow words to be able to change it's attributes.

Change the size to 18 pixels and the choke to 28%.

Now, change the Color by clicking on the small colored square.

I chose a bright orange for this image.

Don't click OK just yet.

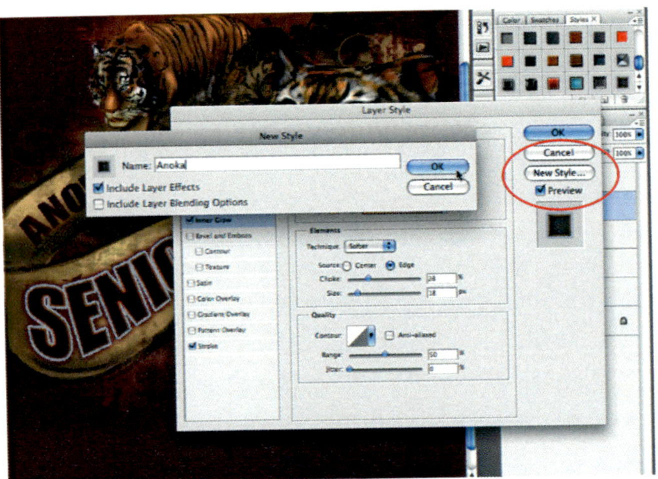

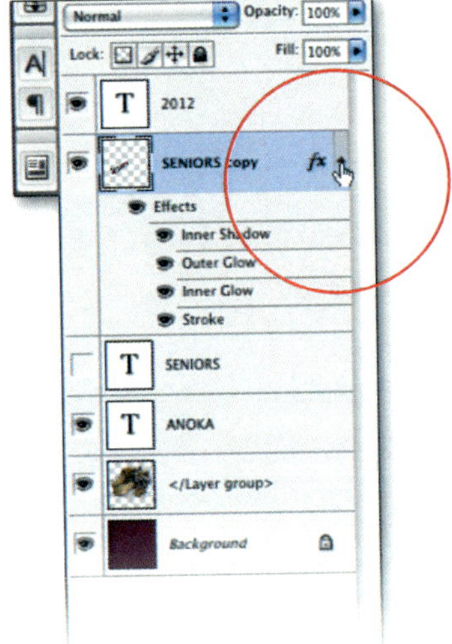

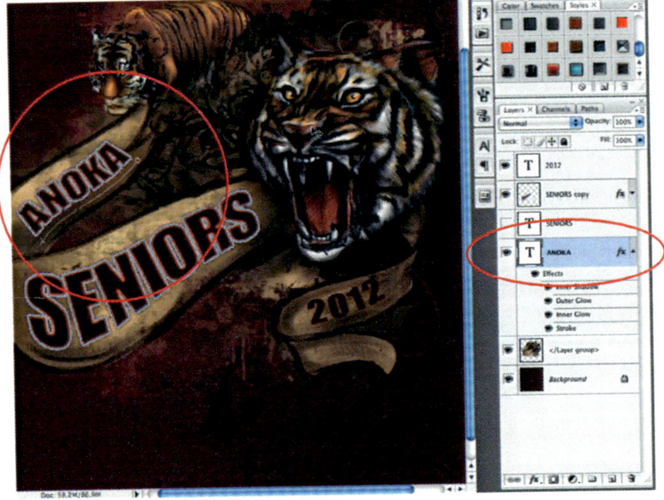

Step 6:

Click on the New Style button.

Give it a name you will remember. Click OK.

Now click OK in the Layer Styles dialog box.

Step 7:

The new Style will be placed at the bottom of your Styles Palette.

Toggle the small arrow to compress the list of attributes in the Layers Palette.

Step 8:

Now in the Layers Palette, click on the next Layer to add the effect.

Simply click once on the New Style button. The Style named is now found at the bottom of the Styles list.

Don't worry if some of the attributes are too big and don't look the same. That will be changed next.

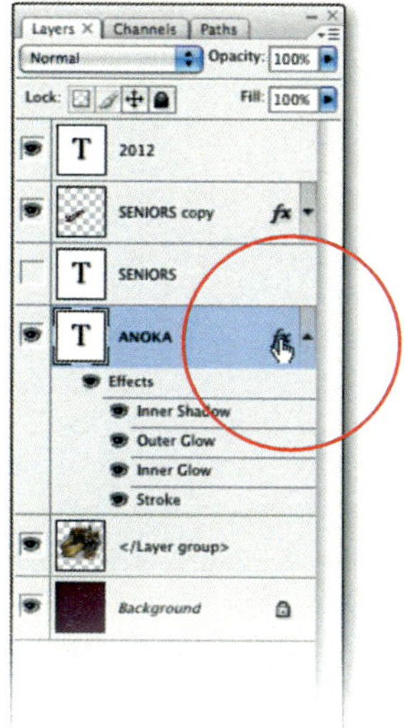

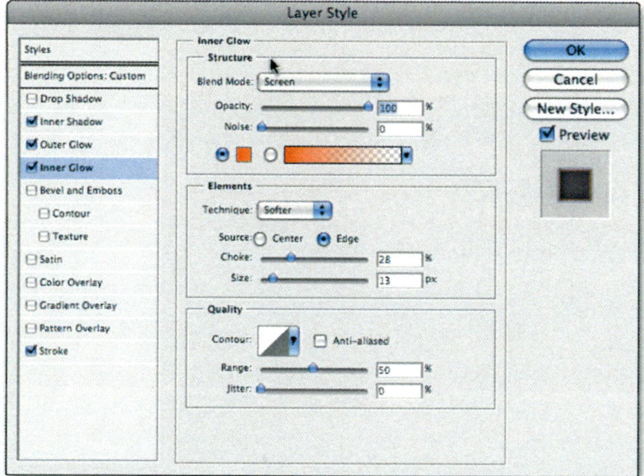

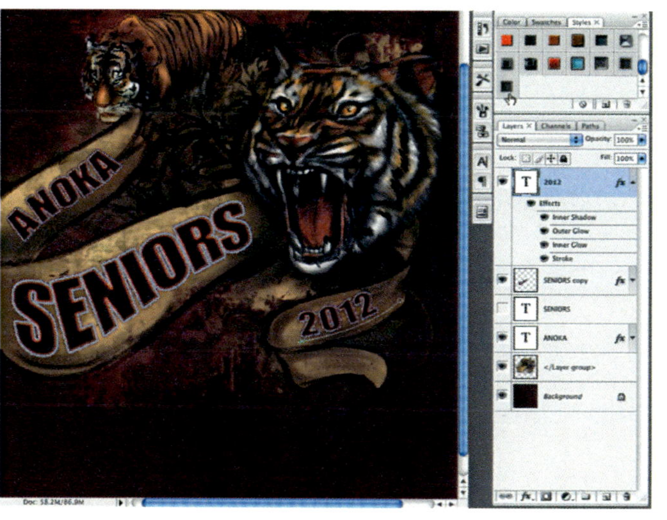

Step 9:

Double click the "FX" icon on the Layer to adjust.

Step 10:

This brings up the Layer Style dialog box.

Click on each Style, and make adjustments.

This is what I changed:

Stroke, from 16 pixels to 13 pixels.

Inner Glow, Size from 18 pixels to 13 pixels.

Outer Glow, Size from 73 pixels to 18 pixels.

Inner Shadow, Size from 133 pixels to 59 pixels.

Click on New Style again to save this adjusted Style. Name it small, or something easy to remember.

Click OK.

Step 11:

Click once on the next Layer to be changed.

Now simply click on the New Layer Style just added to the bottom of the Styles Palette.

Repeat more adjustments if needed.

That finishes out the design rather nicely.

Adding Dimension to Clip Art

In this lesson, I will be adding (painting) some dimension to regular black and white clip art.

If you don't think you can draw, you may surprise yourself with this great, easy lesson. Don't worry! It is not necessary to "really" draw. I will demonstrate how to paint a piece of clip art, so it looks like you did.

You can either use the Clip Art Fish I have here, or use your own. It will work with any image.

Let's get started.

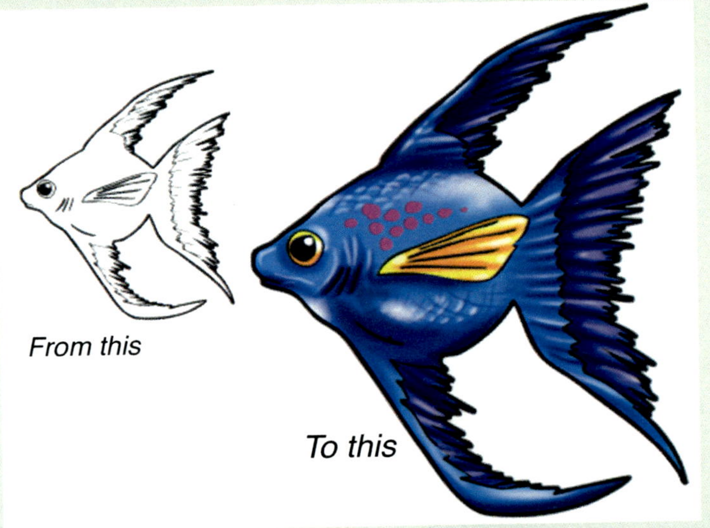

From this

To this

ADDING DIMENSION TO CLIP ART

Step 1: Photoshop CS3 - CS5
Open the clip art file in Illustrator.
Drag select the entire image.
Go to EDIT > COPY.

Now in Photoshop, Go to FILE > NEW. (the file size is determined already by the image copied to the clipboard).
Click OK.

Go to EDIT > PASTE, In the Paste dialog box, choose pixels.

Double click inside the image to accept it.

Step 2:
Now I'll give the image a little breathing room by expanding the Canvas.

Go to IMAGE > CANVAS SIZE

Be sure to check the "Relative" box. Add a 1 in the Width and Height boxes.

Be sure the "Anchor:" is set in the middle.

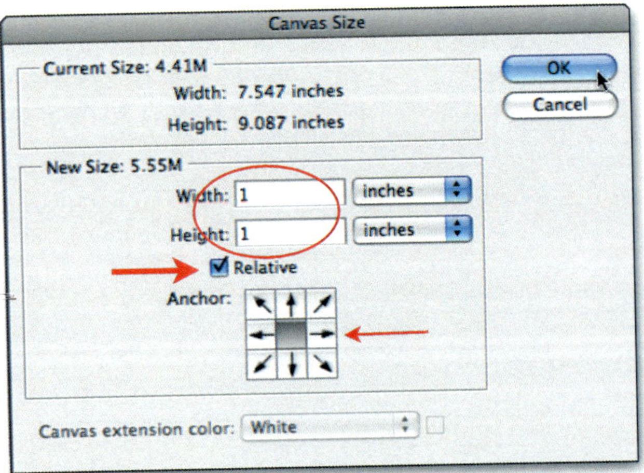

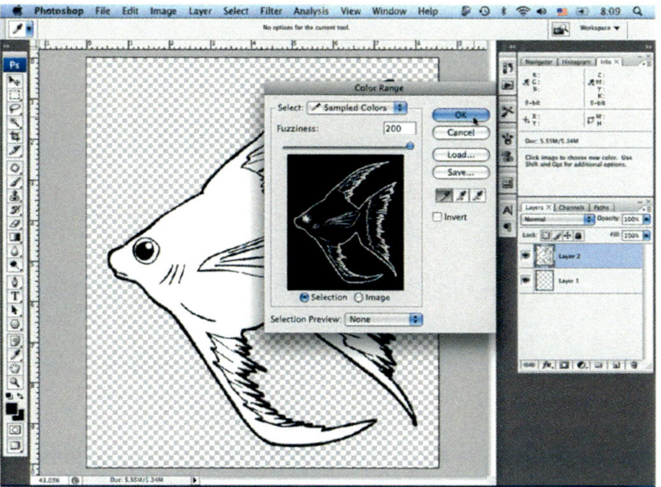

DIMENSION TO CLIP ART continued

Step 3:

With the artwork Layer selected, Go to SELECT > COLOR RANGE.

Click somewhere on a black area in the image.

Click OK

The marching ants should be visible around the black in the image.

Go to EDIT > COPY. Now EDIT > PASTE to put the black outlines on it's own layer.

Step 4:

Now drag the Layer with the black and white image to the trash can icon.

There should be two transparent Layers in the document. One has the outline artwork, and the one below which should be empty.

With the bottom Layer selected, click on the Magic Wand Tool in the toolbox.

In the options bar across the top, make sure "Sample All Layers" is checked.

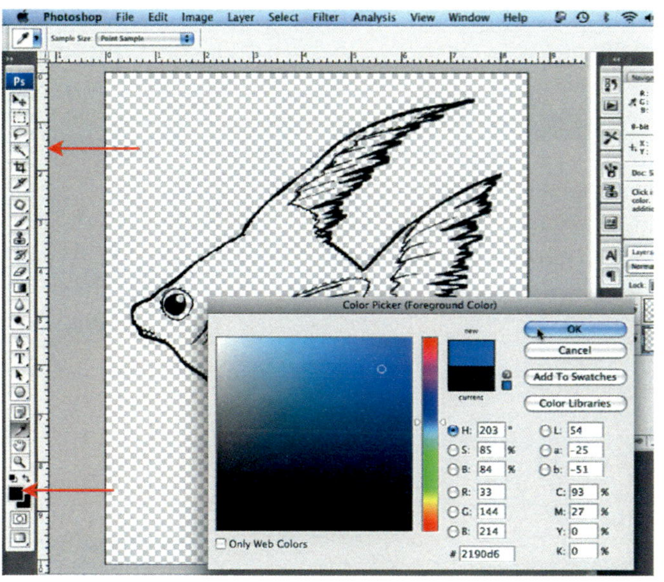

Step 5:

With the Magic Wand Tool, click inside an area of the image.

Click once on the Foreground color square to bring up the color box.

Select a color. I chose a medium blue in this case.

Click OK.

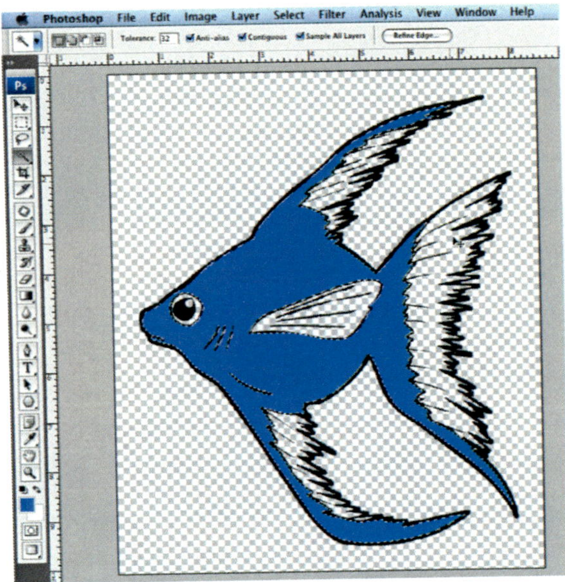

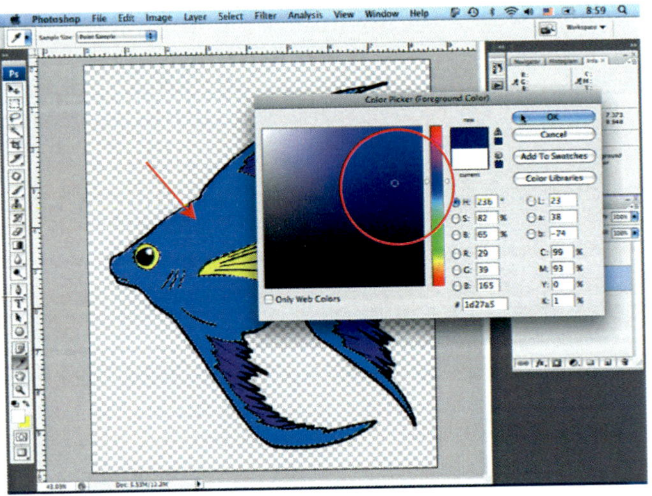

DIMENSION TO CLIP ART continued

Step 6:

Before we fill the selection, it needs to be expanded in order for it to fall under the black lines.

Go to SELECT > MODIFY > EXPAND

Expand by 1 pixel

Click OK.

Repeat these steps until the entire image is filled with solid colors. Change colors as necessary.

Step 7:

Now the image is filled with all solid colors. Choose the Magic Wand Tool and click on the blue area.

This will select that area and allow painting inside.

Step 8:

Click on the Foreground Color box again and choose a darker color than the first one.

In this case, I'll choose a dark blue.

Click OK.

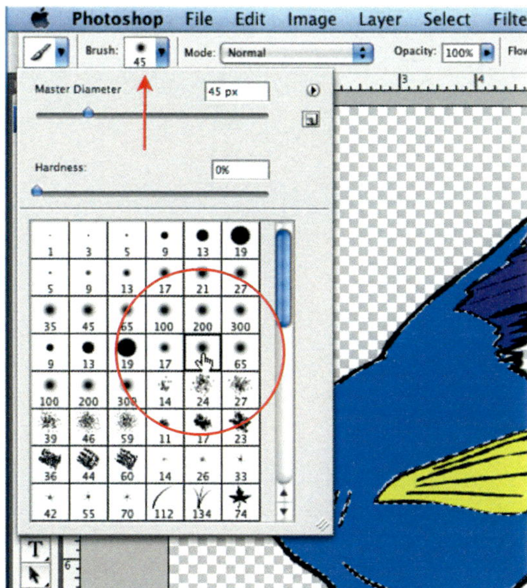

Step 9:

Choose the Brush Tool in the tool box. In the options bar across the top, click on the Brush Preset Picker and select a soft brush.

Select a brush and double click on it.

Step 10:

Press Command-H on a Mac, or Control-H on a PC to hide the selection. The marching ants will disappear. They are still selected. This makes it much less distracting when painting.

Begin painting some shadow areas with the dark blue and soft brush.

This can be done with a mouse, but it's much easier to use a digitizing tablet such as a Wacom Tablet.

The reason to have the areas selected is in order for the selection to act as a mask. This way, all the paint stays where it's supposed to be, and I won't have any clean up after.

Step 11:

Repeat the same steps for all of the other solid colored areas in the image. Just use a darker color than the one that was there in the first place.

It should look similar to mine.

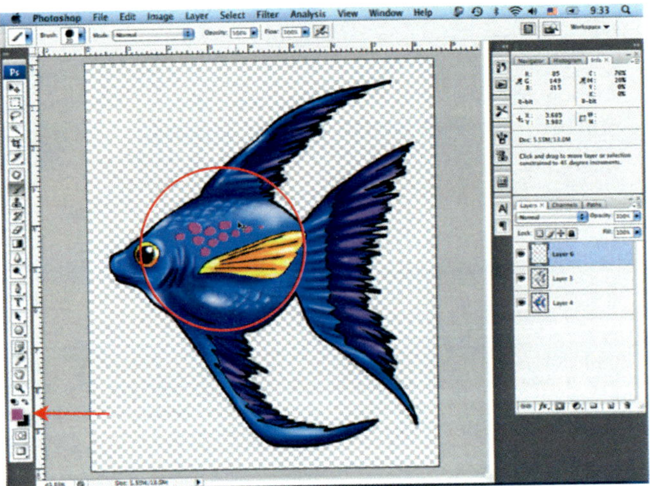

DIMENSION TO CLIP ART continued

Step 12:

Press the "D" key on your keyboard to set the foreground colors to the default Black and White.

Now press the "X" key to switch the two. Now, white should be set as the foreground color.

Click once on the section to add the white highlights to.

Start painting white.

Reduce the opacity in the Options Bar across the top of the screen, if you choose.

Step 13:

Create a New Layer by clicking on the New Layer icon at the bottom of the Layers palette.

Place this new Layer at the top of the Layer stack.

Choose a Brush in the Tool Box.

In the Options bar across the top, click on the Brush Preset Picker and choose a hard edged brush.

Click on the Foreground Color box and choose a bright fun color.

Paint some small spots to add some detail.

Step 14:

The finished design should look something like this.

What do you think? It's a far cry from black and white clip art!

Getting the Most out of Stock Art

Stock artwork allows any decorator, regardless of artistic ability, to create professional, outstanding-looking designs. Saving the customer the time and expense of creating original artwork increases profit.

A major challenge in using stock art is the ability to ensure customers that their product designs will be unique. For example, it would be important for three regional high schools to have uniquely designed images, despite the fact that all three have a tiger as their mascot. The goal is to find ways to take an image and modify it in order for customers to feel they are getting a specially designed product.

The good news is that it is not really too difficult to give stock designs unique looks. By changing elements such as color, size, proportion, texture, background fills, patterns, and even isolating a single element of a design, allows the ability to create many different looks from one piece of art. The most common approach by decorators is to choose a vector outline and simply fill it in with color. A more creative approach using the same piece of art multiple times will maximizing your investment.

I am going to take a basic stock image and change it to create four distinct looks. The goal is to illustrate how the same piece of artwork can be creatively manipulated to become a one-of-a-kind design for a customer. This will enable you to take these principles and apply them to your own collection of stock art.

One way to get the most out of your stock artwork is to start off with one image and change it up to create several unique design looks.

Full Color Lion

This is probably the quickest and easiest way to create a design. The image is already done, all that is necessary to do is to add some text to finalize it.

I will maintain the full color look with this design.

This original Lion image can be found on the companion CD.

Let's get started.

FULL COLOR LION

Step 1: Photoshop CS3 - CS5
Open the image you want to work with.

Step 2:
We need to make room for the text. If the image is large enough, go to EDIT > FREE TRANSFORM and reduce the size.

Or, go to IMAGE > CANVAS SIZE, anchor the image as desired and add as much space as needed.

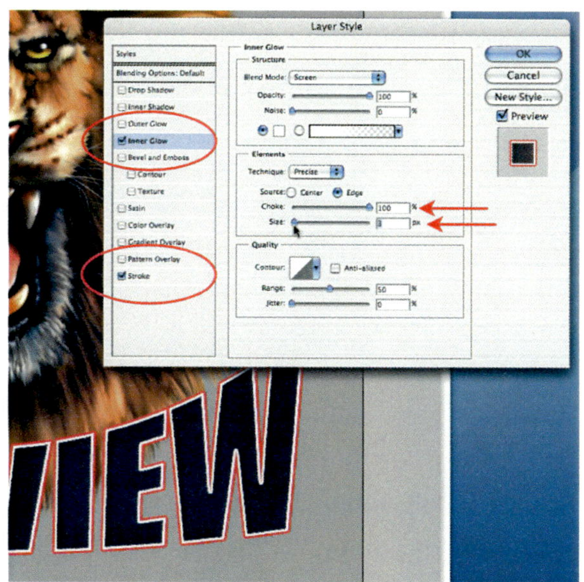

Step 3: Photoshop CS3

Create multiple outline effects on the text using Photoshop's Layer Styles.

Select Inner Glow and change to any color. Set the opacity to 100%, move Choke up to 100%, and adjust the size. Then, select Stroke, and colorize as needed.

Step 4:

Select a different typeface that will enhance the image. Use a Layer Style with textures. Cmd/Ctrl-click on the Layer thumbnail to select everything on that Layer. Choose SELECT > MODIFY > EXPAND to expand the area beyond the text. Fill it with a color. This creates the first outline effect. Create another Layer, repeat the same select and expand step. Fill it with another color. This image uses a white outline, then a red one to get the multiple outline effects.

Step 5:

Create a new layer beneath that one, place a blended bar beneath the text to add the finishing touches to the design..

Gray Lion

In this lesson I'm going to change the design completely. I'm going to change the color of the main element. Although the name of this lesson is Gray Lion, it can be made with any colors. This school's colors happen to be Red and Black.

It will be much easier to complete this lesson with a digitizing tablet. I prefer a Wacom. The tablet feels more natural for "erasing" the jaw and mane.

Let's get started.

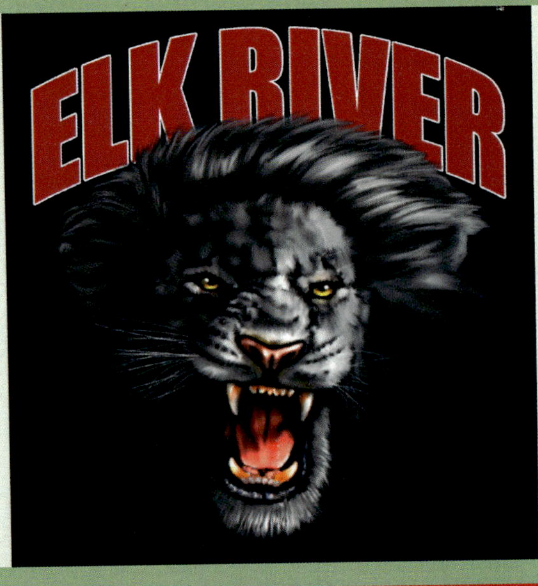

GRAY LION

Step 1: Photoshop CS3 - CS5
Open the original image. Add to the canvas by choosing IMAGE > CANVAS SIZE and expand to make room for the type. Go to IMAGE > CANVAS SIZE. Anchor the image and expand. In this case, I anchored my image at the bottom center and added several inches to the top.

Step 2:
Create a new background layer and fill it with the shirt color (black, in this case). Go back to the first layer and type Cmd/Ctrl-T (or choose EDIT > FREE TRANSFORM) to rotate the image a little just to make it different from the last design.

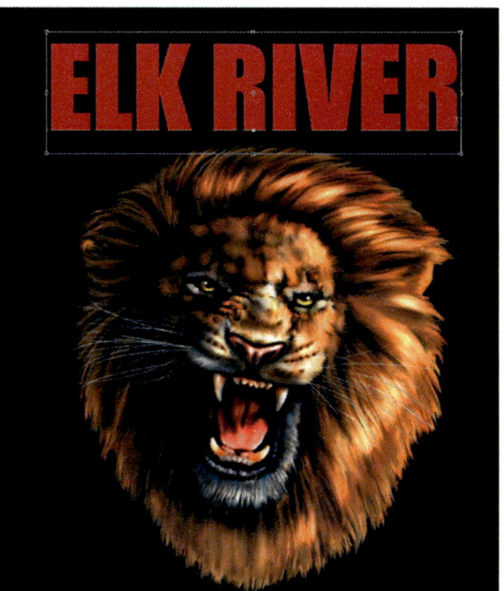

Step 3:

Select the Text tool. Type the team name in the font, color, and type size desired. Use Layer Styles to add a Stroke to the type.

To edit a Layer Style, select the text typed, then double-click the text Layer (or choose Layer > Layer Style). That opens the Layer Style dialog box and you can check any of the effects on the left side. In this case, check Stroke and adjust. It is possible to add / edit multiple effects before closing the Layer Style dialog box.

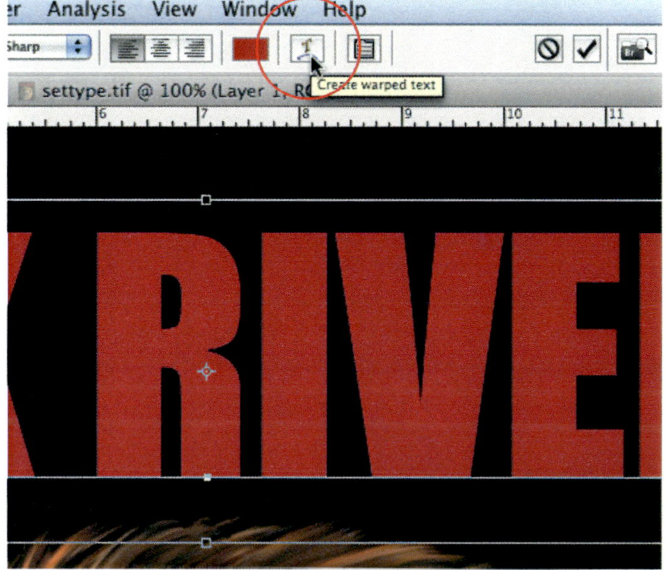

Step 4:

With the Text tool still selected, click the Create Warped Text button in the Options bar across the top of the screen. It's the box to the right of the Text Color, the one with the "T" atop a curved line.

Step 5:

Now, use the pull-down menu to select the warp effect desired. Adjust the look by adjusting the sliders in a positive or negative percentage.

Step 6:

Duplicate the original image layer by dragging that layer onto the Create New Layer icon at the bottom of the Layers palette. Choose IMAGE > ADJUSTMENTS > HUE/SATURATION...from the top menu. In the pop up dialog box, drag the Saturation slider all the way to the left (-100%). Now, with the desaturated layer selected, click on the Layer mask button at the bottom of the Layers palette.

Step 7:

Using the Paintbrush tool, with black as the selected color, "paint" any area of the Layer Mask to reveal the color from the layer below. In this case, I painted black over the eyes, nose and mouth, which makes them "pop" out of the desaturated image.

Step 8:

Merge the two image layers together. First, turn off the preview eyeballs on the other layers. Then, from the top menu, choose LAYERS > MERGE VISIBLE. Now, press the "E" on the keyboard to open the Eraser tool (or just select that tool from the Tool palette.) Use a soft brush on the image layer and erase away the lower, bushy part of the lion's mane. Now, here is another finished design using the same original clip art.

Cropping the Lion

In this lesson I'm going to use only one part of the image, the region around his eyes. I'll use other elements to add interest and complete the image.

It will be easier to complete this lesson with a digitizing tablet, such as a Wacom. "Erasing" lines feels more natural using the tablet.

Let's get started.

CROPPING THE LION

Step 1: Photoshop CS3 - CS5
Open the original image again and use EDIT > FREE TRANSFORM to rotate it. The lion's eyes should be level.

Step 2:
Using the Marquee tool, click and drag a rectangle just around the eyes.

CROPPING THE LION continued

Step 3:

With the eye area selected, choose SELECT > INVERSE from the top menu and delete the rest of the image

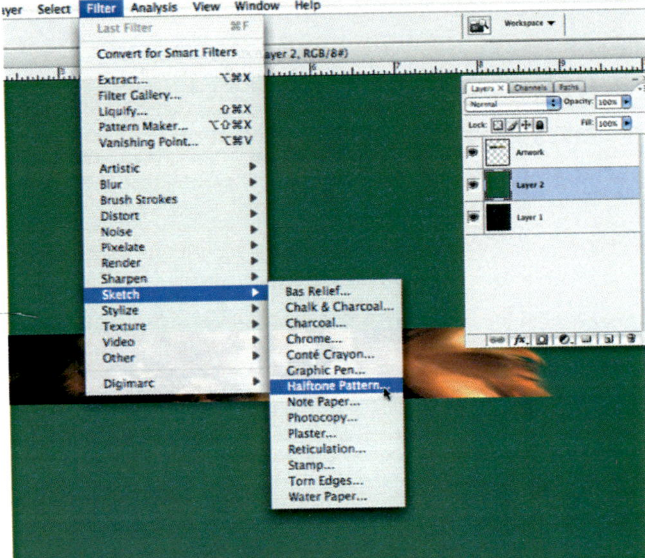

Step 4:

Create a new layer and fill with a school color. With this layer selected, in the Layers palette, from the top menu choose FILTER > SKETCH > HALFTONE PATTERN.

Step 5:

When the dialog box opens, make sure Halftone Pattern shows in the pull-down menu. Then set the Size slider to 3 and Contrast to 50. From the Pattern Type: menu, choose Line.

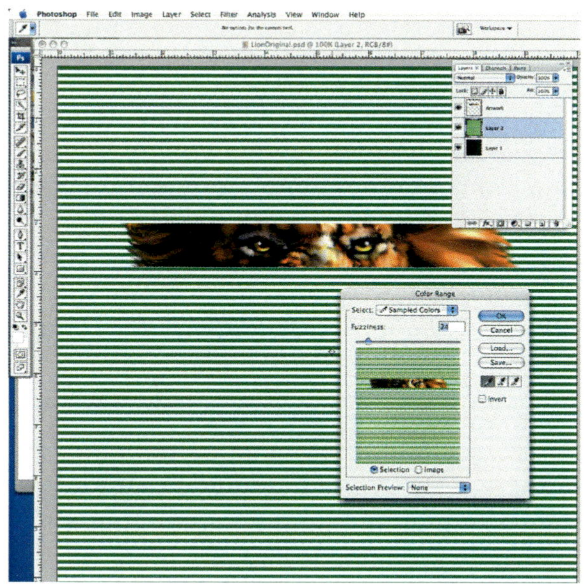

Step 6:

With the halftone pattern layer selected in the Layers Palette, choose SELECT > COLOR RANGE from the top menu. Then click on the white lines to select them and press the Delete key to get rid of them.

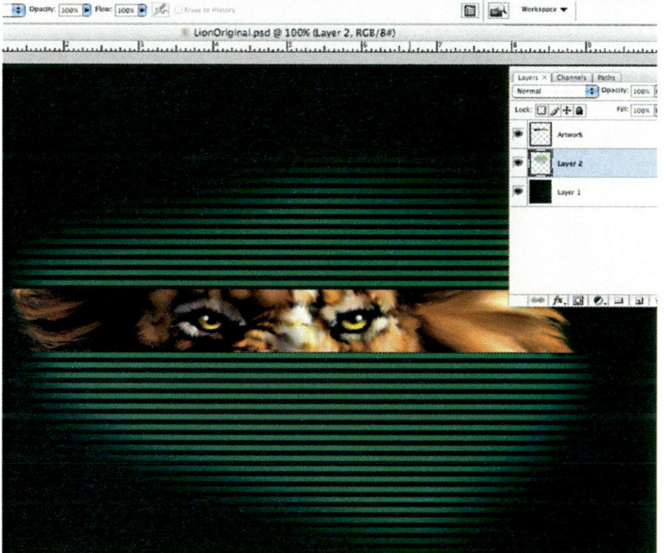

Step 7:

Choose the Eraser tool, change the tip to "brush". Using a soft brush, selectively erase unwanted lines.

Step 8:

Set text as needed. While keeping the text selected, double-click on the Text layer in the layers palette to open the Layers Styles dialog box. Add a black stroke. Next, duplicate the Text layer (LAYER > DUPLICATE LAYER...) move it below the original Text layer and highlight the new layer.

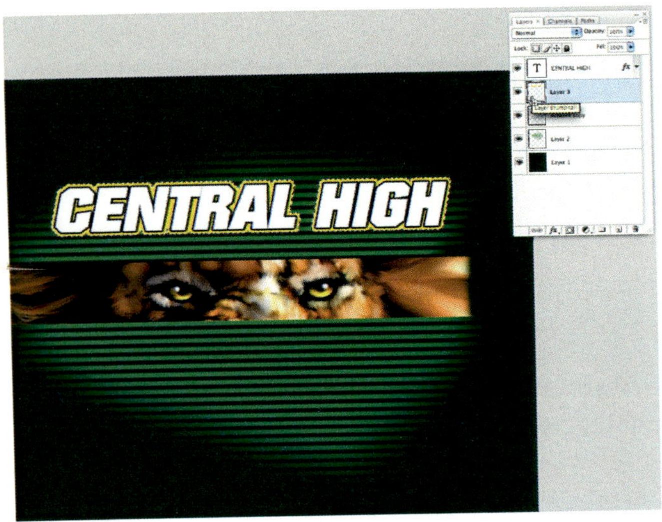

CROPPING THE LION continued

Step 9:

Cmd/Ctrl-click on the new layer to select everything. From the top menu, choose SELECT > MODIFY > EXPAND.In the dialog window, type "6" in the pixels box. Click OK, and fill this selection with yellow.

Step 10:

In this case, I opened a second piece of mascot clip art in Adobe Illustrator and copy-pasted it into Photoshop as a Smart Object. With it selected, I chose LAYER > RASTERIZE > SMART OBJECT and then EDIT > FREE TRANSFORM to resize and rotate it.

Step 11:

I used Layer Styles to add a stroke to it. To finish off this design, I added horizontal bars to frame the eyes. I erased a small green line above and below my new thicker ones, and inserted the text "LIONS" using the same techniques adding the school name above.

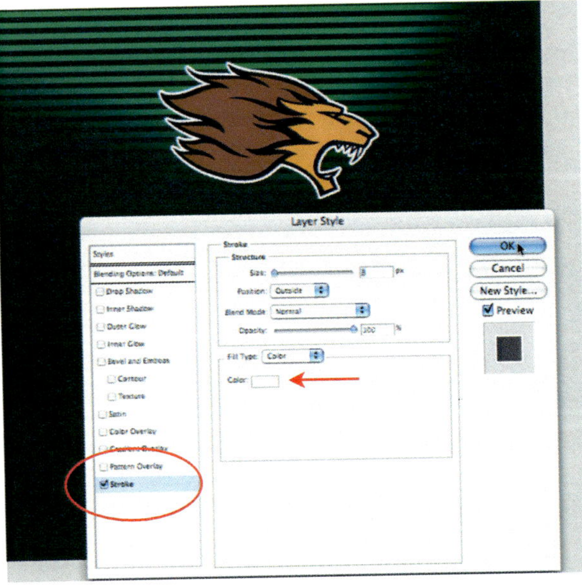

Tone on Tone Lion

In this lesson I'm going to flip the lion to allow him to face the other direction. I'll also colorize him with the schools colors.

If this image were to be screen printed, I would only use four colors (White Base, School Color, Highlight White, and Black). It might be possible to use only one white, but the extra screen will help keep more depth and detail in the image.

Let's get started.

CROPPING THE LION

Step 1: Photoshop CS3 - CS5

Let's open that original clip art image of the lion yet again.

Step 2:

From the top menu, select EDIT > TRANSFORM > FLIP HORIZONTAL to change the image a little.

Step 3:

Now choose IMAGE > ADJUSTMENTS > HUE/ SATURATION. Click on the "colorize" button in the dialog box which will open. The entire image changes to a monochromatic tone.

Step 4:

Control the color of that tone by adjusting the Hue slider. Here are just a few color examples. I use this technique with school colors all the time.

Step 5:

Now, select the Text tool. Pick a font and set the text desired. My text is colored white, and the layer opacity is set to 100%.

Duplicate the text layer by dragging it onto the New Layer icon at the bottom of the Layers palette. Set the new layer's opacity to 80% and choose EDIT > FREE TRANSFORM to reduce the text a little.

Continue duplicating the layer reducing the size of the text using EDIT > FREE TRANSFORM. For each new layer, reduce the opacity 20%. The last layer's opacity is set at 10%.

Color the very last row of words one with 100% white to finish the design.

The Importance of Removing Artwork from a Background

Removing artwork from a background and getting it onto a transparent layer is extremely important. In the printing processes I talk about in this book, it is required in order to print properly. This is true for screen printing and direct to garment digital printing, and basically any printing technique that requires a white underbase with colors on top.

As with anything in Photoshop, there are several different ways to accomplish any task. My favorite is the Alpha Masking technique, because of the accuracy that is achievable with very difficult images. This is the technique I'll show here. It is the one I recommend using for removing backgrounds.

It's one thing to create artwork on a transparent layer. That is what we "should do" if we're creating art from scratch. It is really easy to start art projects this way. I've shown how in this chapter already.

It is quite another if an image is already flattened on a white or black background. If this is the case, it is a must to know how to handle these types of files.

In this lesson we will be removing complex artwork from a background. "Complex" means that the image does not have a hard edge. It will have soft edges, shadows, or anything that is supposed to flow or feather out into a shirt. Removing this type of artwork takes only a little time if approached correctly. Once this technique is mastered it will become invaluable for removing art from a white or black background. Once again, I recommend a digitizing tablet (such as a Wacom) instead of a mouse.

If the image has a hard edge, it may be possible to select the Magic Wand Tool and click in the background by going to Select menu > Inverse. Then, go to Edit > Copy and Edit > Paste in order to put the hard edged object on it's own transparent layer. This, however, is my least favorite way to accomplish this. It just doesn't give much control over detail areas, and the finished result is usually not very good.

Another available technique involves Cutting a Path around the object that is to be removed. This takes only a few minutes, and it is possible to save the path as a selection. This might come in handy for working with that image in the future.

Depending on the image or photo, it may also be possible to use the quick Soft Feathered Vignette edge from Chapter 6.

For the Screen Printer

When creating separations for screen printing the art must be on a black and a white background. The color of the shirt or garment doesn't matter. Black and white backgrounds are what matters.

When creating the white underbase in a separation, the art must be on a black background. This is due to the fact that if the image is on a white background, there will be a large square around the image when printed. The computer is "seeing" this white; therefore, it puts the information on the white screen.

If on the other hand, a white print is created on a black background, the white ink will only be under the actual art elements. The computer doesn't "see" white around the image (because it's black) and therefore puts nothing around the outside.

For the Digital Printer

The same exact workflow is required for the digital printer. Whether making the underbase, or having RIP software create one, the art must still be on a black and white background.

Above: Original artwork on a white background.

Above: Original artwork on a black background.

White is only where it should be in the image. This is correct.

Notice the white box. This is wrong.

Above: A white base created from a file with a White background. Printed incorrectly.

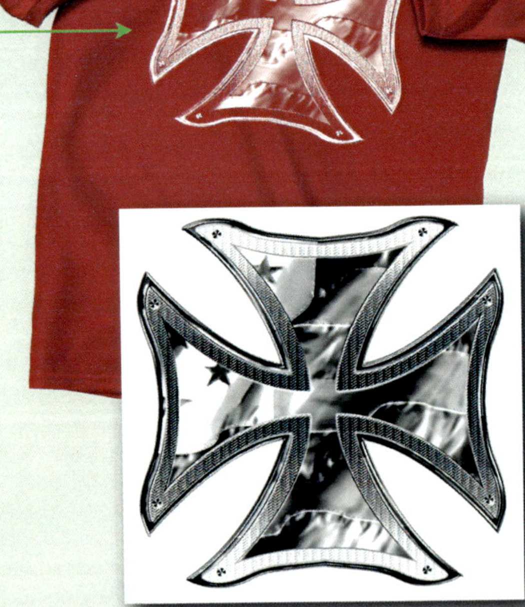

Above: A white base created from a file with a Black background. Printed correctly.

This original Iron Cross file is yours to use and can be found on the companion CD.

Removing Artwork from a White Background

In this lesson I will be removing a complex piece of artwork from a white background and placing it on a transparent layer.

This is a MUST for any printing that requires a white base with colors on top including Screen printing and Direct to Garment digital printing.

This is the technique I prefer, and the one I recommend when receiving a flattened file.
This is the only one I use. It gives me the most control and the best results.

From a White background.

To a Transparent background.

Step 1: Photoshop CS3 - CS5

Bring up the Channels Palette. Go to WINDOW MENU > CHANNELS, if it's not open already.

The file should be an RGB file. There should be an RGB Preview channel and a Red, Green, and Blue channel.

Duplicate the Blue channel by dragging it onto the New Channel Icon at the bottom of the palette. It is the second from the right, next to the trash can.

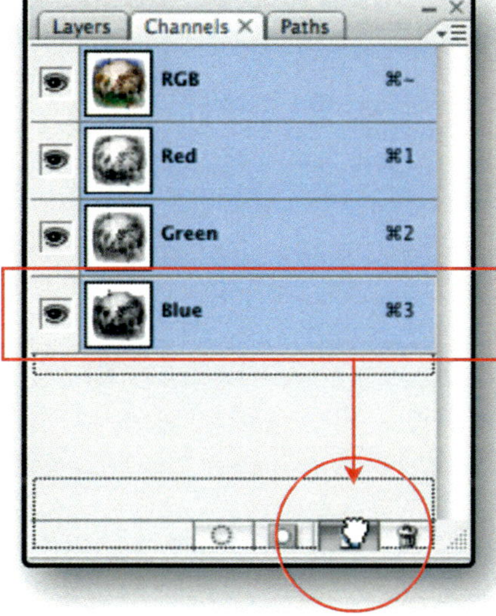

Step 2:

Name this New Channel "Mask". This channel will become the Alpha Mask.

Double click on this channel's preview icon. (The picture, not the eye ball).

Be sure to set the mode to "Selected Areas."

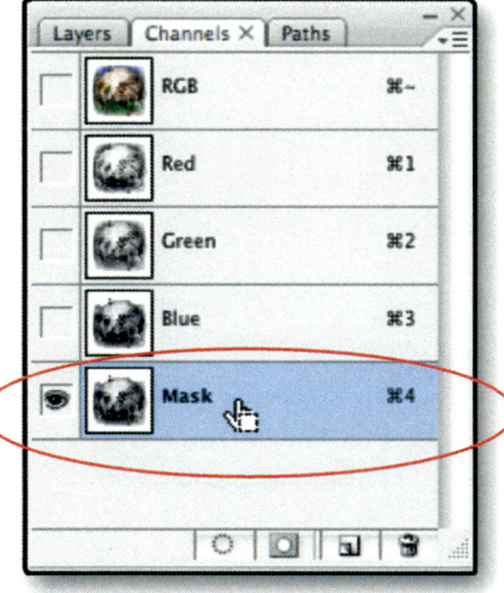

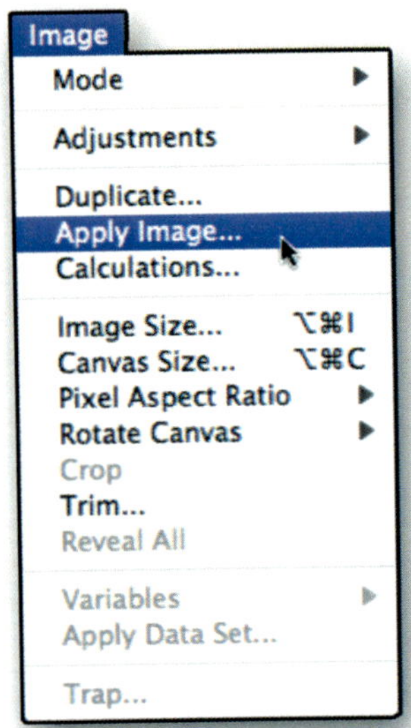

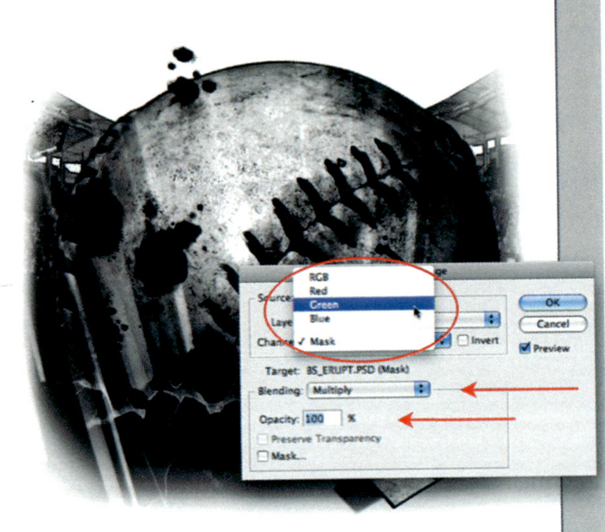

Step 3:

With the Mask Channel selected, Go to IMAGE MENU> APPLY IMAGE.

Step 4:

In the Apply Image dialog box, change the "Channel" from Mask to Green.

Leave the Blending set to Multiply and the Opacity at 100%.

Click OK.

Open Apply Image dialog box again and change from "Mask" to Red.

Click OK.

Step 5:

After all Channels have been applied to the "Mask" channel, the image should look much darker, similar to this one.

I've applied all of the color data in the file onto one channel. The reason white is still visible in the image is due to the fact that the computer sees White as lack of color. That's why I need to paint in the next step.

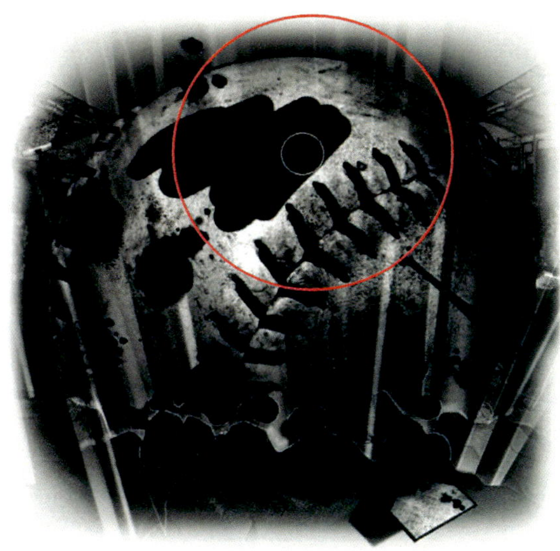

Step 6:

Now I need to "Paint" the middle of the image solid black. I want all elements of the image black, with the exception of any gray areas. Anything that blends into the shirt, or has a soft edge, is considered a transitional element and should be left gray.

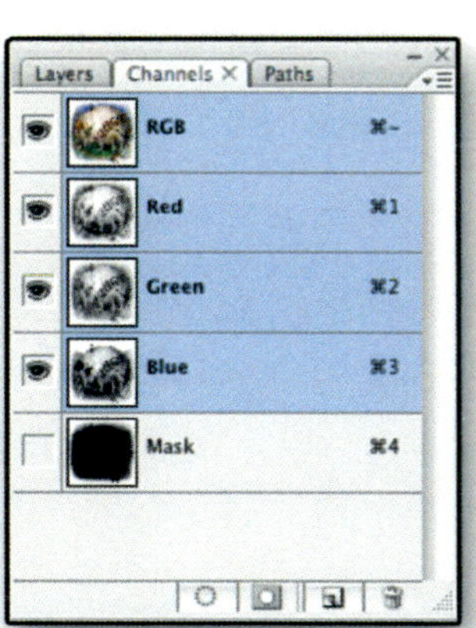

Step 7:

Choose a soft edge brush and begin filling in the middle of the image. Be careful not to paint over the transitional edges.

Once done, the image should look like this.

The main image itself is solid black. The edges that blend into the shirt are soft and gray.

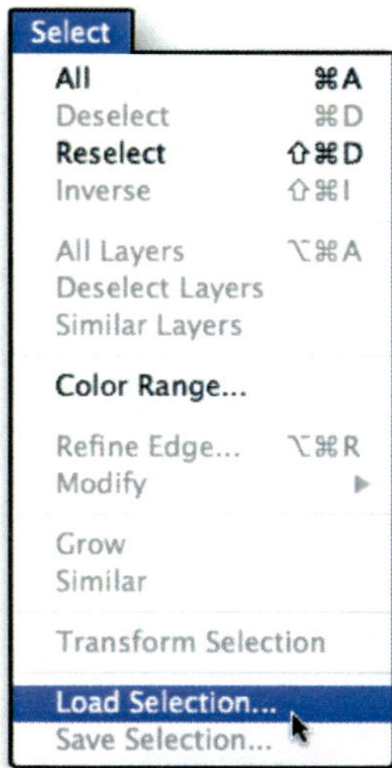

Step 8:

Now click on the RGB Preview channel to select the original art.

Go to SELECT MENU > LOAD SELECTION.

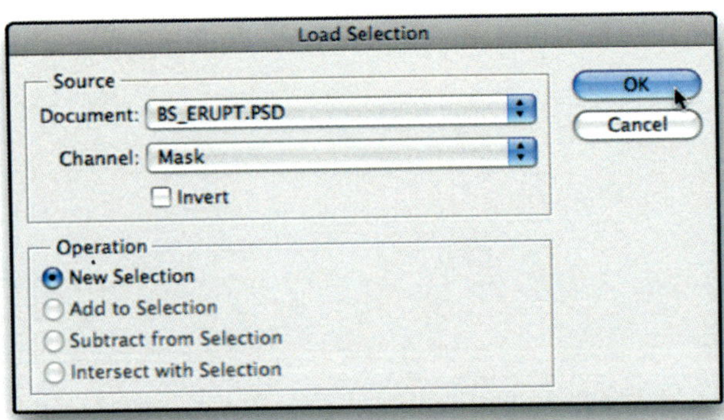

Step 9:

In the Load Selection dialog box, be sure the Mask Channel is selected and the Operation is set to New Selection.

Click OK.

Step 10:

The "Marching Ants" selection should be visible.

Step 11:

Go to EDIT MENU > COPY. Then EDIT MENU > PASTE.

The artwork on the Transparent checkers should be visible. Look at the Layers Palette. There should be a Transparent layer called "Layer 1".

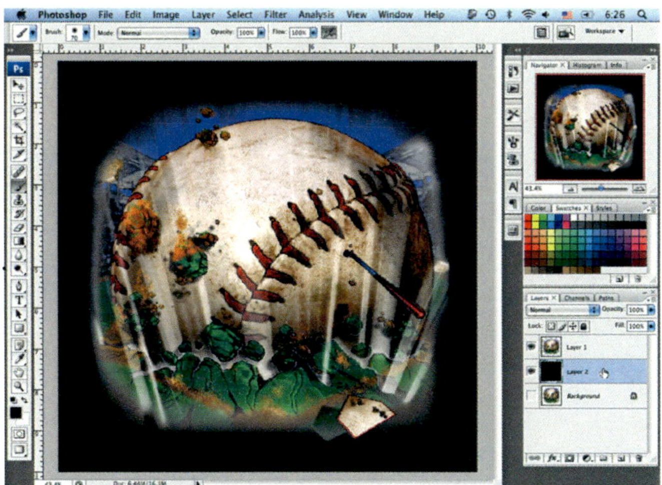

Step 12:

Since I pulled the artwork off of a White Background, I'll place a Black Layer beneath the Artwork layer to see how I did.

Step 13:

Click on the "Layer 1" Layer to select it. Go to LAYER MENU > MATTING > REMOVE WHITE MATTE.

Step 14:

The amount of White "fuzz" around the image disappears. There are no white stray artifacts around the image.

When viewing the art on it's transparent layer, it is easy to see how the edges, the "transitional" areas, blend out softly into the shirt.

This is the only technique I use to remove artwork from a background. I highly recommend you use this one also.

Removing Artwork from a Black Background

In this lesson I will be following the steps outlined in the previous lesson, Removing Art from a White Background. However, it is necessary to do a couple of steps first.

Do steps 1 and 2 of this lesson first. Then follow steps 3 through 11 of the previous lesson.

Steps 12 through 14 of the previous lesson will be changed here slightly because I am working from a Black background.

From a Black background.

To a Transparent background.

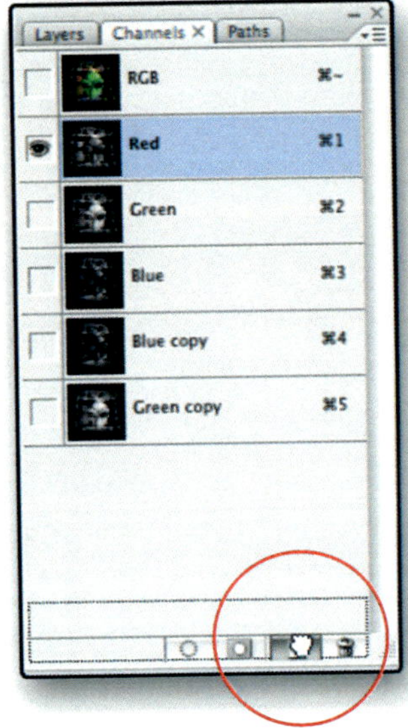

REMOVING FROM BLACK BACKGROUND

Step 1: Photoshop CS3 - CS5
Bring up the Channels Palette. Go to WINDOW MENU > CHANNELS, if it's not open already.

Duplicate each channel by dragging each channel to the New Channel icon.

Double click on these channel's preview icons. (The picture, not the eye ball).

Be sure to set the mode to "Selected Areas."

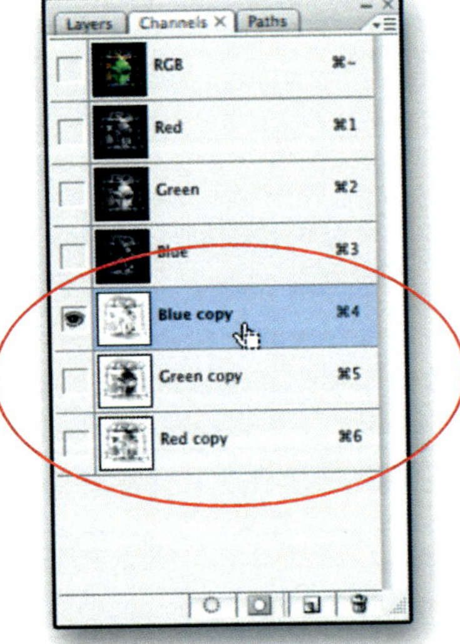

Step 2:
Go to IMAGE MENU > ADJUSTMENTS > INVERT for each channel.

The channels with the white backgrounds will be visible in the small thumbnail icons.

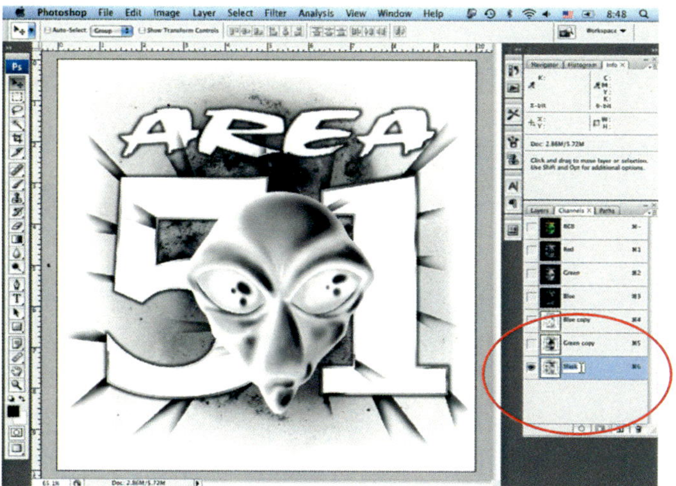

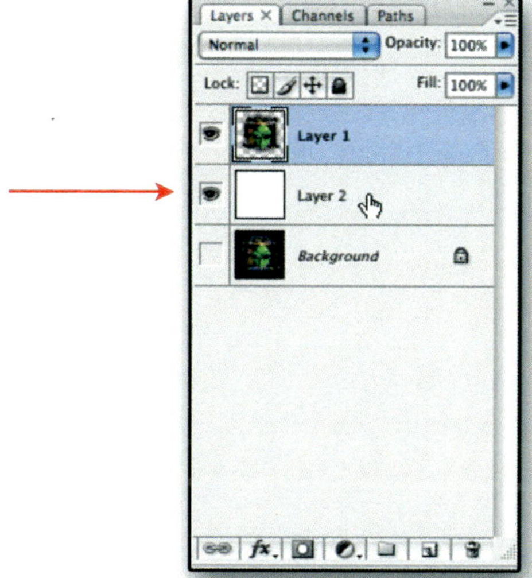

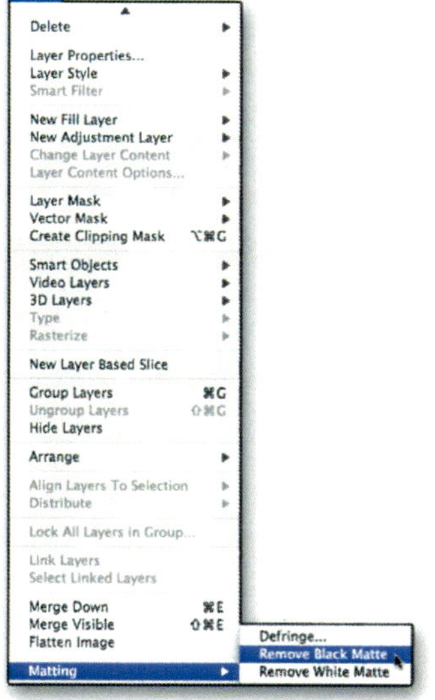

REMOVING BLACK BACKGROUND continued

Step 3:

Change the name of the "RED Copy" channel to Mask. Now I'm at the same stage as I was in the previous lesson.

Follow steps 3 through 11 from the previous lesson (Removing Art from a White background).

Step 4:

Once the previous steps are completed, it is necessary to add a White Layer beneath the Artwork layer due to the fact the art was pulled off of a Black background.

Step 5:

With the Artwork Layer selected, Go to LAYER MENU > MATTING > REMOVE BLACK MATTE.

This is the last step. Most of the steps are identical to removing artwork from a White background.

Cutting a Path

In the previous two lessons I demonstrated my preferred method of removing complex artwork from a background.

In this lesson, I will show how I like to remove objects that have a hard edge. I like the path tool because of the control it gives me, and it usually delivers great results.

Another nice thing about this method is the ability to save the path to use again in the future.

Let's get started.

From a photo.

To a Transparent background.

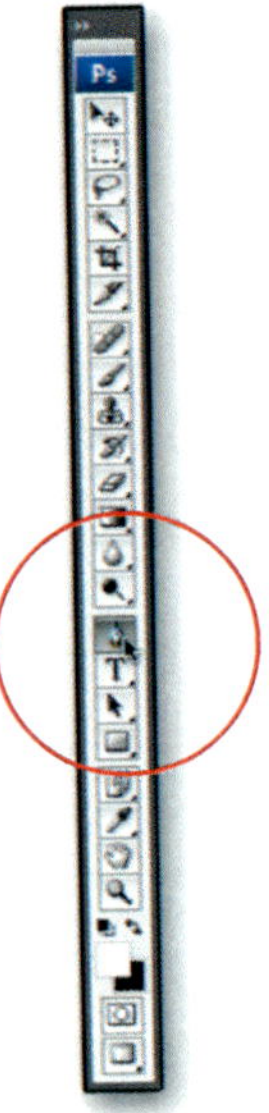

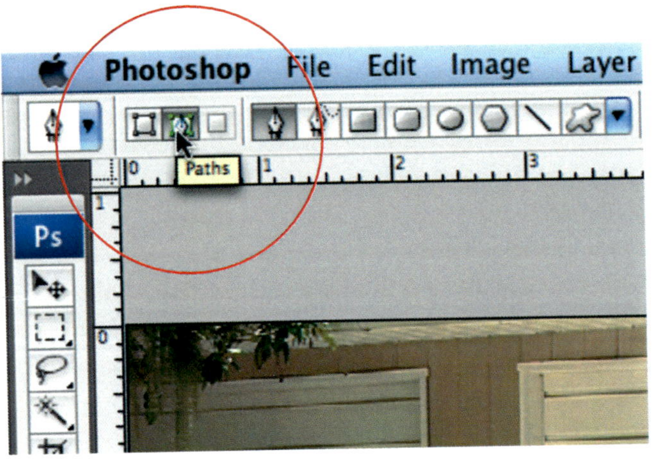

CUTTING A PATH

Step 1: Photoshop CS3 - CS5
Open the photo of the object to be removed.

Select the Pen Tool in the Tool Box.

Step 2:
Be sure the "Paths" button is selected in the Options bar at the top of the screen.

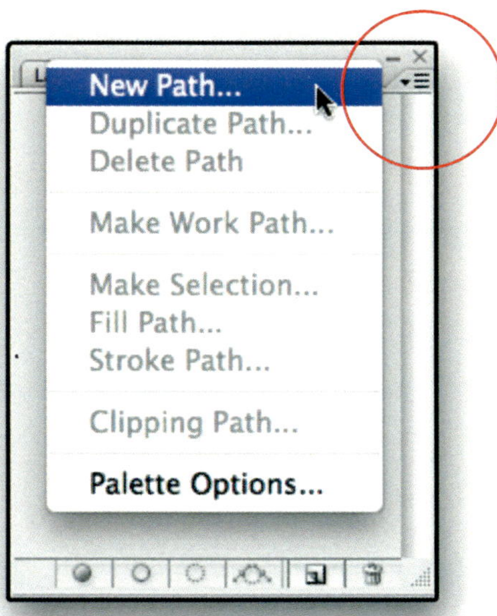

Step 3:

Bring up the Paths Palette. If it's not visible, Go to WINDOW MENU > PATHS.

Go to the small Fly Out Menu in the upper right hand corner of the Paths Palette. Click and hold, go to New Path.

Step 4:

In the New Path dialog box, give the Path a Name. I gave mine Outline.

Step 5:

Pick a starting point on the edge of the object. Click the mouse to place an Anchor Point. Click again further up the object. When clicking the mouse, drag out the Anchor Point.

These are Bezier handles that allow for sculpting the shape and direction of the Path.

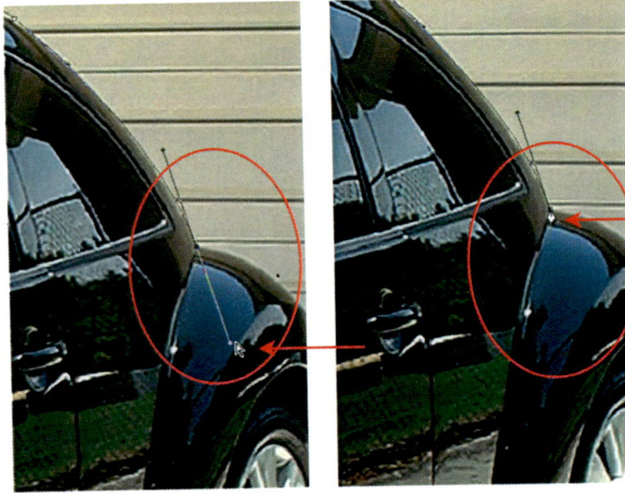

Step 6:

When changing the direction of the path, hold down the Option/Mac, Alt/PC, and click on the Anchor Point of the Path.

The Bezier handle will disappear right back into the point allowing direction change.

Step 7:

Every now and then while adding to the path it will be necessary to make adjustments to it. Hold down the Command/Mac, Control/PC, while grabbing the Bezier handle to move and adjust it as needed.

Step 8:

Continue around the object until it has been completely encircled.

Once this is done, look at the icon in the Path's Palette. It should indicate that it's finished.

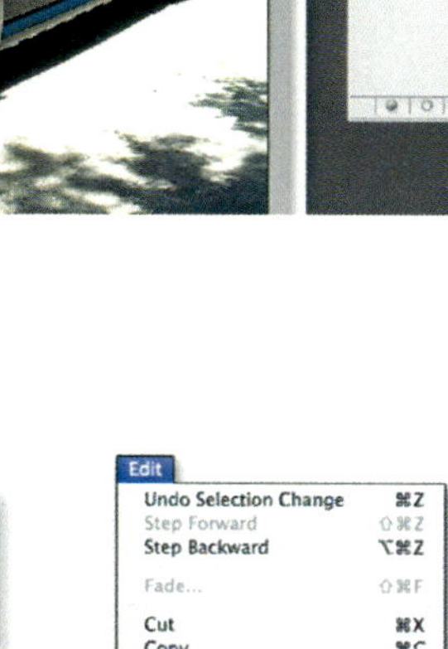

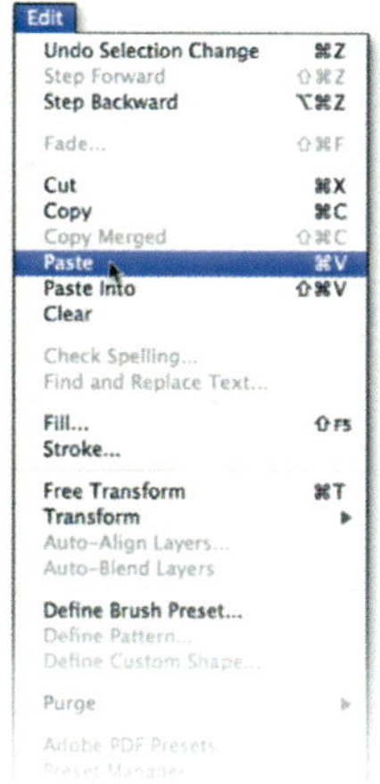

Step 9:

With the "Outline" Path selected in the Paths Palette, Hold Command/Mac, Control/PC, and click on the name of the Path to select it.

The marching ants should be visible around the object.

Step 10:

Click on the Layers Palette.

Go to EDIT MENU > COPY.

Then EDIT MENU > PASTE to put the selection on it's own Layer.

Step 11:

Turn off the Preview Eye Icon from the background Layer in order to see the final image removed.

I strongly urge you to use this method anytime you need to remove objects that have hard edges.

The more comfortable you get with the Pen Tool, the easier and faster these selections will become. This is a simple skill to learn that will go a long way in speeding productivity.

Creating a Distressed Effect

The Distressed Effect technique has been around for quite some time, and shows no signs of going away.

There seems to be no reduction in the popularity of this look.

There are a couple of ways to create this effect. The one I'll demonstrate here is all done in the computer using filters. The second one I will demonstrate in the next chapter.

Let's get started.

The ever popular Distressed Effect.

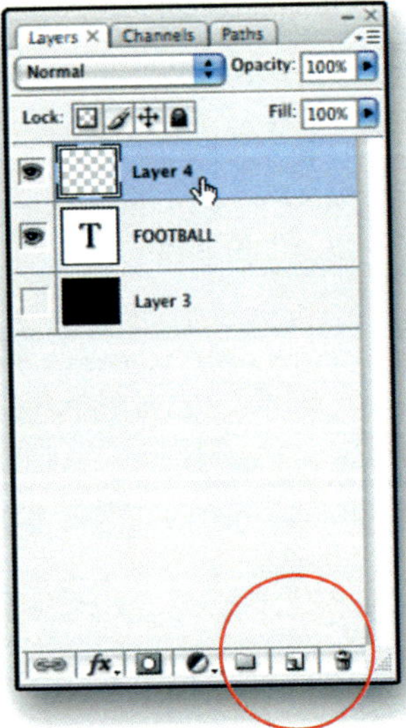

CREATING A DISTRESSED EFFECT

Step 1: Photoshop CS3 - CS5
Open a new document. Using a bolder looking font, set the type to distress.

Step 2:
Create a New Layer by clicking on the New Layer icon at the bottom of the Layers palette.

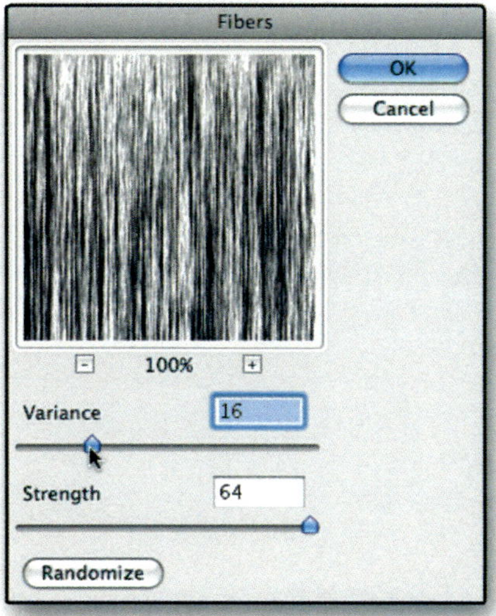

CREATING A DISTRESSED EFFECT continued

Step 3:

Using the Marquee Tool, draw a rectangle selection and fill with black.

Step 4:

With the rectangle layer still selected, go to the FILTER MENU > RENDER > FIBERS.

Step 5:

In the Fibers Dialog Box, experiment with the Variance and Strength. I used a Variance of 16 and a Strength of 64 in this instance.

Click OK.

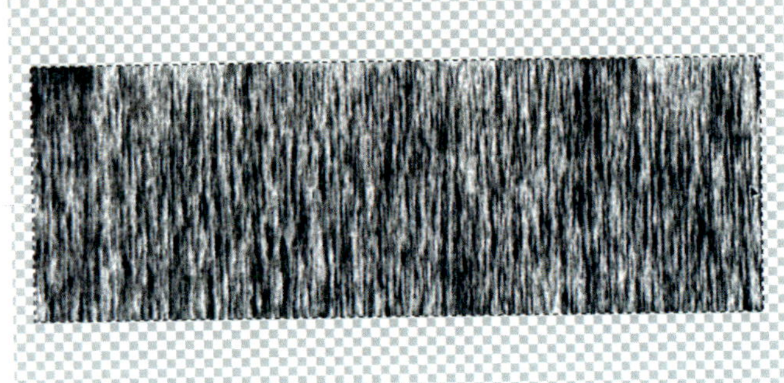

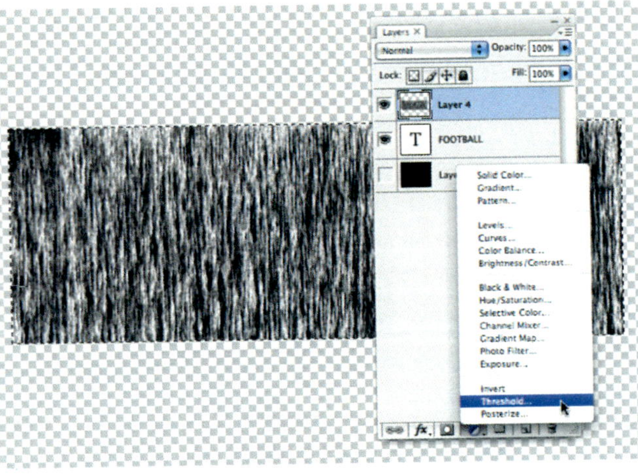

Step 6:

Go to EDIT MENU > FREE TRANSFORM.

Or press Command-T/Mac, Control-T/PC to bring up the Free Transform Command

Step 7:

Grab the right side anchor point and drag out to the right until the text is completely covered.

Double click inside the Transform area or press the Enter Key to accept it.

Step 8:

Using the Adjustment Layer icon at the bottom of the Layers Palette (it's the small circle filled half White and half Black),

Click and hold. Go up to Threshold.

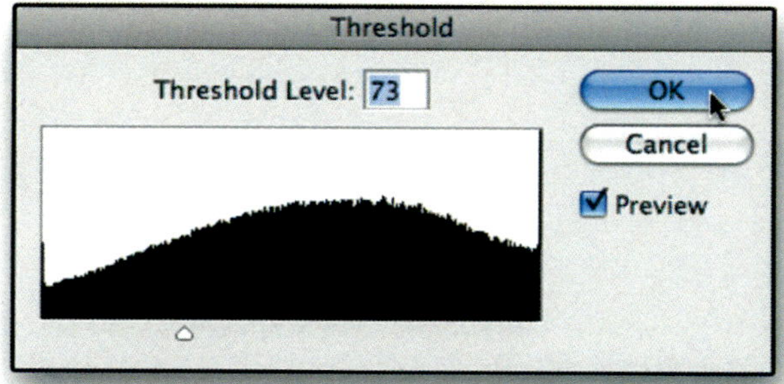

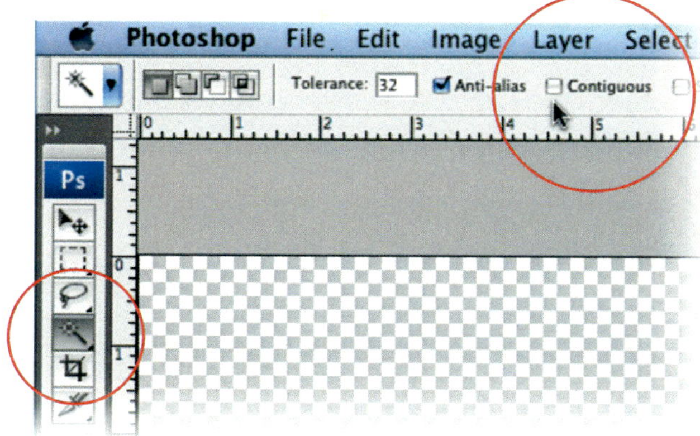

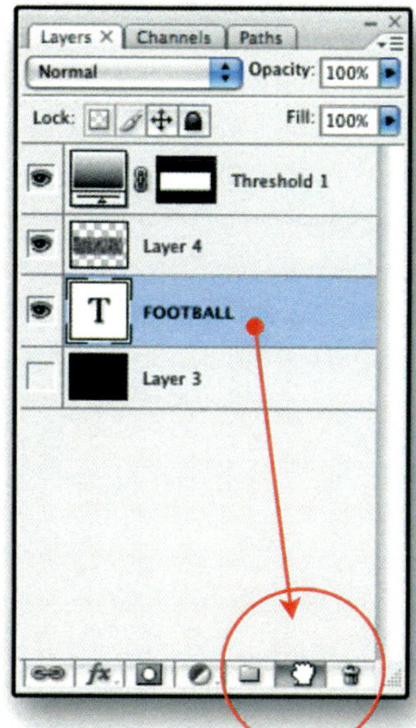

CREATING A DISTRESSED EFFECT continued

Step 9:
Move the Threshold slider to the left to reduce the amount of black just a little.

In this case, I used a Threshold Level of 73.

Click OK

Step 10:
Using the Magic Wand Tool, (be sure the Contiguous box is unchecked),

Click on the black areas in the image to select them.

Step 11:
Duplicate the Text Layer by dragging it onto the New Layer icon at the bottom of the Layers Palette.

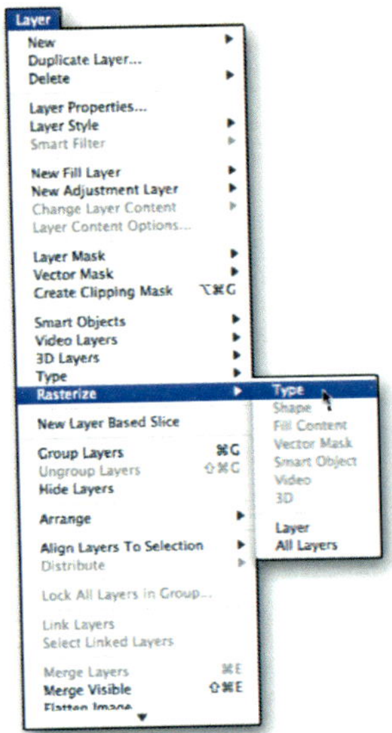

Step 12:

With the New Type "copy" Layer selected, Go to LAYER MENU > RASTERIZE > TYPE.

Step 13:

With the New Text Layer selected, turn off all other Layer preview icons.

While the Texture is still selected, press Delete.

This knocks out the areas beneath the texture.

Step 14:

Go to SELECT MENU > DESELECT to deselect the marching ants from the text.

Turn on a White Layer beneath the text.

This finishes the technique, It's done!

Doing the texture this way also allows for changing the color of the background Layer. It is simple to be ready to create those white underbases for printing those dark shirts!

Creating a Digital Underbase

The secret to producing the best possible quality dark shirt print with a digital direct-to-garment printer relies on the ability to create a good underbase.

Creating an underbase is not difficult, but most people are not aware of how to do it. They tend to rely on their RIP software that came with their printer.

My experience with most of the RIP software that generates an underbase automatically is that they are very weak. If your RIP allows you to bypass the auto generated base and use your own, I would recommend doing just that.

Here's how to make one!

Original

Underbase

Step 1: Photoshop CS3 - CS5

Open the file for which and underbase is needed. Be sure it is on a transparent background. Make the background Black.

Step 2:

Go to IMAGE MENU > DUPLICATE.

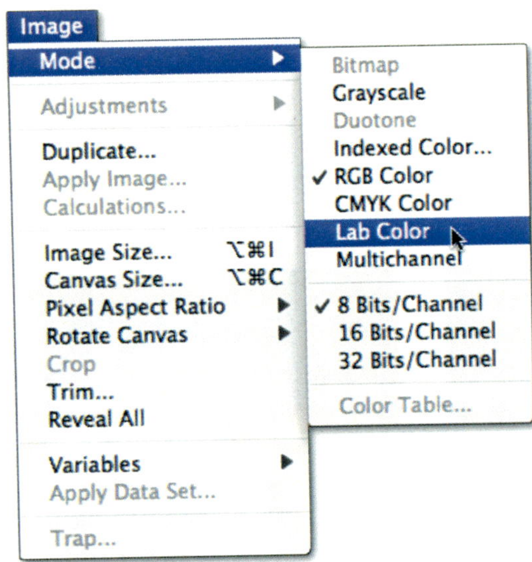

Step 3:

In the Duplicated file, go to IMAGE MENU > MODE > LAB COLOR.

If asked to Merge Layers, click Don't Merge.

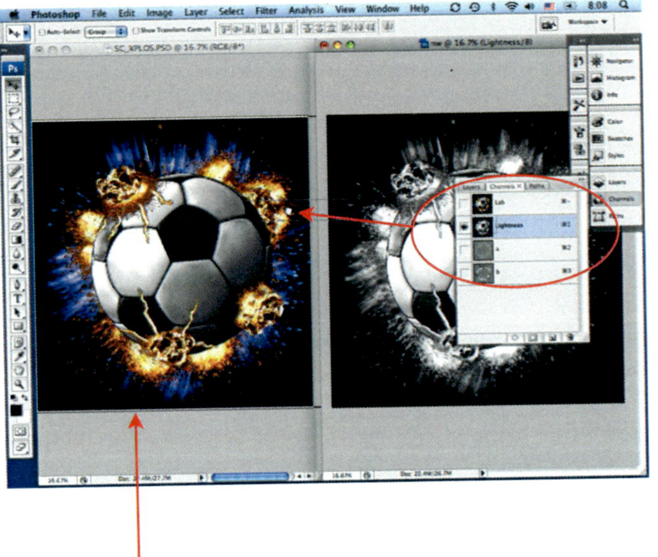

Step 4:

When converting a file's Mode to Lab color, there will be a Lightness Channel in the Channel list. This contains all of the detail in the image. The "a" and "b" channels contain all of the color data.

With the Lightness channel selected, click and drag it to the working document.

There will appear the working document window highlight with a border all around it. Once you see this, simply let go of the mouse.

This places the Lightness Channel inside the working document.

Step 5:

Now, close the Duplicated file. You won't be needing it again. Don't save it.

With the "Alpha 1" channel selected, go to IMAGE MENU > ADJUSTMENTS > INVERT.

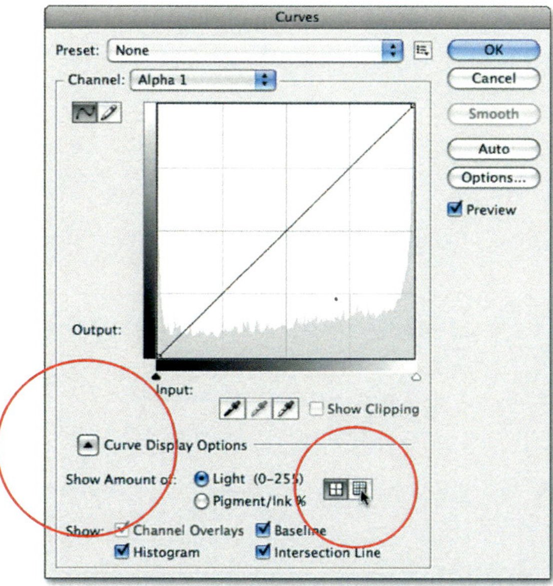

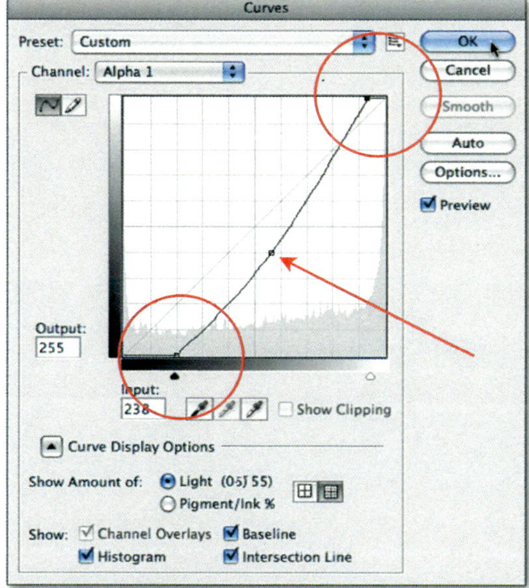

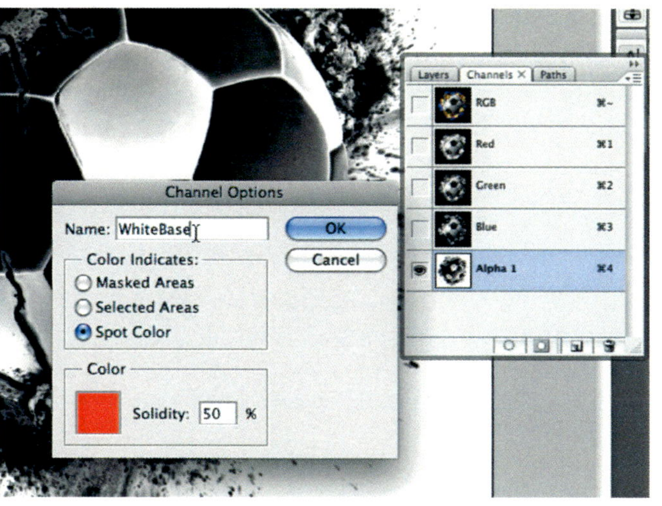

Step 6:

Go to IMAGE MENU > ADJUSTMENTS > CURVES.

In the Curves dialog box, toggle the Curve Display Options arrow.

Click on the little button with the smaller squares on it.

Step 7:

Move the corner point of the line at the Black corner over 2 lines (about 20%).

Now move the top corner, the White corner, to the left about 8% almost to the first line.

Pull the middle of the line down slightly. Recreate the line shown here, and you should be OK.

Each square represents 10% increments.

Step 8:

Double click on the icon of the "Alpha 1" channel in the Channel Options window, and give it a name.

The RIP you use will determine what "Type" of channel to use. Some RIP software requires Spot Color channels, and some don't. Check with your RIP manufacturer.

That's it! The Underbase is done.

CHAPTER 6

WORKING WITH PHOTOS

Working With Photos

More and more these days we see t-shirts and other printable products produced using full color graphics, especially photos. This technique is becoming easier and easier to print.

Back in the early 1990's, it was much more difficult to print full color graphics and photos on shirts. With the emergence of automated separation software, our job became much easier. So much, that today it's really no big deal to print such images. It is pretty much expected that anyone in the business should know how to do it. The separation software gives us a real advantage in doing just that.

Now that there are direct to garment digital printers and the relatively inexpensive dye-sublimation inks and printers, it's super easy to print these images. In fact, with these printers, it's actually easier to print full color graphics or full color photographs than it is to print simple spot color artwork.

Because it is so much easier to print this way, businesses find themselves printing more and more of these for customers.

That is where the strength of his chapter lies. The information I'm going to cover here will help with ALL forms of full color printing. Whether you're a screen printer, direct to garment digital printer, dye-sublimation or large format printer, the techniques I will cover will have the same exact work flow. Follow these techniques in either of the above mentioned printing forms, and the outcome will be success.

The lessons in this chapter will demonstrate methods to deal with some of the most common challenges facing day to day businesses.

A quick look below will show vast improvement and illustrate how necessary these steps are to producing quality prints.

Look at the difference. The Before image is the original photo. With literally, a minutes worth of effort the results are dramatic. Which one do you think would make for a happy customer?!!

Optimizing works on photos and paintings. If creating a digital painting or scanning something. The steps to use are outlined here.

See how it's done in the pages that follow!

Optimizing Your Files

Be sure to Optimize ALL of the full color images. These techniques work for photographs as well as full color paintings.

The steps are always the same. The only difference occurs with the amount the sliders are moved, or the numeric values punched in. The numbers are different from one image to the next, because the color data in each image is unique. These steps allow compensation for those differences.

This technique is easy to do. It will become a habit and allow photos to be fixed in less than a minute!

OPTIMIZING YOUR FILES

Step 1: Photoshop CS3 - CS5
Always optimize your files in the RGB mode.

Go to FILE MENU > OPEN. Find your image.

Go to IMAGE > ADJUSTMENTS > SELECTIVE COLOR.
In the Colors drop down menu, select Neutrals. Change the % in each Cyan, Magenta, Yellow and Black. Start with 3% in each and increase, if needed. (between 3 and 8 usually) Toggle the Preview check box on and off to see what's happening.

This is removing gray matter in the image which will allow bright vibrant colors when finished.

Click OK.

Step 2:
Go to IMAGE > ADJUSTMENTS > HUE/SATURATION. Move the Saturation slider only. (usually between +10 and +40) Numbers may vary depending on the image.

Be sure not to go too far and flatten areas of color. Look carefully at the screen. If small "blobs" of color that have been saturated too much appear, reduce the amount of the Saturation slider.

Click OK.

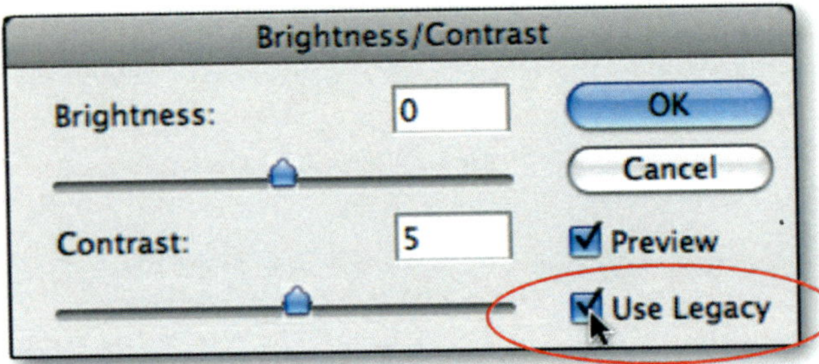

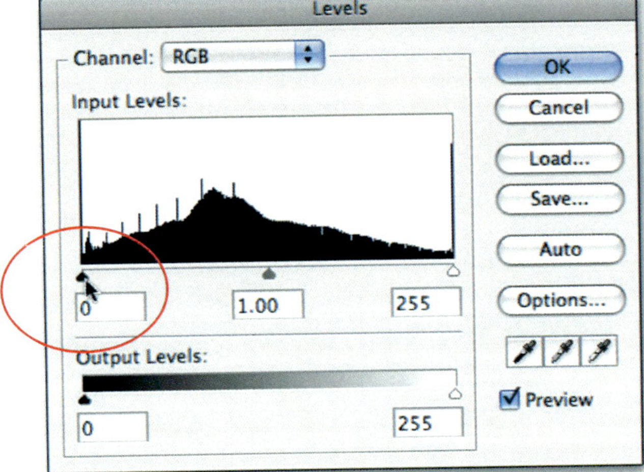

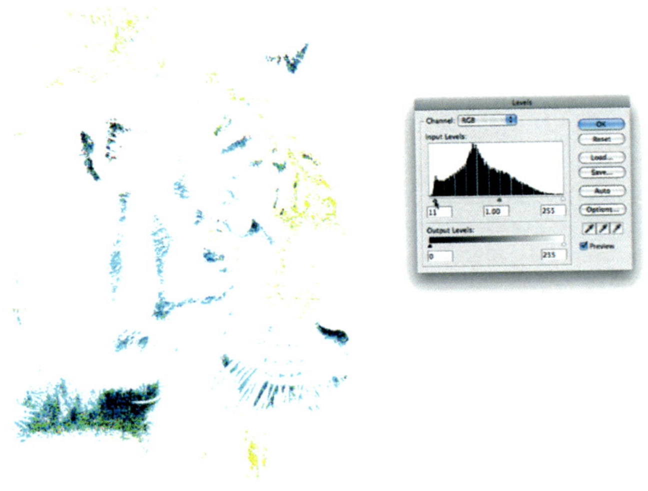

Step 3:

Go to IMAGE > ADJUSTMENTS > BRIGHTNESS/ CONTRAST.
If using Photoshop CS3, click on the "Use Legacy" box. If using any older version, it is not necessary to do this. We actually want to use the "bad" version of Brightness/ Contrast. Adobe really fixed the way this palette works in the CS3 version.

Move the Contrast slider only. Leave the brightness slider alone. Just bump the brightness slider ever so slightly. I always use a number 5. I'm looking for a very subtle increase in the contrast of the image.

Step 4:

Go to IMAGE > ADJUSTMENTS > LEVELS. When the Levels dialog box comes up, hold down the "option/ Mac" or "alt/PC" and move the left black input triangle to the right.

Step 5:

The screen will "freak out" and look like the this. Look for the first area to go completely black. (small chunky areas). Once at this point, release the black triangle.

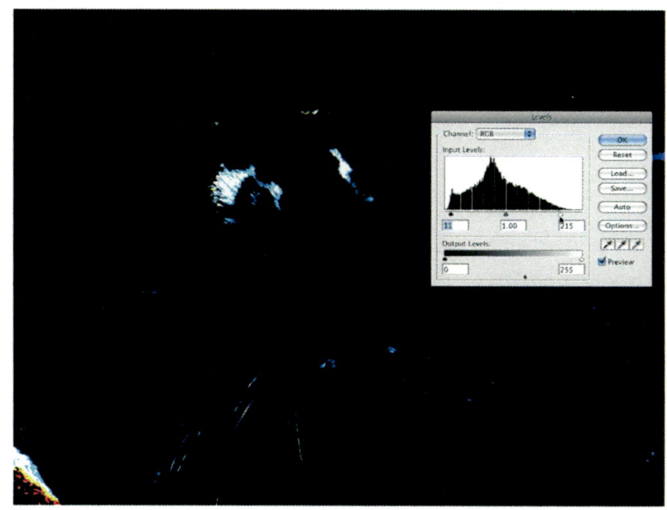

Step 6:

While holding the "option/Mac" or "alt/PC", move the white input triangle to the left. There should appear small, chunky white areas. Once you see this, click OK.

Step 7:

In this step I'm going to Sharpen the image the professional way. This is very quick and easy to do. Go to IMAGE > MODE > LAB COLOR. Be sure the Channels palette is visible. If it's not, (go to Window > Channels to bring it up.)

Step 8:

Select the "Lightness" Channel. The image will change to a grayscale preview. The reason I'm doing this is to sharpen just the detail or tonality of the image without damaging the color. The lightness channel is the detail of the image. The "a" and "b" channels contain all the color.

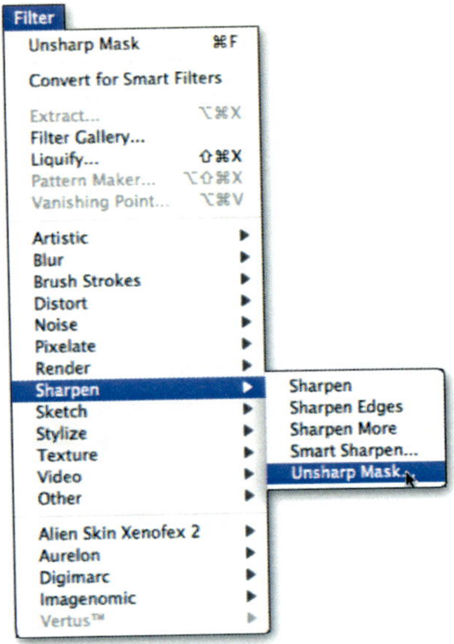

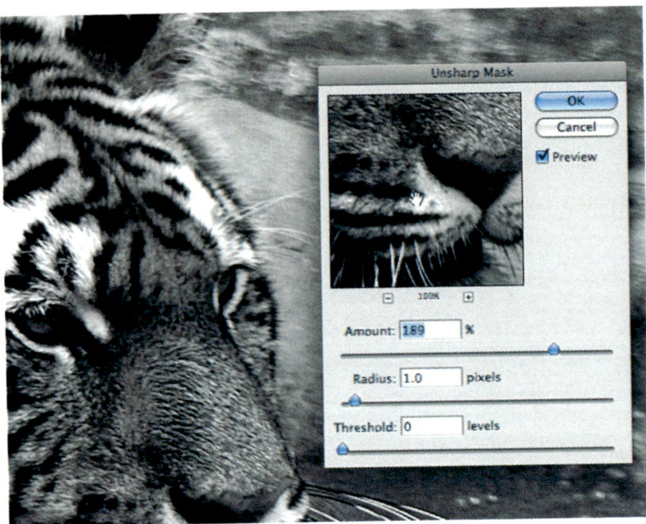

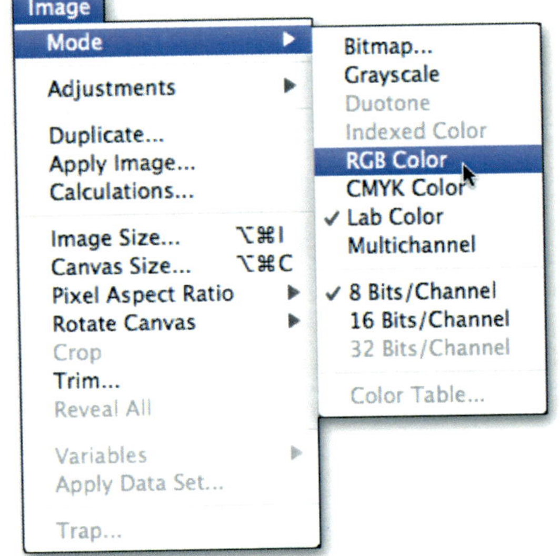

Step 9:

Go to FILTER MENU > SHARPEN > UNSHARP MASK. This will bring up the Sharpen dialog box.

Step 10:

In the Unsharp Mask dialog box, slide the "Amount" slider to the right. Each image is different; therefore, the amount the slider can be moved will vary. In this instance, I moved it to 189. The Radius is set to 1.0 by default, Threshold is set to 0. I usually just leave those as is.

Click OK.

Step 11:

The last step is to convert the file back to RGB mode. Go to IMAGE > MODE > RGB COLOR.

Fixing a Color Cast

When receiving a photo from a customer, don't expect it to always be print ready. In fact, never expect it to be print ready. Go through these steps to quickly improve the image in order to produce a quality print.

Let's get to it!

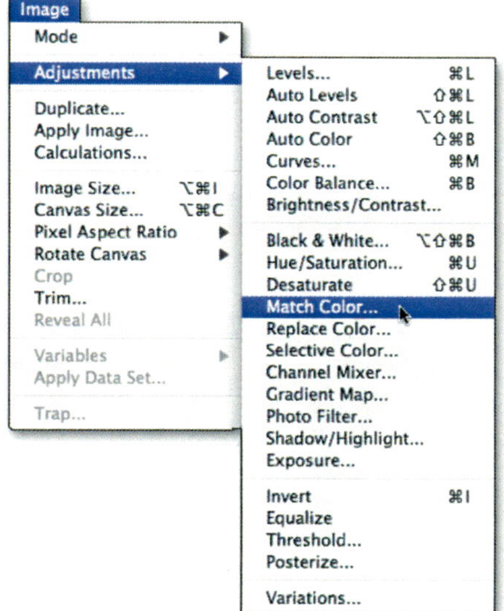

FIXING A COLOR CAST

Step 1: Photoshop CS3 - CS5

This image has multiple problems. First of all, there is a really bad color cast throughout the image. It is very yellow.

Another problem is that the image is too dark.

Step 2:

Go to IMAGE MENU > ADJUSTMENTS > MATCH COLOR.

This little trick works almost all the time.

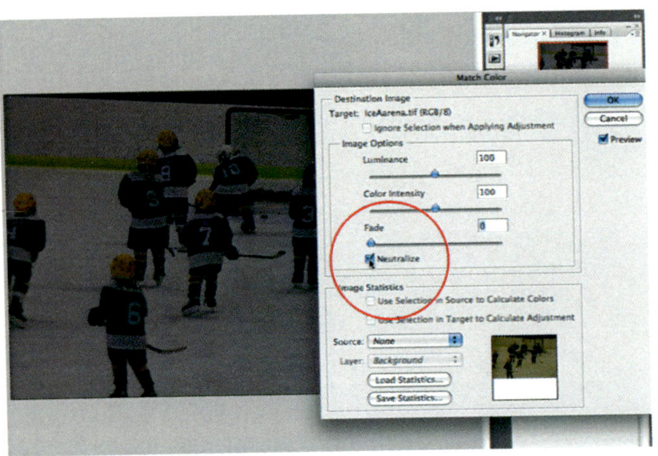

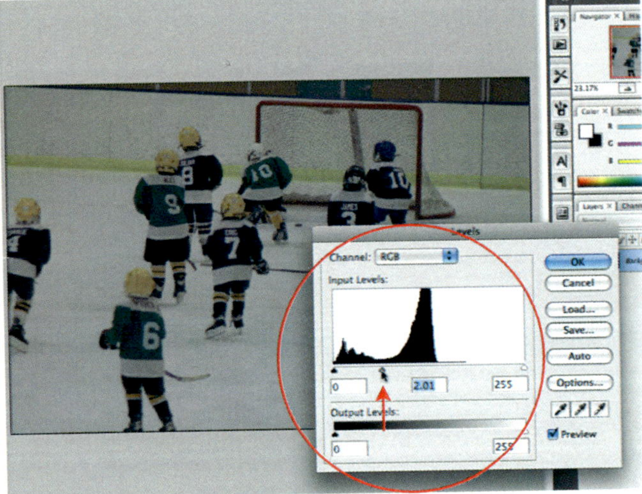

FIXING A COLOR CAST continued

Step 3:

In the Match Color dialog box. Click on the small check box - Neutralize. An immediate change will occur on screen.

The Color Cast is now gone, but it's still too dark. That fix comes next.

Step 4:

Go to IMAGE > ADJUSTMENTS > LEVELS to pull up the Levels dialog box.

Grab the Gray triangle slider in the middle of the Input area of the histogram. Drag towards the Black triangle. This will lighten the image.

Step 5:

Repeat the steps from the OPTIMIZING YOUR PHOTOS lesson here. You'll find the steps on page 143.

Image > Adjustments > Selective Color > Neutrals

Image > Adjustments > Hue/Saturation > Saturate

Image > Adjustments > Brightness/Contrast

Image > Adjustments > Levels. Set Black and White.

Image > Mode > Lab Color. Select Lightness Channel.

Filter > Sharpen > Unsharp Mask

Fixing a Photo That's Too Dark

If an image looks too dark, it will usually print even darker and look muddy. Some adjustments must be made to brighten and clean it up in order for it to print better.

It is necessary to first follow the steps here and then follow the steps from the Optimizing Your Files lesson earlier in this chapter.

Keep in mind, these steps will not create data. They can only help enhance information that is already there.

Here's how to do it!

FIXING A DARK PHOTO

Step 1: Photoshop CS3 - CS5
Go to IMAGE MENU > ADJUSTMENTS > LEVELS.

Step 2:
In the Levels dialog box. Grab the Gray triangle slider in the middle of the Input area of the histogram. Drag towards the Black triangle. This will lighten the image.

This will not create detail in the image. If there is any information in the washed out area, this will help pull it out.

When image is pleasing, click OK.

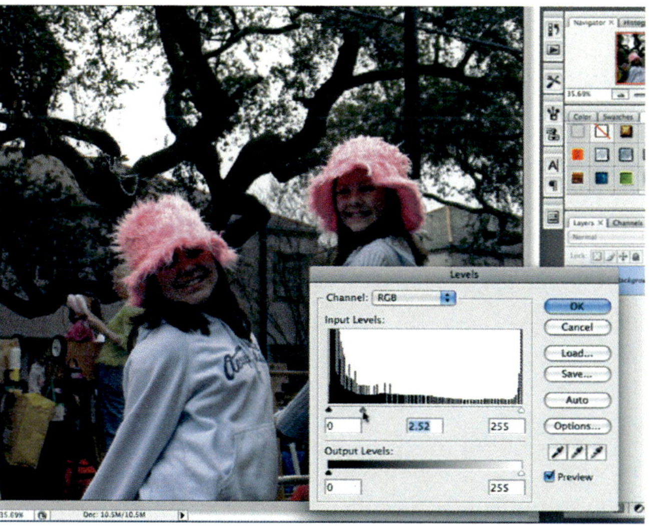

FIXING A DARK PHOTO continued

Step 3:
Finished Image.

Repeat the steps from the OPTIMIZING YOUR PHOTOS lesson here. You'll find the steps on page 143.

Image > Adjustments > Selective Color > Neutrals

Image > Adjustments > Hue/Saturation > Saturate

Image > Adjustments > Brightness/Contrast

Image > Adjustments > Levels. Set Black and White.

Image > Mode > Lab Color. Select Lightness Channel.

Filter > Sharpen > Unsharp Mask

Here are more examples of these same steps. The importance of running these steps on any image becomes obvious.

From this

To this

From this

To this

Fixing a Washed Out Photo

Fixing a photo that is too light or washed out is just as easy as fixing one that is too dark.

As with fixing the dark photo, some adjustments will need to be made to the photo first. Then, the Optimizing Steps from earlier in this chapter will need to be followed to finish the job.

Keep in mind, these steps will not create data. They can only help enhance information that's there.

Here's how to do it!

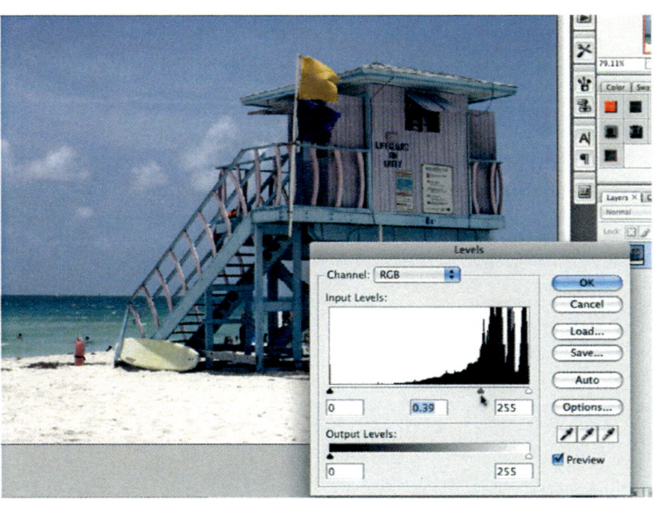

FIXING A WASHED OUT PHOTO

Step 1: Photoshop CS3 - CS5
Go to IMAGE MENU > ADJUSTMENTS > LEVELS.

Step 2:
In the Levels dialog box. Grab the Gray triangle slider in the middle of the Input area of the histogram. Drag towards the White triangle. This will darken the image.

This will not create detail in the image. If there is any information in the washed out area, this will help pull it out.

When you like what you see, click OK.

FIXING A WASHED OUT PHOTO continued

Step 3:
Finished Image.

Repeat the steps from the OPTIMIZING YOUR PHOTOS lesson here. You'll find the steps on page 143.

Image > Adjustments > Selective Color > Neutrals

Image > Adjustments > Hue/Saturation > Saturate

Image > Adjustments > Brightness/Contrast

Image > Adjustments > Levels. Set Black and White.

Image > Mode > Lab Color. Select Lightness Channel.

Filter > Sharpen > Unsharp Mask

Some more examples of these same steps. Just like the photo's that were too dark. I think these images speak for themselves. This only takes a minute to do, why not do them each and every time.

From this

To this

From this

To this

Removing Red Eye

When I see items printed using photos of people that have Red Eye, it really bothers me. There is just no reason this should happen. I have seen Kiosks in malls that print t-shirts, mouse pad, mugs, and other dye sublimated one off products for people using photos with Red Eye. I find this especially true around Christmas time when many vendor's sample items contain Red Eye.

It is easy to fix, so why not do it!

Red-Eye's can ruin a photo.

REMOVING RED-EYE

Step 1: Photoshop CS3 - CS5
Open the photo you want to work with.

Step 2:
Click and hold down the mouse on the Spot Healing Tool. It's the one that looks like a little band-aid.

The tools underneath that one will come out.

The Red-Eye Tool is at the bottom of the list.

REMOVING RED EYE continued

Step 3:
With the Red Eye Tool selected, move the mouse over on of the eyes that needs fixing. The cursor becomes a Plus sign.

Step 4:
Click the mouse once. The Red in the Eye disappears.

Step 5:
Repeat the steps of the other eyes. Click once on each. That's it!

Can you believe it?

Piecing Together Multiple Scans

Sometimes there are situations in which a customer requests an image be printed that's larger than the bed of the scanner.

When that happens, it is necessary to scan the image in in multiple pieces and put it together in Photoshop.

That's what I'll do here!

This image was scanned in two pieces because it wouldn't fit on the scan bed.

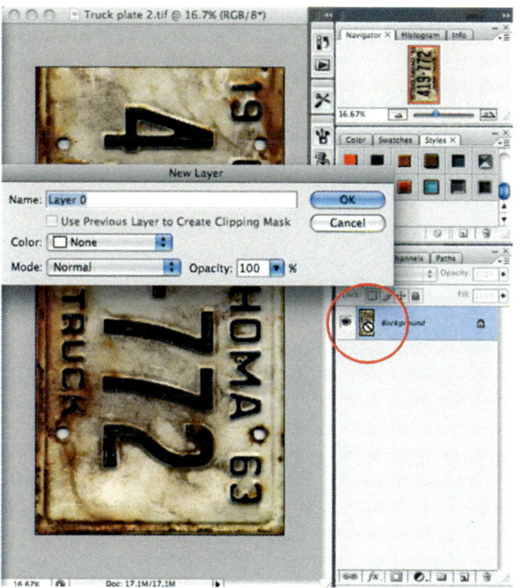

PIECING MULTIPLE SCANS

Step 1: Photoshop CS3 - CS5

This image needed to be scanned in two pieces, because the scan bed was too short. It missed by just under an inch.

With both scans (or more if your image needs it) open. Rotate them to the correct orientation.

Step 2:

Pick one of the files to be the "main" working document. Double click the Layer's icon to make it a Layer that can support transparency.

The Layer name should now read Layer 0.

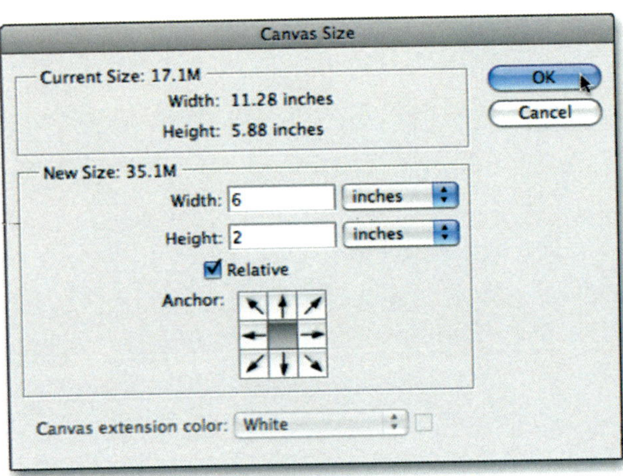

PIECING MULTIPLE SCANS continued

Step 3:

Go to IMAGE MENU > CANVAS SIZE.

Add extra space to have some room to work.

Step 4:

Make the second scan window active. Double click on the background layer icon to make it accept transparency, just like the previous step.

Select the Move Tool and drag the second scan image into the window of the working document.

Step 5:

With the Move Tool still selected, move the image until it lines up with the one beneath it. I like to move it until it is lined up in one direction first. (as shown here)

(See how much of the image didn't fit on the scan bed.)

Step 6:

Reduce the opacity of the top Layer to about 80%. This will allow you to "see" the image underneath and be able to line it up together.

Move up until you believe it is close to where it's supposed to be. Use your arrow keys to "nudge" the top image in whichever direction it needs to go.

Push the opacity back up to 100%

Step 7:

Select the Eraser Tool and make it a soft edge brush from the Options bar across the top of your screen.

Lower the opacity of the brush to about 90%.

Step 8:

With the soft edged Eraser Tool, erase up and down a little at a time until the two scans blend together.

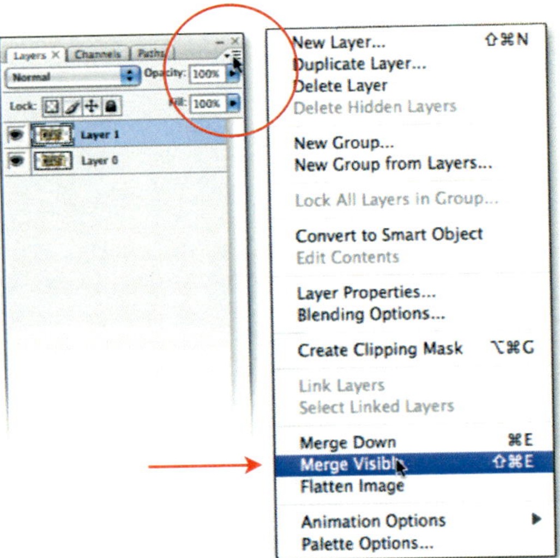

Step 9:
Go to the Layers Palette. Click the small fly out menu.
Come down to Merge Visible.

Step 10:
This image has some holes in it that need to be fixed.
Zoom into that area in order to see better.

Select the Eraser Tool. This time use a Hard edged brush.

Click inside the hole and start erasing.

Repeat these steps for all other holes.

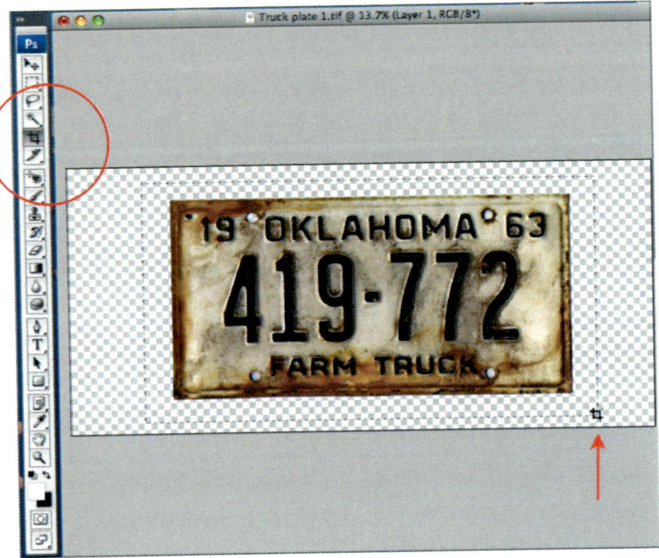

Step 11:
Select the Crop Tool. Drag select the image.
I like to leave a little room around the edges.
Double click inside the selected Crop area to accept it.

That's it!

Using Photo Templates

There are a few companies out there that offer Photo Template Packages in various themes. We are one of them. This photo template is one from our Baseball Sports Package.

If creating your own Photo Frame, do so similar to this one using multiple Layers. Be sure to leave the area you want the photo to go into as a solid black shape. This way you can paste into and adjust easily.

Let's get to it!

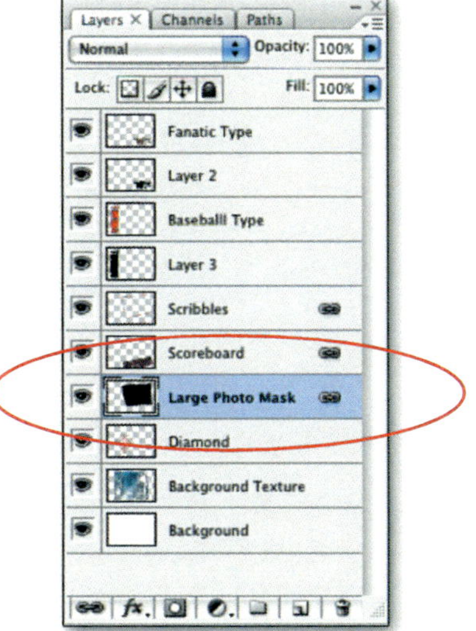

Step 1: Photoshop CS3 - CS5
Open the file you want to work with.

Step 2:
In the Layers Palette, select the Photo Mask Layer, or if working on your own template, select the black shape you want the photo to go into.

Step 3:

While holding down the Command Key/Mac or the Control Key/PC, Double click the Layer icon to select the black shape.

Step 4:

Open the photo you want to add.

Go to SELECT MENU > SELECT ALL

Go to EDIT MENU > COPY

Step 5:

Go to working file window with the marching ants still selected around the black shape.

Go to EDIT MENU > PASTE INTO.

CS5- Go to EDIT MENU > PASTE SPECIALTY > PASTE INTO.

USING PHOTO TEMPLATES continued

Step 6:

If necessary, zoom out with the Zoom Tool.

Go to EDIT MENU > FREE TRANSFORM

Step 7:

Change the size and rotate as needed to fit the frame area properly.

Step 8:

Final Image.

Now you can flatten the image. Save As something else. This way you always keep the original Layered file.

You're ready to print it on something!

Creating a Soft Photo Edge

When a customer provides a photo and wants it printed it on a T-Shirt or mug, adding a simple soft edge can be a quick fix for printing the rectangle around the photo on the shirt. No one wants to wear a squared edge photo!

This simple technique will really finish it off nicely.

This technique takes only a few seconds to create and will make for a happy customer.

Here's how to do it.

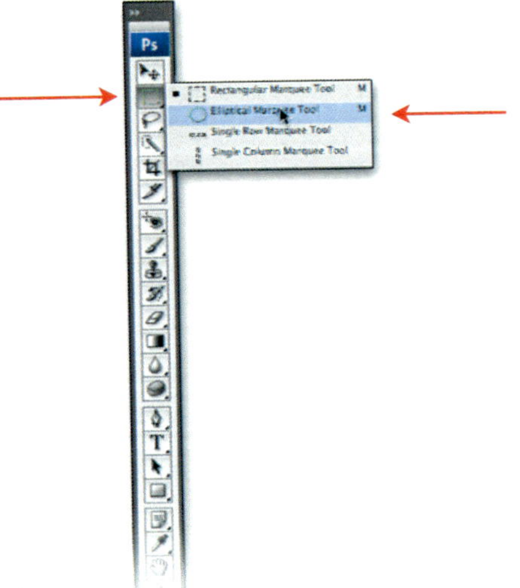

CREATING A SOFT PHOTO EDGE

Step 1: Photoshop CS3 - CS5
Open the photo you want to work with.

Step 2:
Go to the Marquee Tool. Click and hold down the Rectangle Marquee to have the Oval Marquee come out.

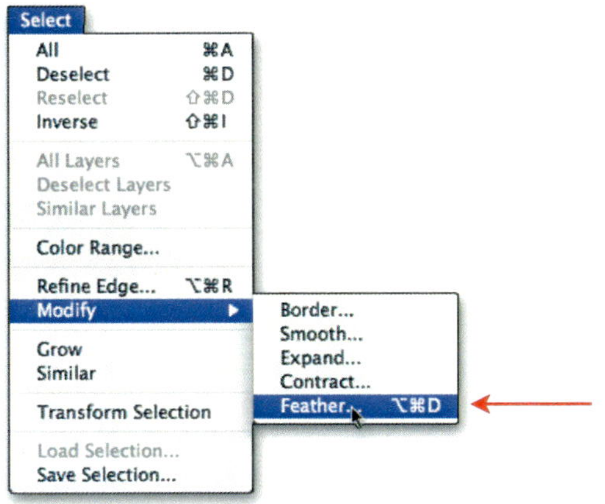

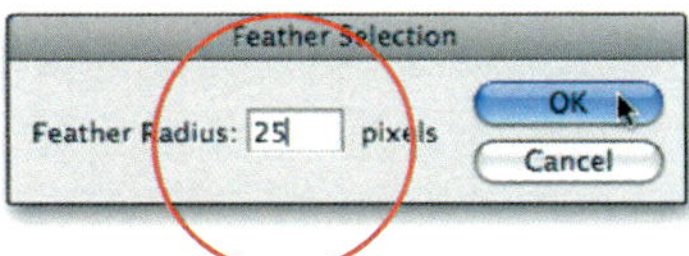

Step 3:

With the Oval Marquee Tool selected, position the cursor in the middle of the area to be kept. Click and drag out until you get the shape and size desired.

Step 4:

With the marching ants selected, Go to SELECT MENU > MODIFY > FEATHER.

In the Feather Selection dialog box, type in 25 pixels. This amount may vary depending on your image.

Step 5:

Go to EDIT MENU > COPY. EDIT MENU > PASTE. This places the image on a transparent background.

Now it is time to change the size, add text, and whatever else needed to finalize the design.

Changing the Color of Something

Every now and then, while working on a project, the color of the image just doesn't seem right. For instance, the image could be a guitar that is a nice light color, but could become an awesome image if it were red. Then make it Red!

Perhaps your wife is getting tired of the color of her car. You both still like the car, but would like it more if it was a different color. Or, maybe once a year, the local Irish pub needed to change the color of it's shirts for a special celebration. Try out any number of colors this way.

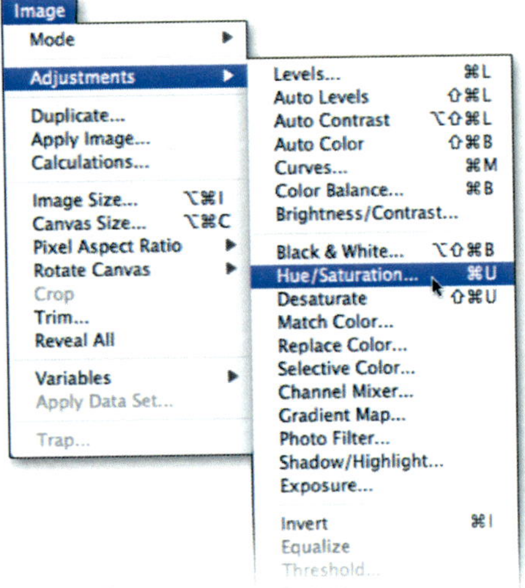

CHANGING THE COLOR

Step 1: Photoshop CS3 - CS5

Open the photo you want to work with.

If it is necessary to change only parts of the image, cut a path around the colored part that needs to change.

In this case, I don't need to do this.

Step 2:

Go to IMAGE MENU > ADJUSTMENTS > HUE/SATURATION.

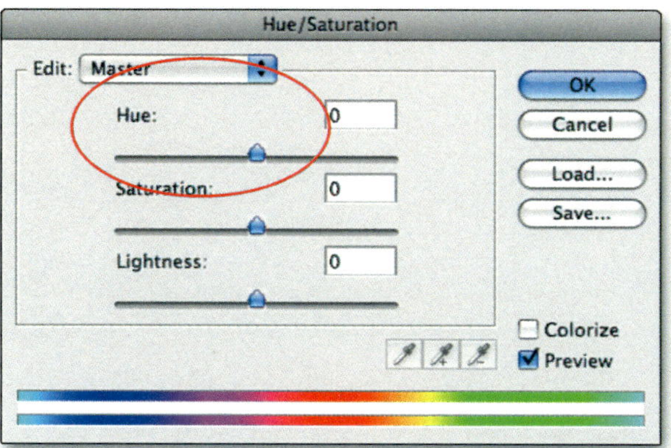

CHANGING THE COLOR continued

Step 3:

In the Hue/Saturation window, it is possible to control many things. The only thing I need to change for this photo is the "Hue". I'll slide the slider until I get a color I like.

Step 4:

Here are some different colored looks created just by moving the Hue slider left and right.

Step 5:

Once the color is satisfactory, click OK.

...I think it's time for one of these!

Scanning Software

The scanning software I'm using came with my Epson Expression 1640 XL scanner. This software has three "modes" from which to operate..

The first is HOME, which is the basic "dummy" scan. It makes all the decisions. The next is OFFICE, which gives a few more options. The one I use is PROFESSIONAL. It gives me more options to choose from, but you'll see that I don't use them. I still want complete control in order to scan in and make all of my adjustments in Photoshop.

Your scanning software may be different, but as long as you make sure the MODE, SIZE and RESOLUTION are set correctly, you will have similar results.

Like everything else in this book, I'm not going to delve into the technical aspects of scanning. There are many other books out there with entire chapters devoted to scanning. This book is designed to show the actual techniques and steps to complete the various projects that come across in everyday business. I will give you a few things to look for when deciding on which scanner to purchase.

When shopping for a scanner, one of the most important things to look for is the Optical Resolution of the scanner. This will determine how crisp your scans are. The next is Bit Depth or Color Depth which will determine how much detail can be captured in the image, especially in the shadow areas. And finally, the Scan Bed size is important. Most entry level scanners have "letter" size scan beds. I recommend a "tabloid" size if you can afford it. The larger the scan bed, the more items that will can scan in in one piece. It won't be necessary to piece together separate scans nearly as often.

Every scanner should have come with tips and instructions that show how to calibrate it. I do recommend going through any calibration suggested by the manufacturer.

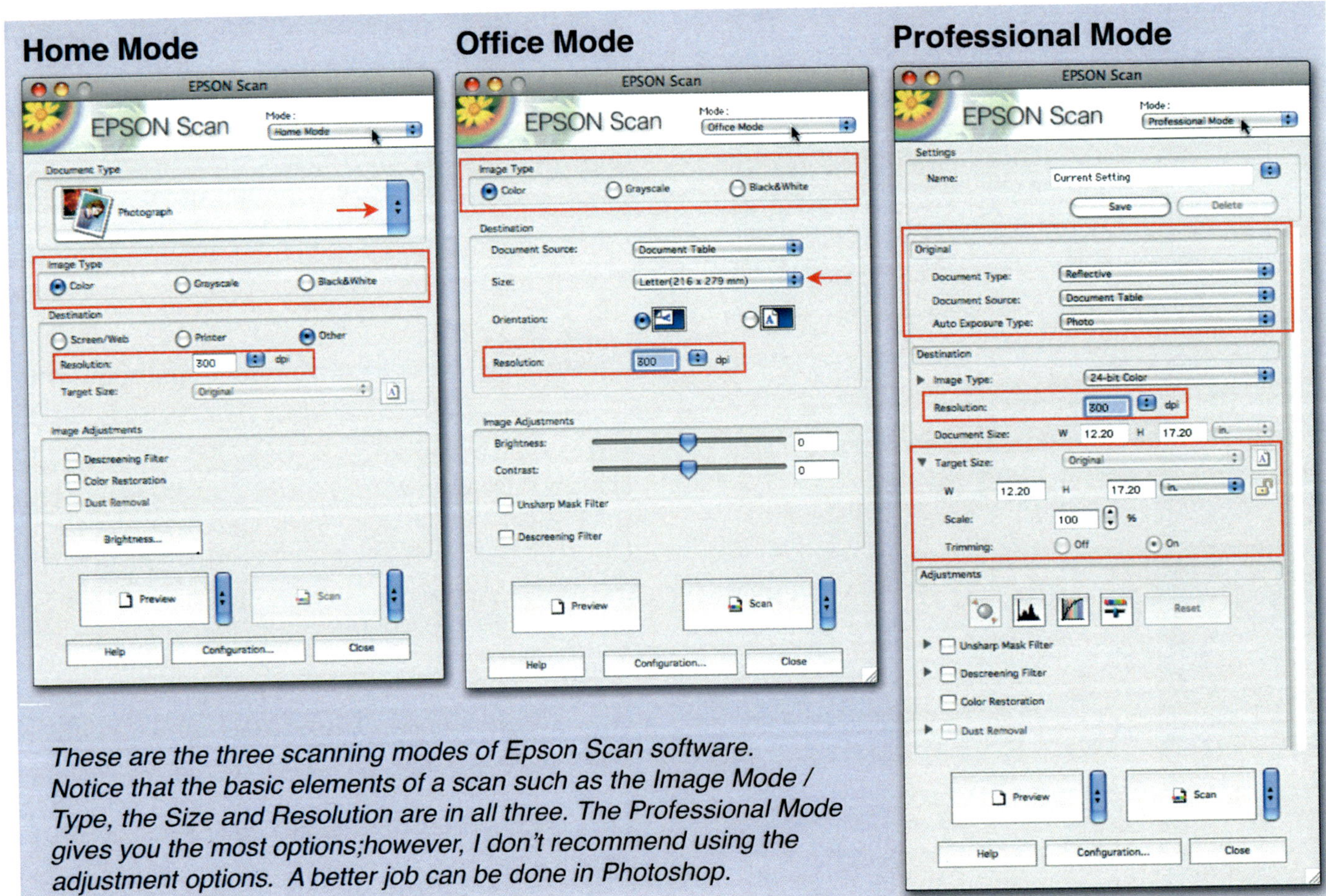

Home Mode

Office Mode

Professional Mode

These are the three scanning modes of Epson Scan software. Notice that the basic elements of a scan such as the Image Mode / Type, the Size and Resolution are in all three. The Professional Mode gives you the most options;however, I don't recommend using the adjustment options. A better job can be done in Photoshop.

Understanding some of the features scanning software provides will help you decide what to use and when to use it.

Document or Image Type
What type of document are you scanning? Is it a color photo? Is it a black and white photo? Is it Line Art? Is it an image that was already printed; such as, a magazine photo for instance? This will determine which option to choose.

Resolution
The resolution of a scanner is known as Samples Per Inch. Most of us refer to it in terms that are more familiar, DPI (dots per inch). While this is technically incorrect, most know what this means and can proceed accordingly.

The type of document will determine the kind of resolution needed. When scanning anything, know what the final size will be and account for it in the scanning software.

 Look at the three scanning modes to the left. It is apparent that the only one that allows you to specify an exact size is Professional. This is the main reason I use this mode.

If scanning in a color photograph that is 4"x6", but needs to be printed at a full front image size of 12" wide, enlarge the scale in the scanning software. Also, scan it in at 300 dpi. This will give plenty of resolution.

Adjustment Features
Most scanning software will offer some image adjustment features, such as Unsharp Masking and Descreening. The Professional mode that I use also offers Color Restoration and Dust Removal.

Unsharp Masking
Don't let the name fool you. Unsharp masking is what is used to "Sharpen" an image. Always sharpen a scanned image.

Descreening Filter
If you ever need to scan in something that has already been printed, such as a photograph in a magazine, use the descreen filter in the scanning software.
This will help eliminate any moiré patterns that might occur from the screens that were used when printing the image.

Dust Removal
Dust removal is a filter that helps to eliminate small imperfections such as dust and scratches in an image. Some of these can come from dust, dirt, wrinkles and any cracks on the original print. Others can come from the scanner's glass. Even though efforts have been made to keep the glass clean, sometimes dust can be on the inside of the glass. There it can't be cleaned easily.

Preview Button
The preview button allows you see a Pre-Scan. This is a low resolution quick pass of the scanning element. Normally, this will show up in a preview window. Once the image is visible, drag selection around just that area and scan that part only.

Histogram Adjustment
Is a poor attempt at Photoshops Levels command.

Tone Correction
Is a poor attempt at the tone Curves in Photoshop.

Image Adjustment
This allows control of the contrast, saturation, and color balance in an image. Once again, this is a poor attempt at Photoshop's tools.

Although these built in features might be helpful if image editing software isn't available, I just can't recommend using them Photoshop is available. Photoshop allows much more control over all of these things.

The only thing I might use from this list would be the Descreening Filter. If I scan in an image that was previously printed, I would normally use this feature, and save the other features for Photoshop.

Scanning Tips

Photographs
Scan in photographs,(Black and White and Color) at 300 dpi. Be sure to scale the image up to the required final size at the time of scanning.

Line Art
If you are starting out with camera ready "clean" line art, then scan it at 1200 dpi or higher if the scanner allows. This will produce a clean crisp image.

If the image is not the cleanest in the world, scan it in at 300 dpi and choose Grayscale as the mode. There are many more tools, such as curves, dodge and burn and brushes available to you in Photoshop to clean up the image.

FPO Logos
FPO Logos or "For Position Only" means recreating this artwork in the computer. Scan these types of images at 100 dpi but scale it to it's final size. Redraw these logos in Photoshop or Illustrator.

How to Scan a Photo

With the popularity of full color printing these days, it is often necessary to reproduce photos of people, places and things! You'll learn how in this lesson.

Scanning software is different depending on the brand of scanner, or the scanning software. However, the basic elements of scanning are the same.

Mode, Size and Resolution are the most important. As you follow along with me, look for these three things and you should be successful.

Here's how to do it!

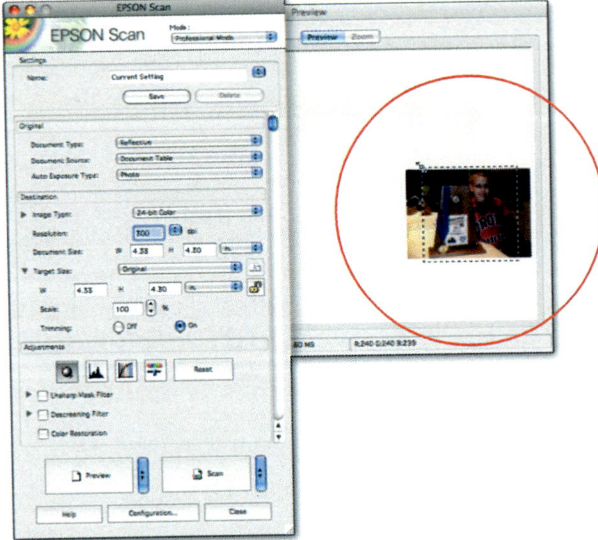

HOW TO SCAN A PHOTO

Step 1: Epson Scan Software
Place the photo you want to scan face down on the scan bed.

Open your scanning software.

Mine has a "Preview" button, If yours has one, click it.

Step 2:
The image will appear in the preview window.
Click and drag a marquee selection to "tell" the scanner what to scan. I've cropped the image slightly as you can see here.

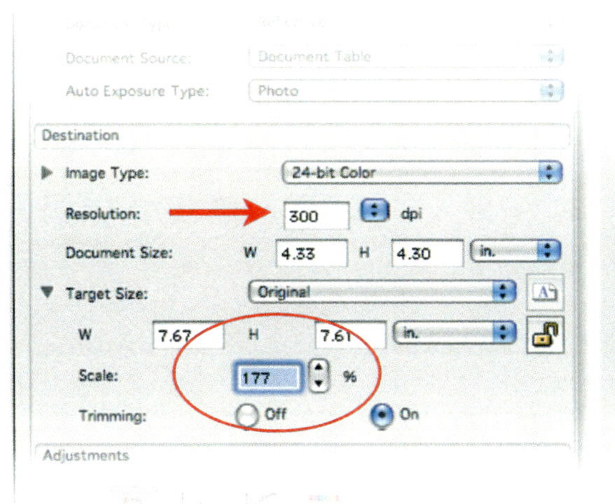

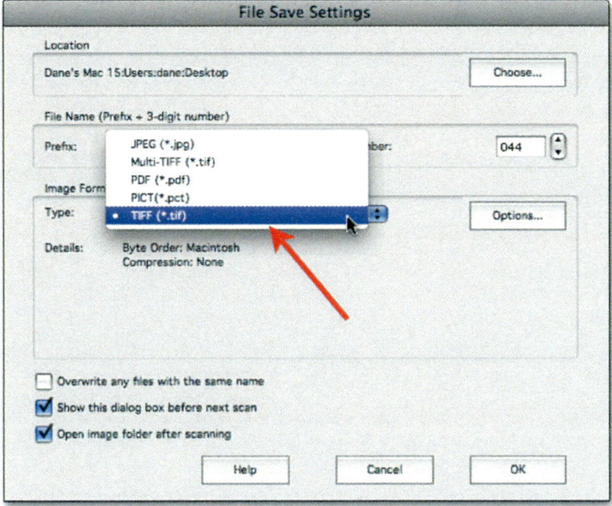

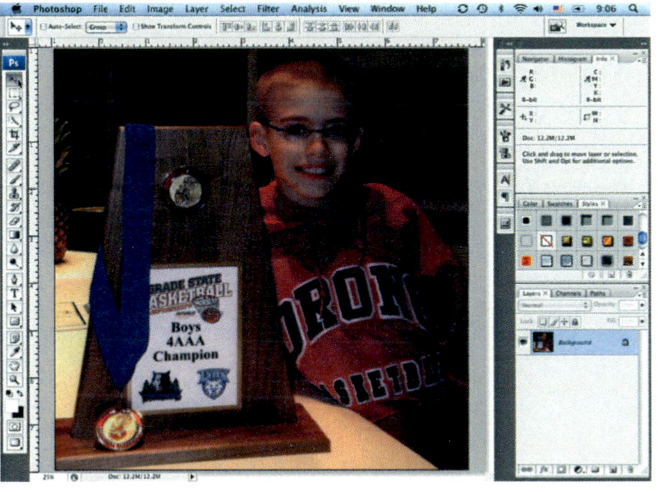

Step 3:

Set up the scan as needed.

I have a Basketball Photo Frame for this photo. I measured the size of the area for the photo. This helps me determine the size and resolution I need.

I put my resolution at 300 dpi and enlarged the image 177%.

Now that everything is set up properly, I'll click OK.

Step 4:

Before the scan is actually done, this software will give a File Save Settings window.

In this window choose the location to put the file. Give it a name. It puts a number after the name, and you can choose the type of file to use.

I chose TIF because it is easily handled in Photoshop, and it won't lose data when I save it like a JPEG does.

Click OK.

Step 5:

This is the file opened in Photoshop.

Now I need to perform the "Optimizing Your Files" steps on this image. These steps can be found at the beginning of this chapter. These steps will remove the magenta color cast and make this photo overall much better. Look at the image at the top of the previous page to see the difference.

After the steps are performed, this image will be ready to be placed in the Photo Frame.

How to Scan a Logo

In this lesson I will show how to scan in a "Camera Ready" logo. This means that the customer was able to provide a very clean print of the logo.

This is used for the type of image on the the right. It works perfectly for a sponsor's uniform back, or anytime when a clean edged logo or graphic is needed.

 Scan this way when there isn't much to clean up or do to the logo or image.

It's really easy. Here's how to do it!

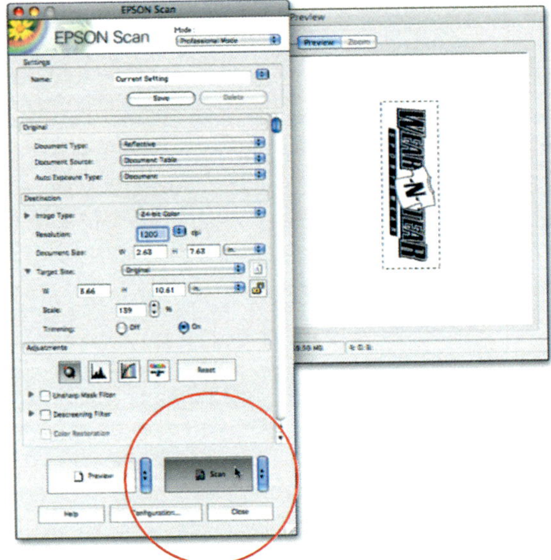

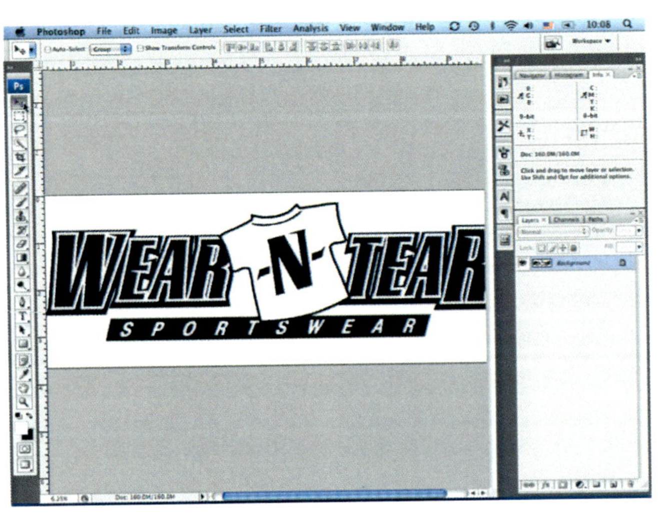

HOW TO SCAN A LOGO

Step 1: Epson Scan Software

Place the logo face down on the scan bed.

Click the Preview button. Drag select the logo to scan. If this is not done, the scanner will scan the entire scan bed resulting in an unnecessarily large file. Most of it will be blank white space.

If the scanning software has an option for line art, choose this option. If it doesn't, it will still work. Follow the steps below either way.

Change the size and resolution. Since I'm going to use this logo as is and don't plan on spending time re-creating or cleaning it up, I'll change the resolution to 1200 dpi.

It may take 5 minutes or so to finish this scan because of the high resolution.

Step 2:

This is the file opened in Photoshop. Now it's ready to be placed in the sponsor back file!

How to Scan a FPO Logo

In this lesson I'm going to demonstrate how to scan in a FPO (For Position Only) logo. This means that the original probably isn't very good, and I will have to rebuild the entire logo in a vector program.

This scenario is commonplace in a business. You will (I promise) be asked to create a t-shirt design from a customer's business card. More often than not, it will be torn, tattered, and worn.

When presented with one of these, this is what you do!

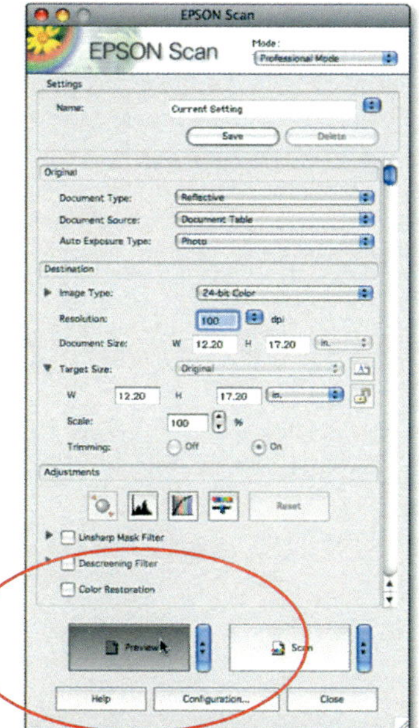

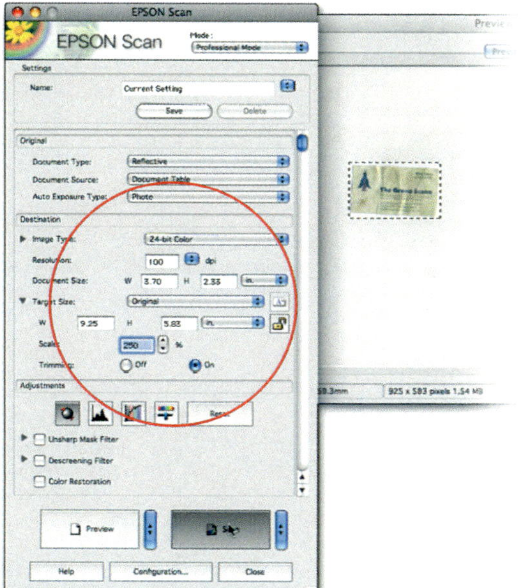

HOW TO SCAN A FPO LOGO

Step 1: Epson Scan Software
This lesson will be completed in Chapter 4.

Place the business card face down on the scan bed.

Open the scanning software, click Preview.

Step 2:
Drag a marquee selection around what is to be scanned.

Check the size, and be sure to enlarge it as needed here in the scan.

Only use 100 dpi for this type of scan. I will be placing this scan in Illustrator and tracing over it to create a quality vector file.

Click Scan.

Creating a Distressed Texture

I like to call this technique my "Old School" Distressed technique. It has been around a long time and I have my doubts that it will ever go away.

If using an older version of Photoshop, then this one for you. The distressed texture in Chapter 5 was created using a Photoshop filter new to CS3 called Fibers. This technique requires no filters, just a piece of paper and a scan.

It's really easy, here's how you do it!

DISTRESSED TEXTURE

Step 1: Illustrator and Photoshop CS3 - CS5

Open Illustrator and create a new document. Choose the Rectangle Tool from the Tool box.

I just used a regular Letter sized document for this, not my template file as I normally would.

Step 2:

Drag select a box that fills most of the page. Using the Fill box at the top left of your screen, fill the box with Black.

It is also possible to create a black page in Photoshop and you will not need to use Illustrator.

Step 3:

Print out one sheet of paper with the solid black box. It should look like the one here.

Step 4:

Crumple the sheet into a small ball as seen here. Unfold the paper and crumple it again. Repeat this several times.

Step 5:

After crumpling the paper several of times, unfold, roll, and twist it. Twist it really tightly. Unfold it and repeat.

Repeat these steps several times.

The objective here is to have a very wrinkled and "distressed" piece of paper to use as the basic texture for the effect.

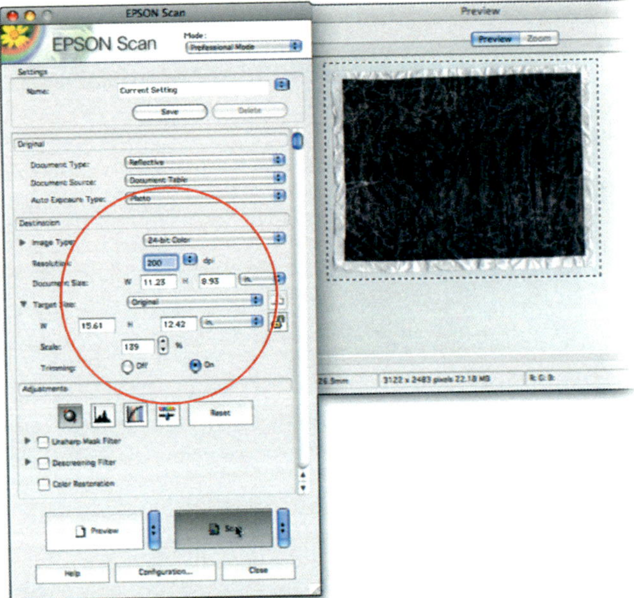

Step 6:

The paper should look something like this one.

When it does, scan it into the computer.
This scan only needs to be 200 dpi since there is no
real concern for much detail.

Step 7:

Place the paper face down on your scan bed.

I scanned this at a resolution of 200 dpi and enlarged
the page, so that it would fit over most of the designs
I'm choosing.

This one was enlarged 139% and the final size was
12" x 16".

Step 8:

With the scanned image opened in Photoshop, select
the Crop Tool from the Tool Box.

Drag select as much of the black distressed area as
possible.

Double click inside the area or press the Enter Key to
accept it.

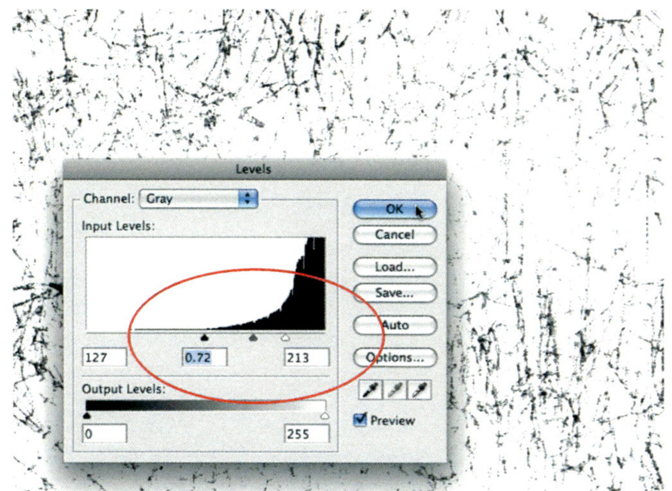

DISTRESSED TEXTURE continued

Step 9:

Go to IMAGE MENU > ADJUSTMENTS > INVERT.

This will invert the texture as seen here.

Go to IMAGE MENU > ADJUSTMENTS > LEVELS to bring up the Levels dialog box.

In the Levels dialog box, compress the range to give the distressed information more contrast. Do this by sliding the Black triangle towards the White one and the White triangle towards the Black one.

Step 10:

Open the image to be Distressed.

Open the Distressed texture at the same time, side by side.

Drag the Texture Layer into the Artwork file. Notice when you click and drag a layer to a new file, a Black border around the window of the new file will appear. Let go of the layer.

This moves the texture from one file to another.

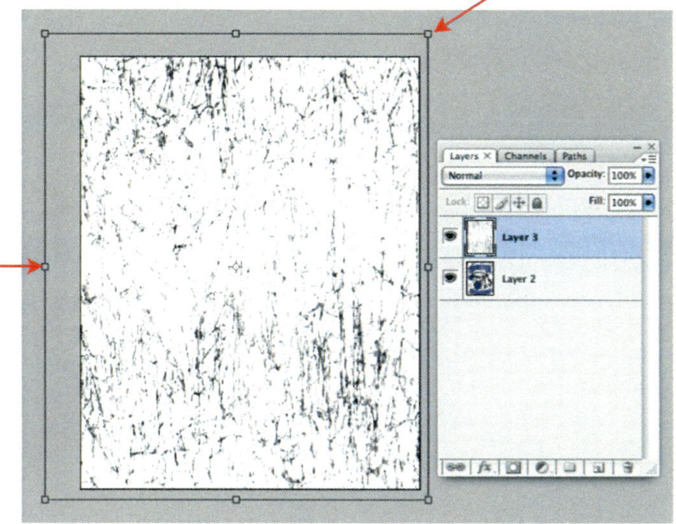

Step 11:

Zoom out a little. Go to EDIT MENU > FREE TRANSFORM.

Grab the anchor points and reduce the size of the texture. I "squeezed" mine in from the left and right. Be sure all of the image to be distressed is covered.

Press the Enter Key or Double click inside the Transform.

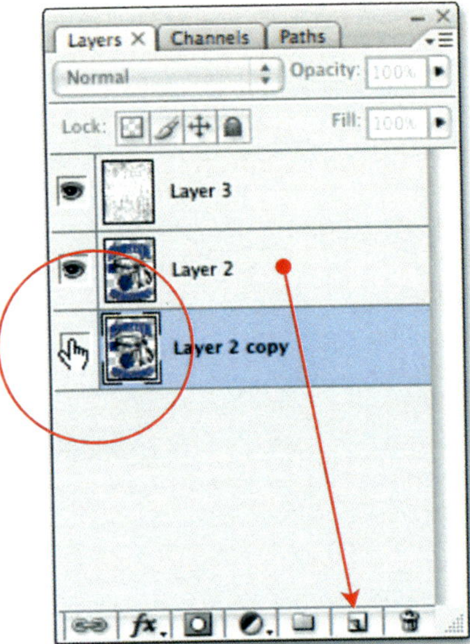

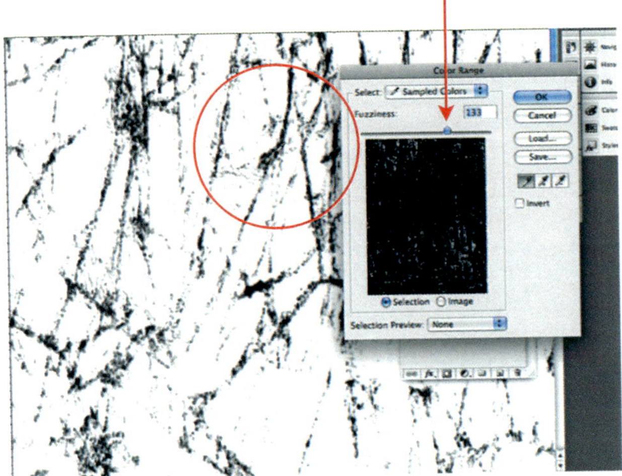

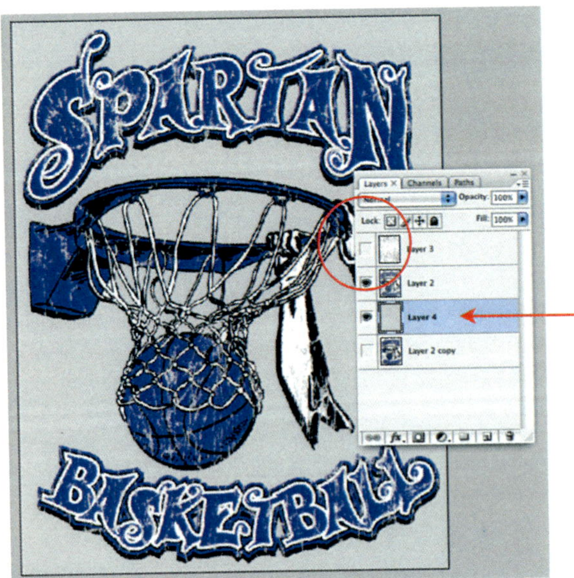

DISTRESSED TEXTURE continued

Step 12:

Copy the Artwork Layer for safe keeping by dragging it onto the New Layer icon at the bottom of the palette.

Turn off the Preview Eyeball for the Artwork Layer underneath.

Step 13:

Select the texture layer by clicking on it once.

Zoom in really close to get a good view of the texture's color.

Go to SELECT MENU > COLOR RANGE.

Click on a dark area of the texture. Adjust the "Fuzziness" Slider.

Click OK.

Step 14:

With the Marching Ants still selected, turn off the Preview Eyeball for the Texture Layer.

Select the Artwork Layer by clicking on it once.

Press the Delete Key to knock the texture out of the image. Deselect the texture.

I like to put a light gray Layer at the bottom of the list in order to see how the design will look.

Creating the textures this way will allow you to change the background layer's color. This will enable the use this technique for screen printing or digital printing on any color garment.

Saving Texture for Future Use

Save your Distressed Texture for use with other images in the future.

You may want to create a few different textures this way. (some with little distressing, others with really heavy distressing)

Keep the Textures in a folder close at hand in order to get to them quickly.

This is how to do it!

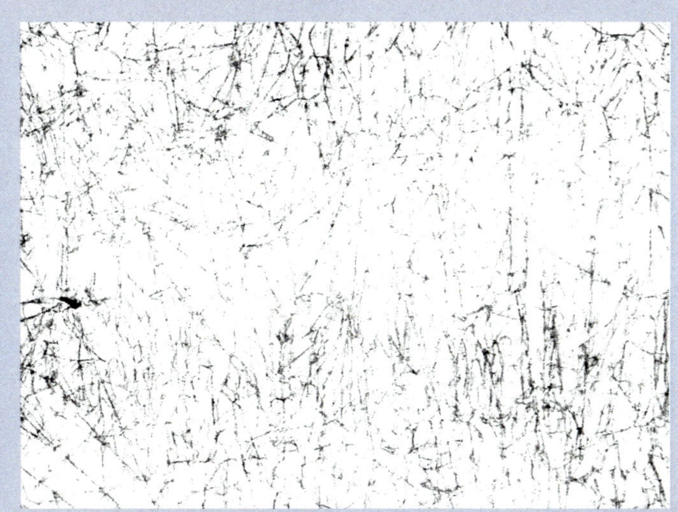

SAVING TEXTURE FOR FUTURE

Step 1: Photoshop CS3 - CS5

I've opened the Texture image used in the previous lesson. It was saved as a Grayscale document. I need to make it a Bitmap document. That way I can use it really easily in Illustrator.

Go to IMAGE MENU > MODE > BITMAP.

Step 2:

In the Bitmap Window, leave everything set as default. Whatever the resolution of the file is, that's what will appear in the Resolution Output box.

Use the Diffusion Dither as the Method.

Click OK.

When saving the file, save as a TIF.

That's it! It's ready to use in Illustrator!

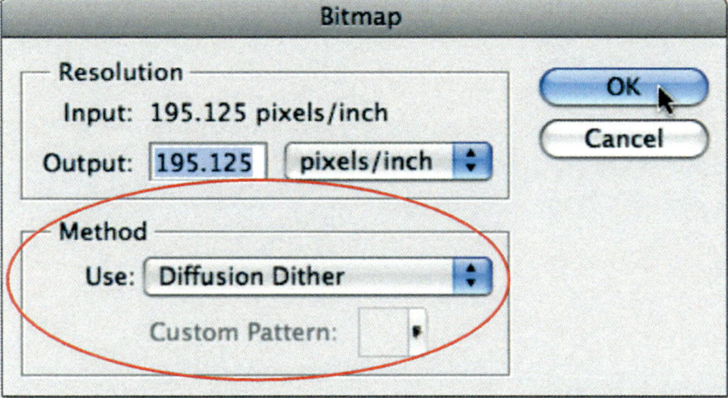

Masking Part of a Photo

In this lesson I'm going to show how to remove part of a photo, so it can be placed on top of another background. This technique will allow endless possibilities for creating almost any situation for your images.

I'm going to place this little guy into a Photo Frame with a completely different background.

Here's how!

MASKING PART OF A PHOTO

CS5- This lesson does not apply. Adobe removed the Extract Plug-in.

If you'd like, you can download the Extract Plug-in from the Adobe website and use it in your CS5 version. Visit www.adobe.com and search for Extract Plug-in. Download and install it.

Step 1: Photoshop CS3
Open the file you want to work with in Photoshop.

I'm going to get rid of the distracting background and place him in a Photo Frame. I'll use this image to print some cool shirts.

Step 2:
Go to FILTER MENU > EXTRACT.

T-SHIRT ARTWORK SIMPLIFIED · Using Adobe Photoshop and Illustrator   **CHAPTER 6**

MASKING PART OF A PHOTO continued

Step 3:

In the Extract Window, select the Edge Highlighter Tool. The tool at the top of the Tool Box.

Photoshop explains what this tool does next to it. This tool says "Marks the edge of the areas you want to retain."

Use this tool to "Draw" around the image. Zoom in on the image when needed by using the magnifying tool.

"Split" the difference along the edges, and be sure the brush goes over both sides of the edge of the image.

Step 4:

Select the Fill Tool, the paint bucket tool just below the Edge Highlighter Tool.

Photoshop now says "click the Fill Tool in the areas you want to retain."

Step 5:

Click the mouse. The image should fill with blue.

If the entire window fills with blue, the highlighted edge is not closed. Press Command / Control -Z to undo and close the open gap.

If it looks good like this one, click OK.

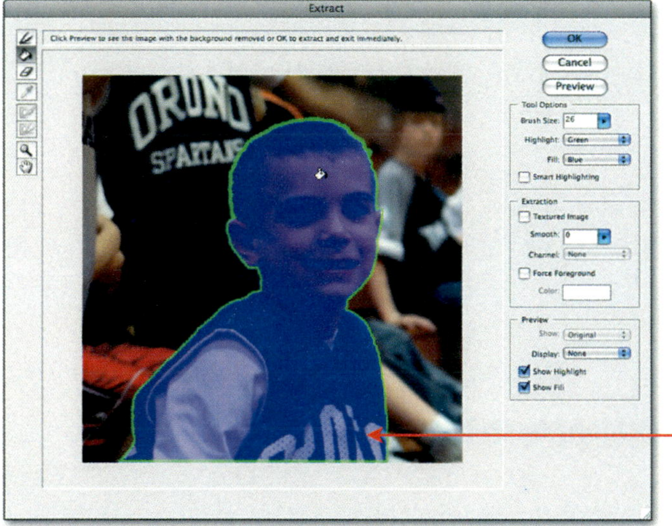

Step 6:

The image should be visible on a transparent background in Photoshop.

There may be some weird looking artifacts around the edges. This is normal, and they need to be cleaned up.

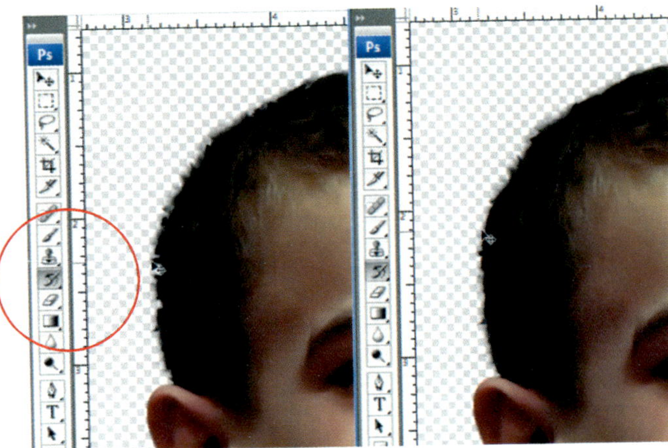

Step 7:

Zoom in on an edge to see what needs to be cleaned up.

If the image has any missing gaps or holes, select the History Brush Tool. It's the brush with the little swirling arrow on it. The History Brush lets you "Paint" back in from the original photo.

Clean up any missing gaps and holes throughout the image.

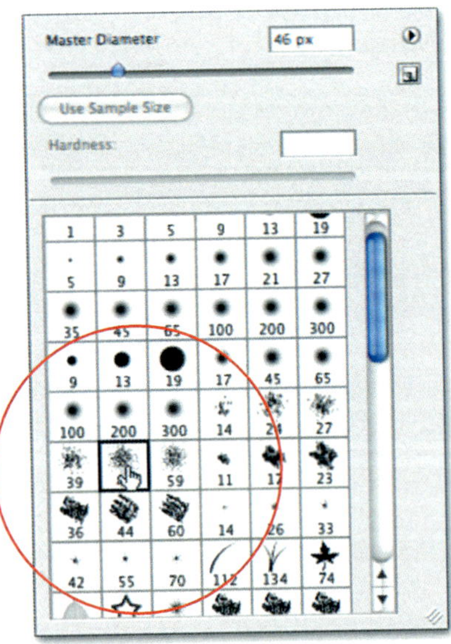

Step 8:

Choose the Eraser Tool to erase elements that are floating around the edges. If it is a softer or more random edge as seen around his hair, choose a rough edged brush similar to the one here.

MASKING PART OF A PHOTO continued

Step 9:
Go around the entire edge of your image. It should look clean, like this one here.

Step 10:
Command / Control click on the Layers icon to select everything on the Layer.

Go to EDIT MENU > COPY.

Step 11:
This is one of our Photo Frames. I selected the Black Mask layer and went to EDIT MENU > PASTE INTO.

This put the photo inside the shape I wanted.

Resize and adjust as needed using the Free Transform tool.

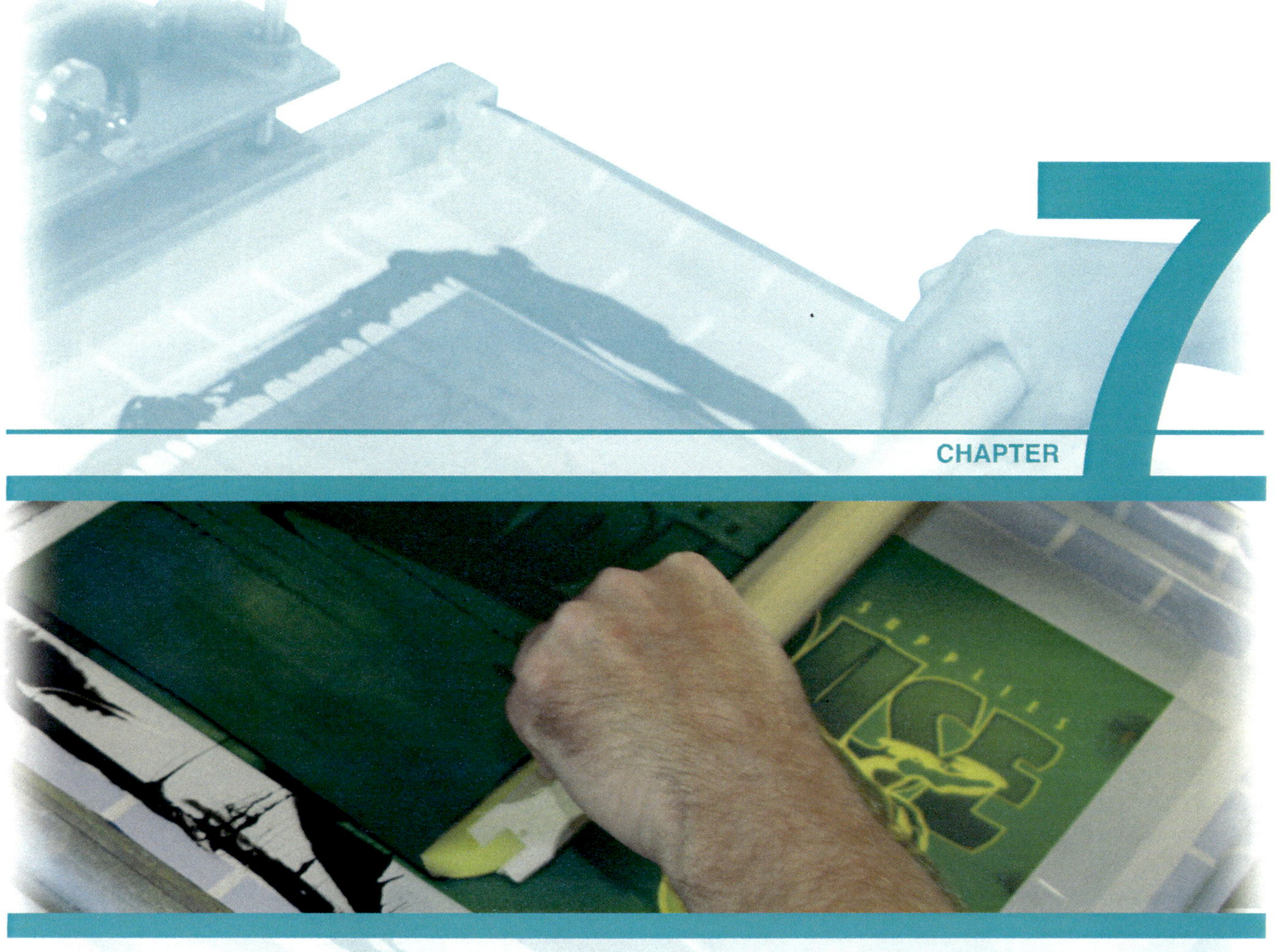

SEPARATING YOUR ARTWORK FOR SCREEN PRINTING

Separating Your Artwork for Screen Printing

Separations are the process of breaking down the colors in an image. This is necessary in order to screen print something in multiple colors. It is necessary to have one color per screen. These screens are set up on press and contain one ink color. At that time each screen/color is printed, one after another in order to finish the print.

Before today's sophisticated separation software appeared in the marketplace, decorators could spend literally days creating a single set of separations. Thankfully, industry-specific software has made the job much simpler. In fact, an experienced decorator can create separations for a job in minutes. With that in mind, the average businessman might be wondering whether he should now bring the job of creating separations in house.

For the uninitiated, the thought of doing separations may be about as intimidating as the prospect of building an automatic press from scratch. In reality, it is not as overwhelming as one might think. Undoubtedly, it takes practice and skill to make high-quality separations that create great-looking prints. But, armed with the right tools and knowledge, it's a job that's well within anyone's reach.

The Fundamentals

Screen printers with any experience at all know that when artwork has multiple colors, each color requires its own screen. This requires "disassembling," or separating, the artwork by color. For instance, a black and green image would be separated into two screens — one for black ink and the other for green.

They would also be aware that the artwork is either in a raster or vector format. Raster, or bitmap images, are pixel-based and generally used for artwork such as photographs, full-color paintings, and illustrations. Vector images are made of geometrical shapes based upon mathematical equations that represent images in the computer.

Ironically, although vector artwork is simpler to create than raster, it can be harder to print. Depending on how large an image's elements are, it is possible for them to bleed together. Meaning it will be necessary to "flash" in between colors, or at least every other color. With raster artwork, the white underbase can be flashed, and everything else can print wet on wet when separated properly. If the setups aren't perfect, it is less likely to be noticed.

Some jobs may require separating raster images, others might involve separating vector images, while still others may involve a combination of the two. For instance, a printer may have an image of a full-color raster mascot along with the word "Eagles" in vector. Combining both techniques achieves the best of both worlds. Ultimately, whether using vector or raster depends on the artwork the customer provides. If presented a photograph of his hot rod, it wouldn't be scanned, traced, and turned it into a line drawing. It needs to be scanned, separated, and printed.

Vector-based software

Adobe® Illustrator includes the capability to do spot-color separations for vector artwork. (Technically, spot-color separations can be created in Photoshop, although that is not really advised.) While these programs aren't technically separation software, they will do the job just fine for vector-based images. Nothing else is needed to create separations for this type of artwork.

Raster-based separation software

Unlike vector separations, those for raster images require industry-specific applications. Additional money will need to be spent on a stand-alone program or a separation plug-in for Photoshop. These include Spot Process / Separation Studio, T-Seps, or Quick Seps. Prices for most separation applications range from around $350 to $895.

Taking a Test Drive

If you're not sure which stand-alone separation program or plug-in to use, visit supplier Web sites and look for trial downloads. You can find a fully functional trial version of the separation software that I choose to use in my studio, Spot Process, at my website. Download the software, and give it a shot. This way, you can spend a few weeks test driving the programs and find out which one best fits your needs. There is a learning curve on all of them. They are all capable of getting the job done with some better than others. Therefore, it is ultimately a matter of your likes and dislikes.

A test drive is even more important for a non-artist without graphics training. Creating separations is a mechanical process, not necessarily an artistic one. An eye for recognizing what looks good, and knowing the goal to achieve on screen as adjustments are made is essential. This doesn't require an artist. It's really about numbers and percentages.

Fortunately, even the most complicated separation software is not very difficult to learn. Perfect results right off the bat are not likely. However, looking over the directions, watching the training videos, and reading through the manual will cut the learning curve in half or more! I cannot stress this enough!

There is an important caveat to this, however. The graphics software must be mastered first, and then the separation program should follow. In other words, if purchasing a separation plug-in for Photoshop, the first step is — not surprisingly — to learn Photoshop. (The exception here is Spot Process, which is a stand-alone separation program. There is no additional graphics software to learn.)

Another training option would be to have an artist create separations for you (generally at about $20 to $25 per color) and print them out. Then try your hand at creating separations for the same artwork. Compare your work to that of the artist. How did he create the separations? What percentages did he use? How did the printed results from his separations compare to those of yours?

Color Considerations

Given that separations are all about "splitting" an image into separate colors for separate screens, one may wonder if it is necessary to have any kind of formal color training. Fortunately, that's not required. For starters, it is T-shirt printing, not fine-art posters on paper. While the goal is to create the image as close to the original as possible, the detail will never match perfectly.

What is seen on screen is generally very close to what will result on press. Of course, that's not always the case. Sometimes it is possible to print out the film, burn the screen, put it on press, and have it looks nothing like the original. The blue may be too strong, for instance. Or, the red isn't strong enough. Here again, it's important to try demo versions of the various separation applications in order to see for yourself whether one does a better job producing colors accurately.

The bottom line is that as complicated and confusing as doing separations may appear at first, it isn't rocket science. Expect to spend about one to three weeks perfecting the technique. Start with a relatively simple image, separate it, print it, and take a critical look at it. Once you see what has happened on the press, go back to the art room and make some adjustments. Darken or lighten certain channels. It may be necessary to repeat

this print/adjustment cycle two or three times before getting it right, but you'll get there.

With enough practice, you will reach a point when the most you may have to do is darken or lighten the ink color. Everything else is perfect, right off the bat.

Spot Color

Spot color images are probably the most commonly printed images for screen printing. Usually they involve a limited number of colors that can be separated and printed easily. Sometimes they will have a black outline with colored fills. They usually can be printed with basic colors right out of the bucket. The only exceptions might be a need to match a corporate color.

Process Color

Process color images contain four colors. (Cyan, Magenta, Yellow and Black). Often referred to as CMYK or Full Color, Process color is used to print a full color photographic type of image. Each screen is created with halftone dots and blend the colors together, usually in a rosette pattern, to achieve the finished print.

Because this process uses transparent inks, process color prints usually only work well on light colored shirts. In most cases that is a stretch. In order to get a really nice, rich print it is usually necessary to add bump or extra screens in order to achieve this. So in my opinion, why bother.

Simulated Process Color

Simulated process on the other hand is nothing like true process color. It uses spot colors, opaque plastisol inks for vibrancy. When separated properly, this type of printing will be very forgiving and easy to print. It uses halftones. Although, there are instances when it is married with vector elements. The halftones are printed out at the same line screen and angle. This process requires printing wet-on-wet. The only exception being if it is on a dark garment. Then print a white underbase and flash cure just that one screen. Print the rest of the colors on top, wet-on-wet.

For more information on Spot Color, Process Color and Simulated Process Color see the section dealing with working with color in chapter One.

Indexed Color

Indexed color images can contain from 2 to 256 colors. There is no screen printing press that can print 256 colors; therefore, the colors must be cut down to something manageable, depending on the press.

It uses a dithered dot, not a halftone dot. In order to reproduce an image of a green leaf radiating from dark green to light green, it will be necessary to print with three different greens. (one dark, medium, and light) In order to achieve quality prints with this technique, a press must have many heads.

Working with Vector Separations

When working with vector art and creating separations, it is important to consider a couple of things. If using more than one color in the image, it is imperative to create some type of registration. Registration is the accurate aligning of one color on top of another when printing. This prevents any unwanted overlapping of colors or gaps between colors.

Registration assures that all of the elements in a design will be printed in the correct place.

Keeping these examples in mind, it would be assumed that you would be printing Spot Colors from your vector files. These types of registration will not work with Process files.

When working with vector artwork, there are three main types of registration to consider, TRAP, BUTT, and GAP.

Trap Registration Is probably the most common form of registration in the industry today, and probably the one that should be used the least. It consists of one color expanded slightly by a thin line or color called a stroke. This line, usually 1 point thick, is overprinted in order that a small overlap of colors will occur. This type of registration helps prevent any gutters from occurring between colors. However, if the colors tend to "bleed" or expand when printed, this may not be the best type of registration to use. If there is too much bleeding, colors will begin to mix and look muddy or may actually change color.

If this is the case, there are a couple of things to do. It may be necessary to flash cure in between each color. This, however, can slow production down to a crawl. Butt registration may be worth a try.

I believe the reason that TRAP registration became so popular is that most presses are not in tune. Most people don't know how to level the palettes on their presses. With most manual presses, for instance, if the head is in the raised position, the screen should not move even if wiggled just a little. Manual presses contain little plastic bolts, some are plastic bushings, that hold the screen head in place when it is laid down to start printing. These are plastic because they are supposed to be replaced when they wear out. It is cheaper than having something metal wear out in the head. I would guess that these plastic bolts are worn out on most presses, which would allow large amounts of movement! Required maintenance is often not done. If leveling the palettes and otherwise keeping equipment tuned up isn't done, the printer will often just "stroke" a little extra around this element and overprint it. This results in a little fudge factor with the registration. This lack of attention to detail has taken on like wild fire in out industry. It seems everyone is using this type of registration.

Butt Registration is the type of registration to achieve when screen printing. If done properly, it is possible to print really long runs without having to clean the buildup on the back of screens and flash in between colors. With this type of registration, the colors touch one another with no overlap. This helps prevent too much mixing of colors if they should bleed. However, because there is no overlap, there is the chance that if the registration is off, small gaps could show up between the colors allowing the shirt to show through.

Gap Registration is used less than the other two, but is still necessary in certain situations. With this type of registration it is necessary to begin with a small gap between the colors. This is useful using inks that will expand. These would include puff inks or other specialty inks that may contain a blowing agent that would cause the ink to expand up as well as out.

Halftones

Vector files sometimes limit the the number of colors that can be used in a one particular design. One way to add a color to the design is to utilize the shirt's color. Another way is to use halftones. A halftone is a series of small dots lined up in rows, which when printed will produce a tint of the color.

Halftones are referred to by percentages. A 50% halftone of black will produce a grayish tone midway between white and black. The smaller the percentage the lighter the tint will become. The higher the percentage, the darker the tint.

It is recommended never to go below 15%; otherwise, you will begin to lose dots. This means that the dots will be too small for the screen to hold, and they will not show up in the print. It is also suggested never to go above 80% which will result in dot gain. Dot gain refers to how much a dot bleeds when it hits the substrate on which it is being printed. With a halftone above 80%, all the dots could expand, filling in most of the open space creating a solid, and thus defeating the purpose of the halftone.

It is also possible to create colors by mixing different colored halftones. For example, if printing yellow and red inks in a design, create an orange by overprinting a red halftone over a solid yellow colored element.

When using halftones, there are three variables to consider: LINE SCREEN, SCREEN ANGLE and DOT SHAPE.

Line Screen or Frequency

Line screen is the number of rows of dots per square inch. It is referred to by frequency or lines per inch (lpi). The example above is 10 lpi. The higher the frequency, the more rows of dots there will be. Thus, in order to fit more rows of dots per square inch, the smaller the dots need to be.

This is important to understand because higher frequency line screens produce finer, smoother looking prints But, they are much harder to print. When there are many more dots at such a small size there is less control. When it comes to burning screens, it becomes harder to hold the dots on the screen.

If new to printing with halftones, you may want to try a 35 to 45 lpi frequency. If you have had some experience and a quality exposing unit, try moving up to a 50 to 55 lpi frequency. I don't recommend going above these numbers. The print will only become harder to achieve and will not look any better.

Screen Angle

The second variable to consider when setting up halftones is screen angle. Screen angle is the angle at which the rows of dots are aligned. The angle that I prefer to use is 61°. It reduces the likelihood of a moiré pattern resulting. A moiré pattern is a pattern of lines that results on a printed piece due to an improper alignment of the halftone on the screen.

The examples given above shows two screen angles that should always be avoided, because we print through mesh, a weaved fabric. The green lines in the example represent this mesh. If a 90° angle is used, there is a chance that the monofilament "thread" of the mesh will "clip" a row of dots. If this happens, the resulting print will have a moiré pattern. If a 45° angle is used, the same thing may occur at the knuckle or area that the horizontal and vertical threads meet.

Dot Shape

The third variable to consider is the dot shape. There are several different shapes that can be used, but I recommend the elliptical dots. They naturally take up

more area, since they are longer than round dots. This allows for more of the dot to be printed instead of being clipped off by screen threads.

Top Row: Shows the printing process. One color per screen.

Second Row: Shows the result of each pull of the squeegee from the photos above.

Right: Shows the close up of the halftone gradient as it was printed.

Setting Up a Template

Follow these easy steps to create a master template that will help set up and register jobs faster, while also offering some visual references to trouble shoot on press.

Having a predesigned production template is a must for any shop that wants to be productive, speed up setup times, and catch film problems early in the process. Templates are not hard to make and can be done using Illustrator very easily.

> **Having a predesigned production template is a must for any shop that wants to be productive,**

Graphics programs were designed for offset printing, not screen printing on textiles. Therefore, there are some changes that need to be made in order to make the file work for textiles. The first thing to change is the page size. Whenever a new file in a graphics program is opened, it defaults to a pre-set size. For example, many programs default to 8 ½ b 11 inches.

It is important to create a custom template, so that your computer opens up at a size you typically use for most jobs. It might be 13 by 13 inches, or 13 by 14 inches, or even 15 by 16 inches. Whatever your shop's requirement is for production.

Once the page size is set, create your own registration marks and gray scale bar. This will enable work to start immediately every time a new file is opened. Simply save your document as a template and set Illustrator to open it by default each time the program is opened. At the very least you should be able to choose it as File > Open New from Template. This will get you right to work.

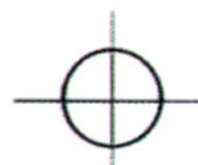

The Problem With Standard Registration Marks

Because the registration marks that come with graphics software are designed for the offset industry, it is necessary to create your own. Offset registration marks consist of small, thin lines that are difficult to hold on screens. They are also located in the four corners of the page. There is a challenge with this registration mark placement. If, for instance, there is no text in a design that can be read, it would be easy to expose one of the

film positives upside down and never realize it until the job is complete. The registration marks might line up, but the actual artwork contained on the page will not.

In order for something to be in register, three points of register are needed. Four are not necessary. Therefore, if you create your own registration marks, you can put two of them north and south right in the middle of the document, and then one more over to the top right. The two down the center of the page will help locate the center of the palette on press. This method ensures that none of the films are upside down and get burned incorrectly onto a screen. If one piece of film is accidently placed upside down on the exposure unit, the third mark does not line up with your template.

Illustrator has a special color called "registration color". Colorize the registration mark you create with this color. This will ensure that the marks print out on all of your separation films. I have seen many shops spend up to 20 minutes or more making the registration marks on the red film, red; and the marks on the blue film, blue in order for it to print out on each color separation. Just choose registration color, and it instantly colorizes all the marks so they print on each film. It saves a lot of time.

A typical registration mark has a circle with two cross hairs in it. I like to colorize each line a different thickness. For instance, make the circle 1.5 points. Make the horizontal line 1 point and the vertical line .5 points. This will help the printer see if there is a properly exposed screen. If one or more of these lines are missing on the print, it is necessary to revisit the exposure time.

The last thing needed to create for the template is a grayscale bar. This is a bar that starts at 5% and increases to 10%, and then in 10% increments all the way to 100%. This should also be colorized with registration color.

Example of a Grayscale Bar

Setting Up a Template

Using a production template in your shop for every print will improve production set up speed and quality control. The template should be used even for one color prints! The simple, quick visual references for the center of the design (the center registration marks and the grayscale bar) help to visualize improperly burned screens.

This only takes a few minutes to put together, and it's a one time thing. Simply save it as a Template once you are done, and you'll always have it.

Here's how to do it.

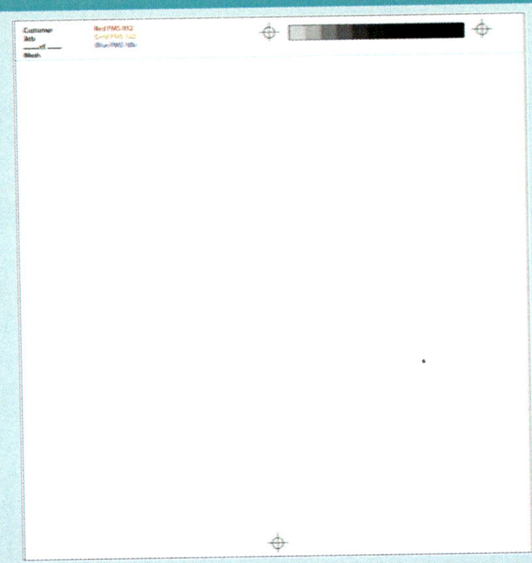

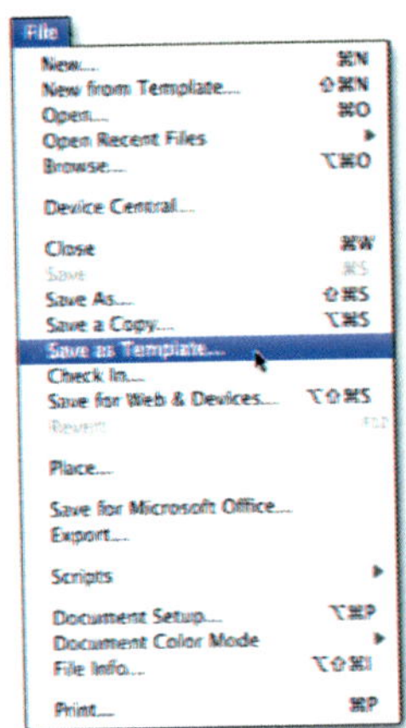

SETTING UP A TEMPLATE

Step 1: Illustrator CS3 - CS5

In Illustrator, Go to FILE MENU > NEW.

Change the page size to a Custom Size. I chose 13" x 16".

Give the file a name you intend to use.

Click OK.

Now save the file as a TEMPLATE file to be opened and used as often as needed.

Go to FILE MENU > SAVE AS TEMPLATE.

Illustrator puts it in a Template folder. It is possible have as many templates as needed in there.

Step 2:

Click on your Swatches icon or Go to WINDOW > SWATCHES to bring up the Swatches palette. The "REGISTRATION" color will be needed for the next few steps.

Registration Color is the icon in the upper left that looks like a small registration mark.

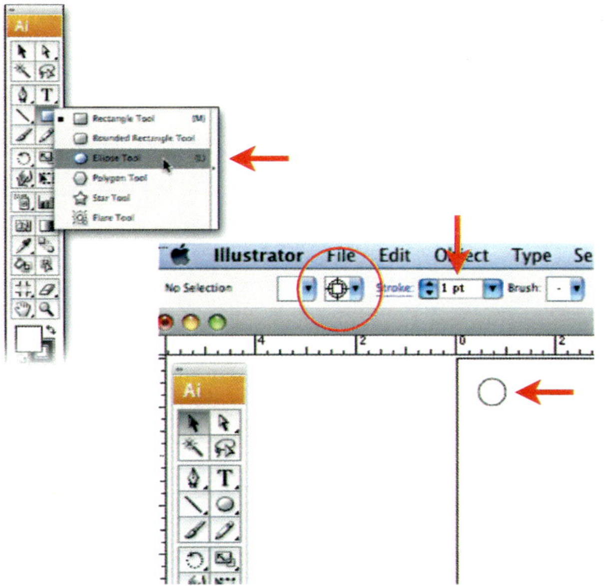

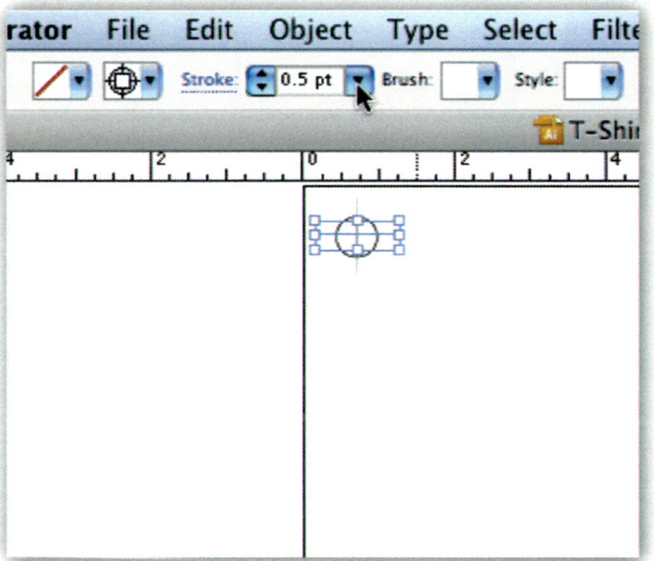

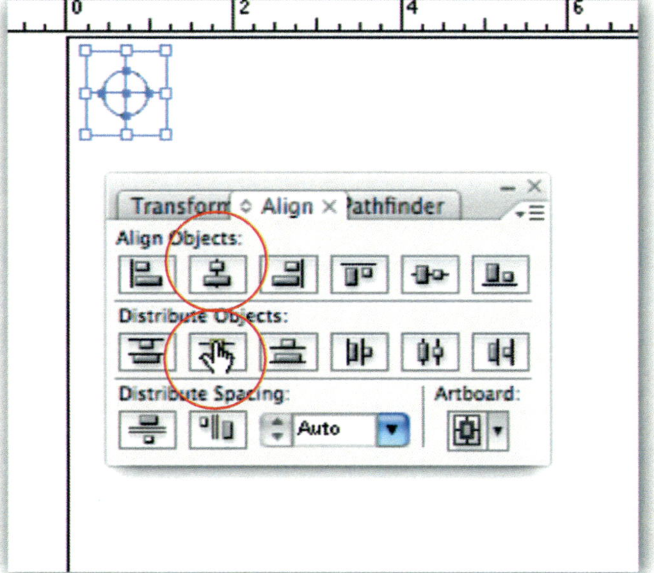

SETTING UP A TEMPLATE continued

Step 3: Creating the Registration Mark

I'm going to make my own Registration Mark now. In the tools box, click on the rectangle Shape Tool and hold for the other Shape tools beneath. Select the Ellipse Tool.

Drag out a small circle. While dragging the shape, hold down the Shift key to constrain the shape to a perfect circle.

Colorize the stroke with Registration Color, and set a point size of 1 pt for the line weight.

Step 4:

Now Go to the Line tool. This is the one located next to the Rectangle Tool in the tool box.

Draw a Vertical line and Stroke it with a quarter of a point, or .25. Colorize it with Registration Color.

Now, draw a Horizontal line, Stroke it with half a point, or .5pt. Colorize it with Registration Color also.

Step 5:

After you have the circle and both lines drawn, drag select them all.

Go to WINDOW MENU > ALIGN to bring up the Align Palette. Click on the Horizontal Align Center icon located in the top row, second from left. This centers everything Horizontally.

Now click on the Vertical Distribute Center icon located one below the Horizontal Align Center icon.

Now Go to OBJECT MENU > GROUP in order to Group everything together as one unit.

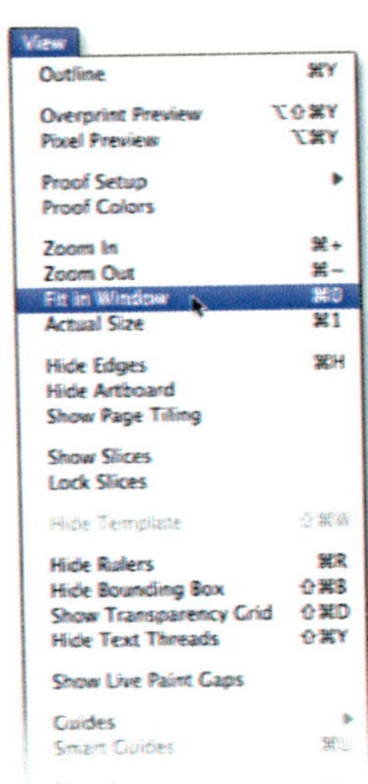

Step 6:

Now it is necessary to see the entire page. Go to VIEW MENU > FIT IN WINDOW. This will reduce everything so the full page can be viewed.

CS5- VIEW MENU > FIT ALL IN WINDOW.

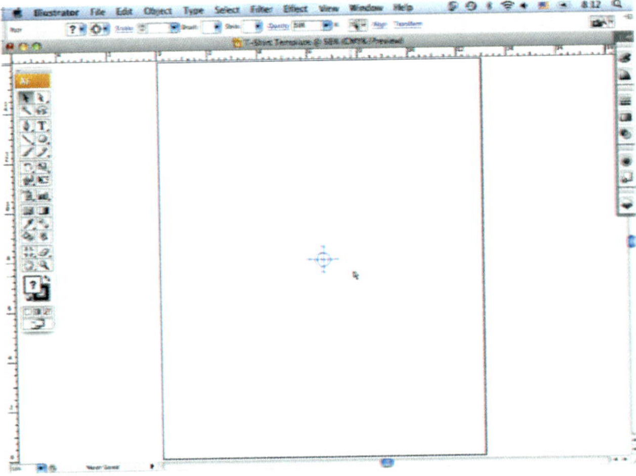

Step 7:

Make sure Registration Mark is still selected. If it's not, click on it until the light blue lines with end points appear.

Go to EDIT > CUT to cut the Mark to the clipboard.

Out of habit I usually Hit Command-0 (Mac) or Control-0 (PC). This is just like going to the View Menu > Fit in Window. I want to be sure the document is viewed this way. It's very important.

Now Go to EDIT > PASTE and see the Registration Mark pasted "Dead Center" of the page. That's why it was so important the View Fit in Window was correct.

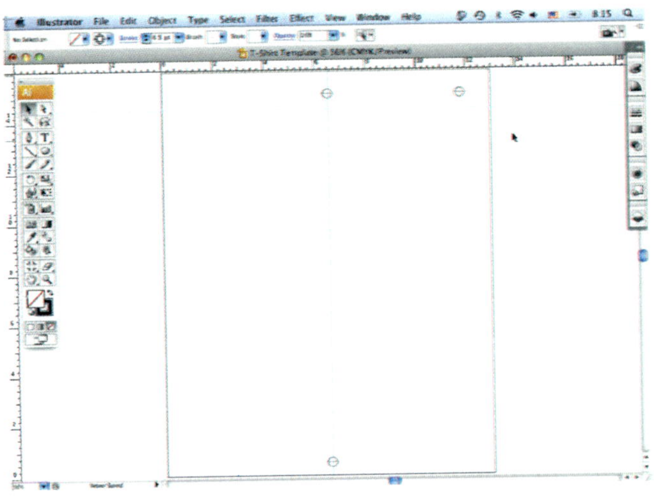

Step 8:

While holding the Shift key down, click and Drag the Registration Mark up to the top of the page. Holding the Shift key keeps it on a straight line. Release the Shift key and mouse now.

Hold the Shift key down again and Drag the mark to the right. (while still holding the Shift key, hold down the Option/Alt key) then release the Mouse first, then the other two keys. This duplicates the Mark to the right.

Repeat the same thing and Drag the center mark to the Bottom of the page.

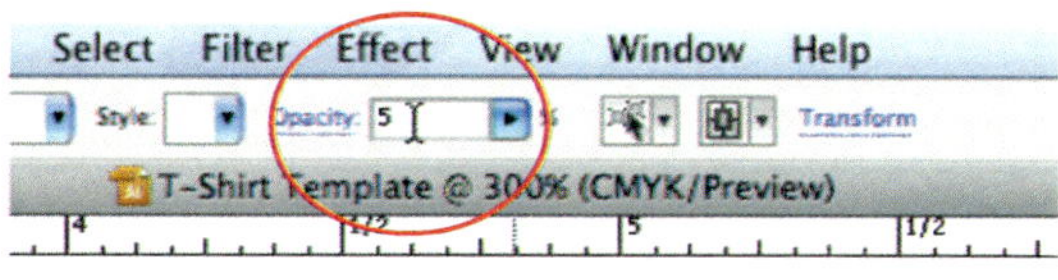

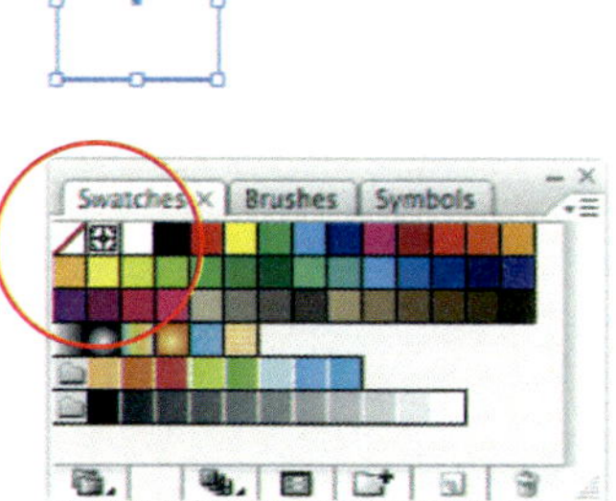

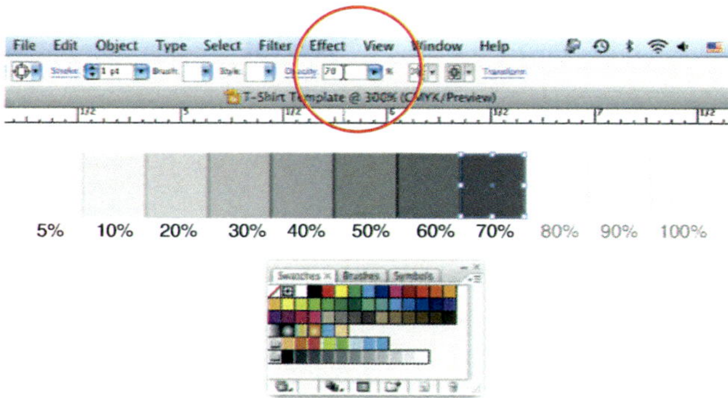

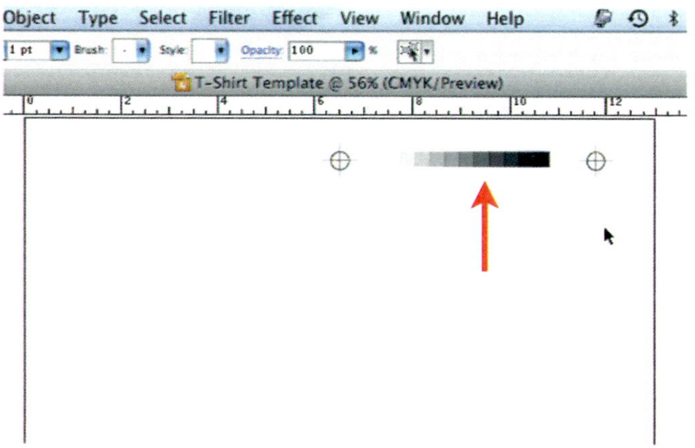

Step 9: Making the Grayscale Bar

Using the Rectangle Tool in the Tool Box, Drag out a small square. Hold the Shift key to keep it square.

Select Registration Color, and in the Options Bar set the Opacity to 5%.

Step 10:

Duplicate the square by Selecting it. Hold the Shift key and drag it over to the right. While still holding the Shift key, hold down the Option/Alt key.

Once the second square is done, simply press Command/Control -D key to duplicate. Keep pressing Command-D for as many squares as needed. You need a square from 5% color, 10% color and 10% steps all the way to 100%. You should have 11 squares total.

Change the Opacity amount for each square created.

Step 11:

After finishing the squares, Drag select them and Group them together as one unit.

Now move the position of the bar to the empty space between the top two Registration Marks.

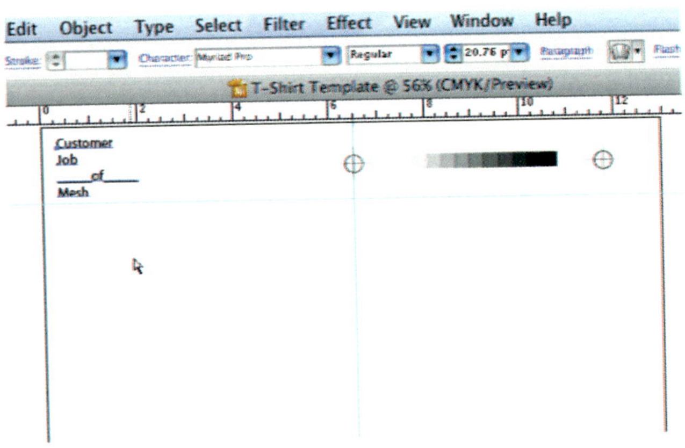

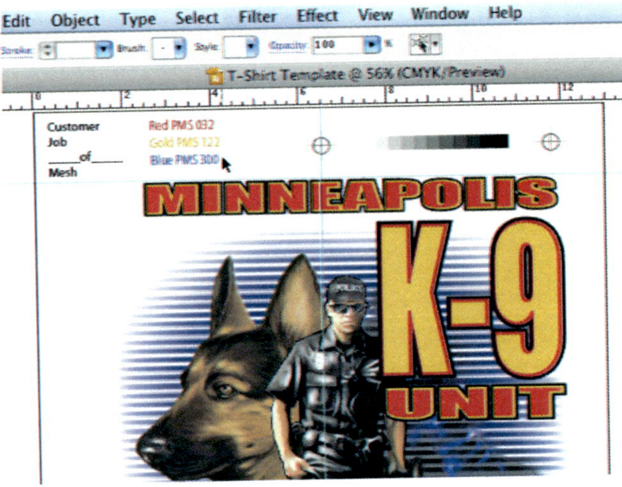

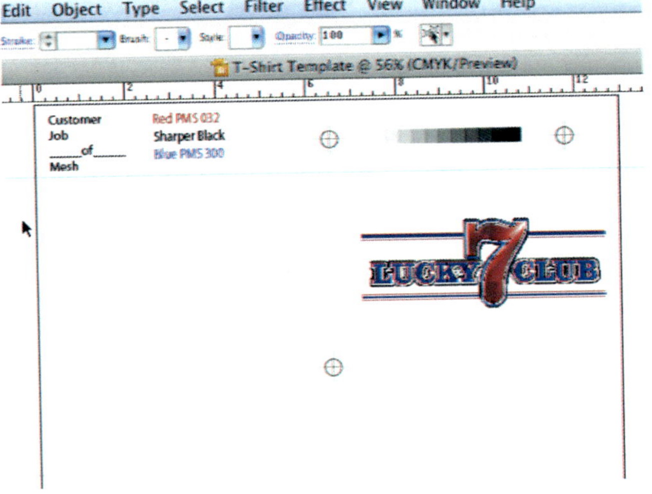

Step 12:

It is necessary to add some identifying information to the films.(ex. Customer, Job, Number of Films, Mesh Counts etc). Type this information in the upper left corner of the Template. This is not a live area and is the perfect location for such info.

Colorize this with "Registration Color". Write the Customer name, number of screens etc. on the films with a sharpie or type it here. If you type everything here in Illustrator, be aware that whatever is Registration Color will print out on ALL films.

Step 13:

Once you Place a DCS file into your Template, it is possible to type a color box with the name of the colors in it. Colorize this with the Spot Colors that came with the DCS file, and the color names will print out on the correct films.

Step 14:

The same Template is used when printing Left Chest designs as well. Simply move the bottom Registration Mark to just below the image.

Remember to hold the Shift key while moving it, and it will stay centered in the document.

I know this looks like a lot of steps, but it's not really. I just had to create a few things in order to get it done. This work only needs to be done once, now that it's saved it can be brought up each time Illustrator is opened by using File > New from Template. Now it's done and ready for the next job.

Saving a DCS 2.0.eps File

If you are a screen printer and are not using DCS2.0 eps files for your separations, then pay attention. This file format is a screen printer's best friend when trying to marry both vector and raster elements together in one design. If needing to create an image using a full color raster image while applying clean crisp vector text to it, then this format is for you.

A DCS 2.0 (desktop color separations) eps file is a "fancy" eps file that lets you contain spot color alpha channels inside it. Place one full color preview into Illustrator. Once you print your films, the separations are pulled from the DCS 2.0 file.

This file format works only with raster artwork and is only needed by screen printers. It's also only needed for jobs with two or more colors.

Before DCS2.0 files were available, when designing a multicolor job for output, each color or channel would have to be done one at a time. So let's say an artist is doing separations for an eight-color job. First, he would separate the artwork into eight channels in Photoshop, and then "split channels" into eight individual TIFF files, one for each color.

It is necessary to create individual pages, and later on, Layers in Illustrator to contain all the information the file needs, and keep the colors together. It would first be necessary to put the black channel (color) TIFF along with any type that was to print black on the page. Next, the page would have to be duplicated, and the black Tiff and the White Tiff would have to be changed or re-linked. Then, whatever text was to print white on this

page would be added. Finally, it would be saved in order to move on to the next color. It would be necessary to do this for all of the colors in the job.

The challenge with this method is the ease of getting confused and/or forgetting to link images together. This might result in having two colors (one green and one blue image) in a design that both print in blue, because the link of the two images was not changed. This probably wouldn't be noticed until it got to press.

When DCS2.0 files came into the mix, this allowed the artist to create separations and place or import one full color preview, (the DCS2.0.eps file) into the document. When this happens, all of the colors (in the example case, 6 colors) will come into the color swatches palette. This would make it possible to create the text needed using the colors that came in with the placed image and print them. This allows for saving all the time and hassle of creating individual pages. Saving separations in this format is fairly easy to do; however, it is done slightly differently on a Mac vs. a PC, because some information must be specified while saving the file.

If using a RIP software to print films to an inkjet printer, for instance, it isn't necessary to save the halftone screens and screen angles in the file. Just skip that part. However, to insure the file will print with the line screens and angles specified, inbed that info into the file, as in our example. It doesn't hurt to have that info in the file. It will override your RIP specifications. This file format is used for spot colors only. Four-color process is not done using DCS2.0 files.

**DCS 2.0.eps file
A Screen Printer's Best Friend**

Left: The initial channel separations in Photoshop.

Left: The original artwork in Illustrator. Showing a raster image combined with vector text.

Saving a DCS 2.0 File

If you're a screen printer this should be one of the most used files in the Art Department. It takes a few steps to create, but it is well worth it ! Wow!

If using a RIP software, skip the part about assigning a halftone and frequency to it. The RIP can take care of that. I still recommend saving the file with ALL of these steps. It won't hurt anything, and it will guarantee the file prints as expected.

This original K-9 file can be found on the companion CD.

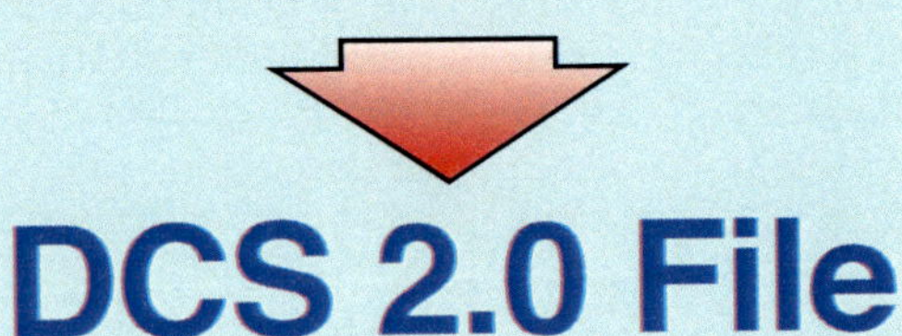

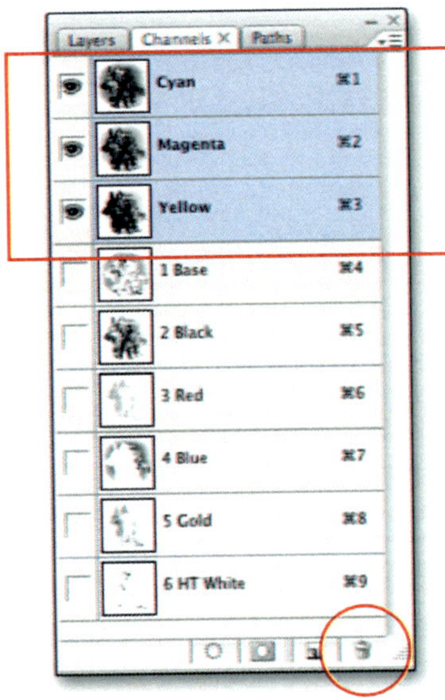

SAVING A DCS 2.0 FILE

Step 1: Photoshop CS3 - CS5

With your initial separated file open.
Go to IMAGE MENU > MODE > MULTICHANNEL. If asked to flatten layers, click OK.

If the file still has the colored RGB artwork in it once the mode is changed to Multichannel, it will be necessary to delete the remaining RGB channels. The Channels palette should look like this one. Simply drag the Cyan, Magenta and Yellow channels to the trash. The Trash can icon is at the bottom right of the channels palette.

Step 2:

In the Channels Palette, double click the top channel's "preview icon", not the name to bring up the Channel Options dialog box. Select "Spot Color" for the channel type. Click OK. Do this for all channels in the document.

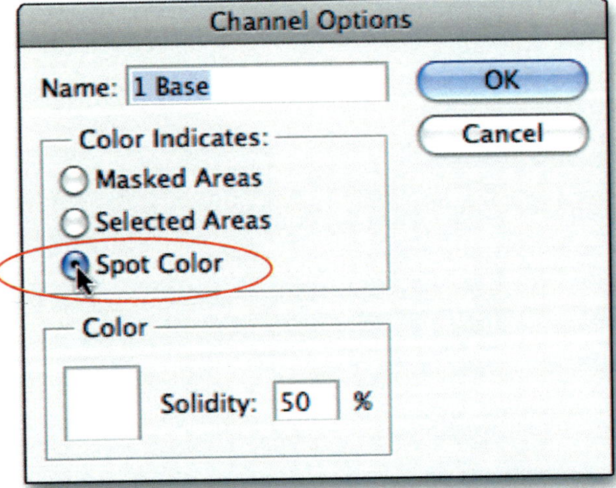

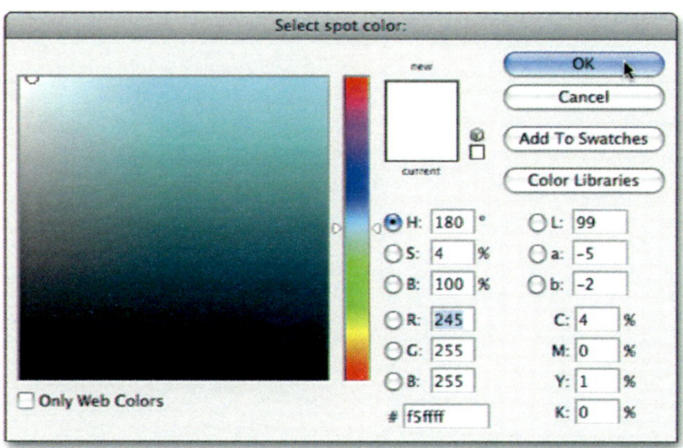

SAVING A DCS 2.0 FILE continued

Step 3:

If White ink channels is needed be sure to "colorize" the preview color with a color other than RGB settings of 255, 255, 255. This is seen as white to the computer and indicates a lack of color. Nothing will print out on the separations. I like to make my White base color RGB-245, 255, 255. and the Highlight White RGB-255, 255, 245. Now they will both print correctly.

Step 4:

Go to FILE MENU > SAVE AS.
In the Save As dialog window, select the Format: drop down menu and select Photoshop DCS 2.0.

Click Save.

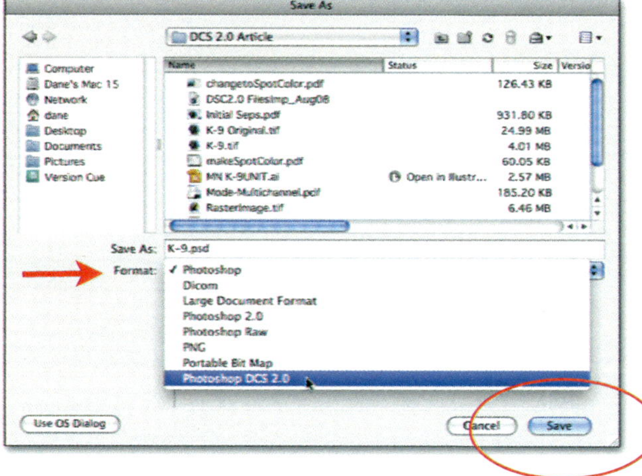

Step 5:

In the DCS 2.0 Format window, select the DCS: drop down and choose "Single File with Color Composite (72 pixel/inch).

Check the "Include Halftone Screen" and "Include Transfer Function" boxes.

Click OK.

I left my Preview and Encoding drop downs set to default. Some Mac users may want to select "binary" encoding. Windows 98 and 2000 users should use "ASCII" encoding and the "Preview:" set to TIFF (8bits per pixel). If using Windows XP and having trouble importing the file into the drawing program, try re-saving the file and using the ASCII encoding.

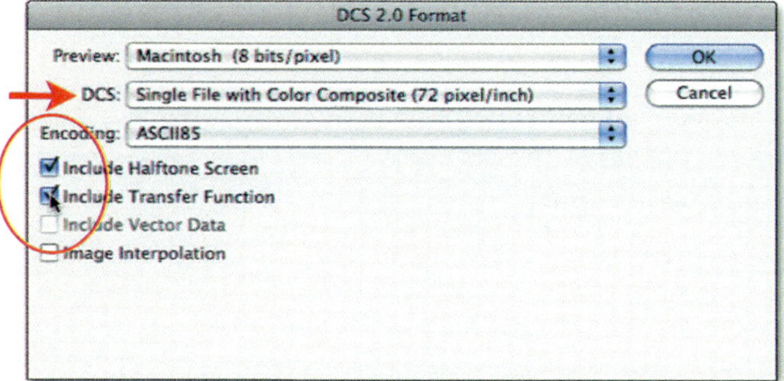

Placing a DCS 2.0 Into Illustrator

Once the DCS file has been created and saved, it must be placed into Illustrator a certain way. This allows the separation colors to be carried into the swatches palette.

At right is the Original artwork in Illustrator. This design consists of a Raster image with Vector text. After the DCS file is in place, use the colors that came in with it to colorize the vector text. This way there will be clean, crisp text on the same films as the image!

It's easy to do, heres how.

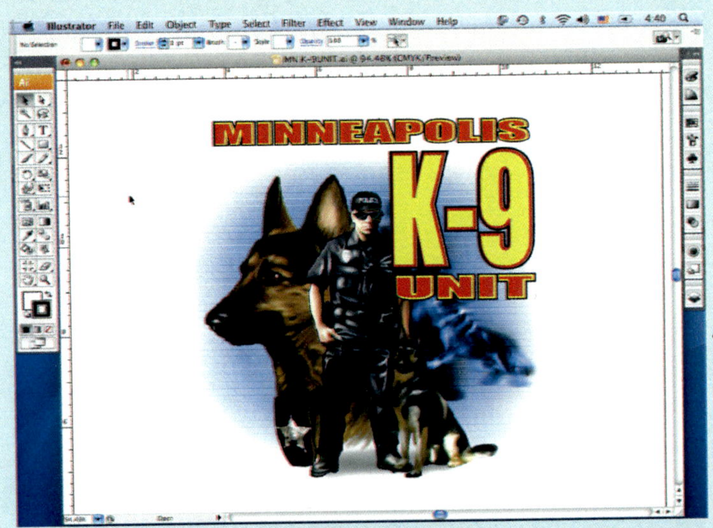

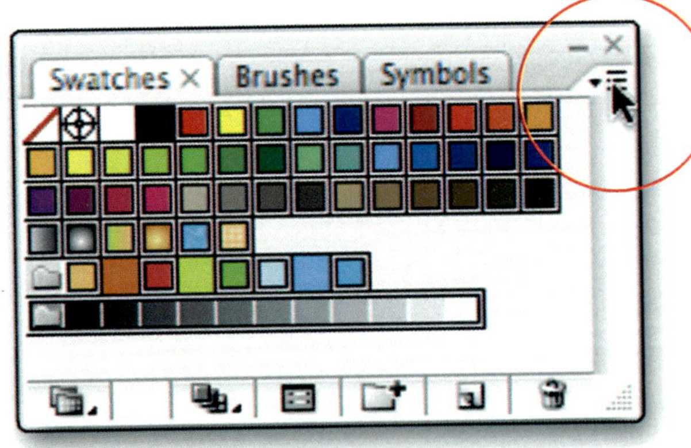

DCS 2.0 INTO ILLUSTRATOR

Step 1: Illustrator CS3 - CS5

Click on the Swatches icon, or Go to WINDOW MENU > SWATCHES to bring the palette up.

Click on the little "fly out" icon in the upper right hand corner of the palette to bring up a drop down menu.

Go to Select All Unused.

Step 2:

You should now see all of the Unused colors selected in the palette.

Click on the "fly out" icon again.

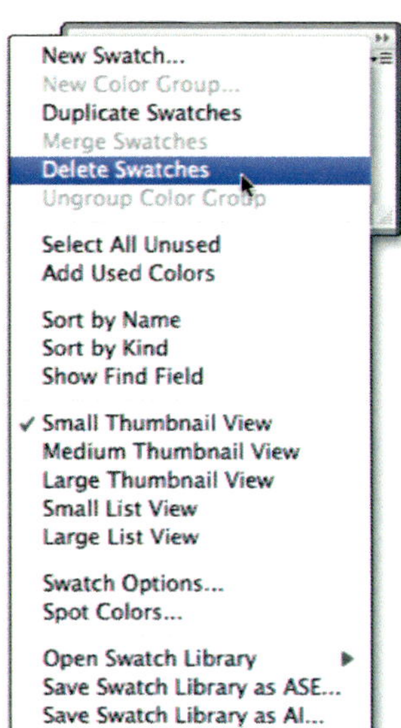

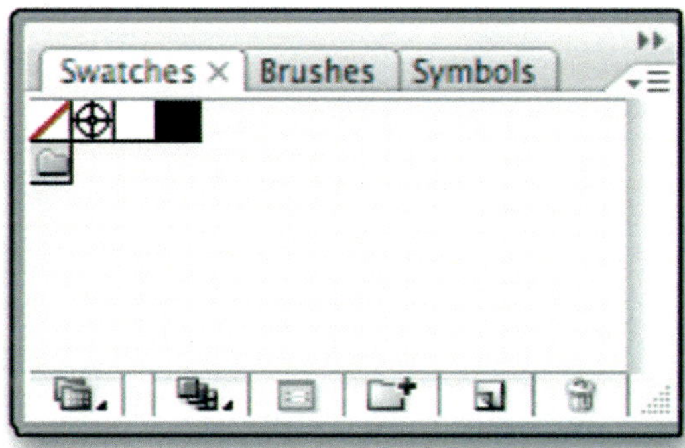

DCS 2.0 INTO ILLUSTRATOR continued

Step 3:

Go to DELETE SWATCHES.

Step 4:

Your Palette should now look like this.

Sometimes Illustrator might leave extra colors in it. Just select those colors and delete them a second time. What I want to leave in the palette is the default colors only.

The NONE, Registration, White and Black colors only.

Step 5:

Now, go to the artwork itself. Click once on the art to select it.

What I want to do here is "link" the original artwork with the separated DCS 2.0 file just created.

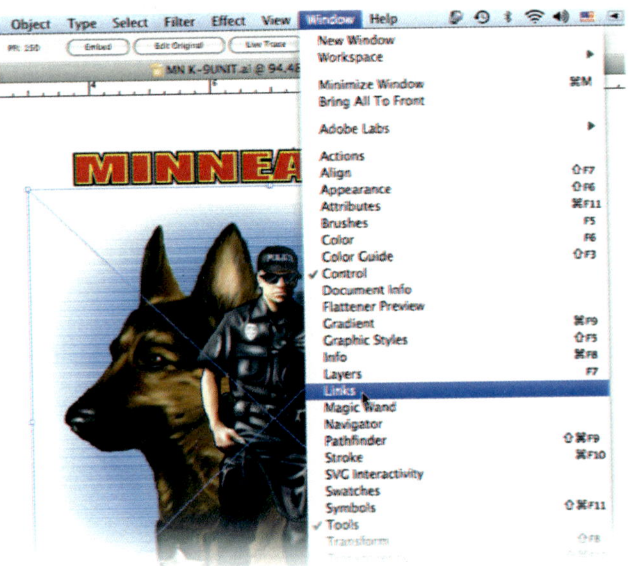

DCS 2.0 INTO ILLUSTRATOR continued

Step 6:

Go to WINDOW > LINKS to bring up the Links dialog box.

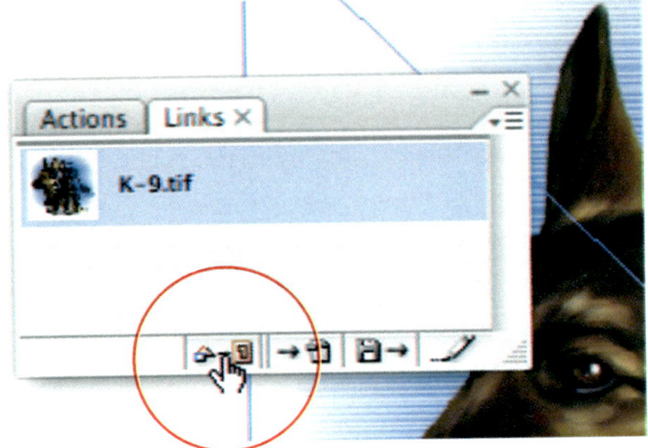

Step 7:

When the Links dialog box comes up, Click on the Re-link button. The icon at the bottom left of the palette.

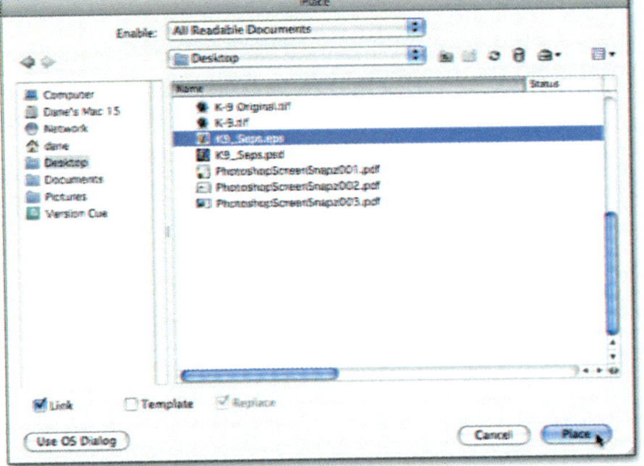

Step 8:

In the Place dialog box, be sure "link" is checked at the bottom left of the palette.

Browse to find the eps file to be brought in.

Click Place.

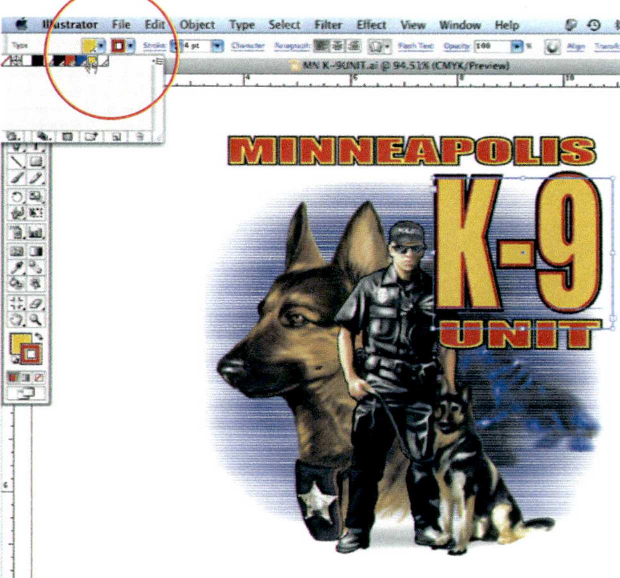

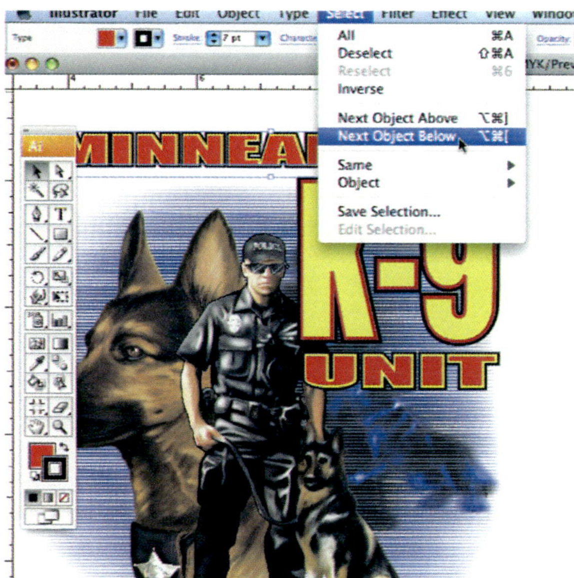

Step 9:

When the link update finishes, notice a change in the art. This is the separation file.

Look at the Swatches palette. The colors in the separated file (the alpha channels) should populate the Swatches Palette.

Step 10:

Click on a text element to change it's color. Notice the Options bar at the top of the screen. You should see the Fill and Stroke colors.

Click on the Fill color first, and the Swatches palette should pop up below it. Select the color to use. Notice that the small color icon has changed to a "spot color" icon. It has a little white triangle at the bottom of the color square with a small black dot in the middle.

Change the Fill and Stroke of all the text to your Spot Colors.

Step 11:

In this example, we have a copy of the text with a thick black outline below the colored type.

Go to SELECT > NEXT OBJECT BELOW to select this element.

Once selected, colorize with the Black Spot color from the separated file.

Repeat these steps for all of the colors in the image.

When finished, you are ready print out the separations to film.

Printing Out Separations

With the artwork opened, and the text colorized with the Spot Colors from our DCS 2.0 file, it is time to print out separations.

Always print separations this way from Illustrator. Never print the DCS files directly from Photoshop. Photoshop doesn't do that very well. The percentage value of the data is not correct.

This is easy, here's how.

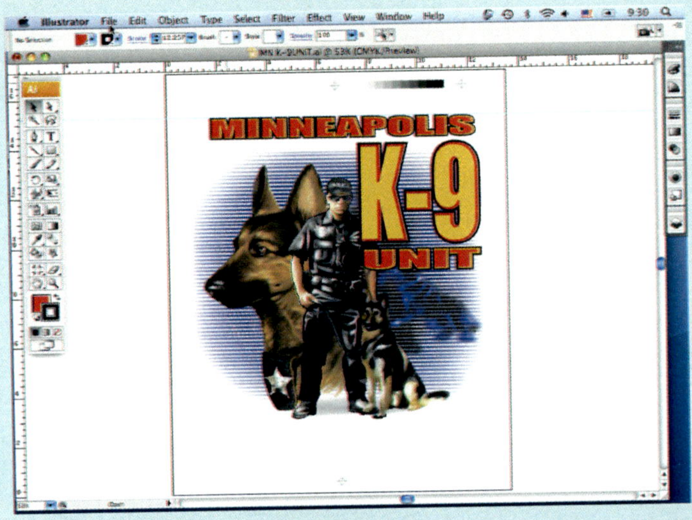

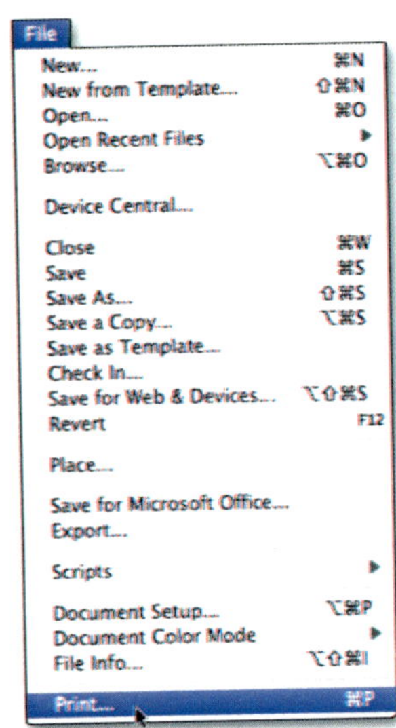

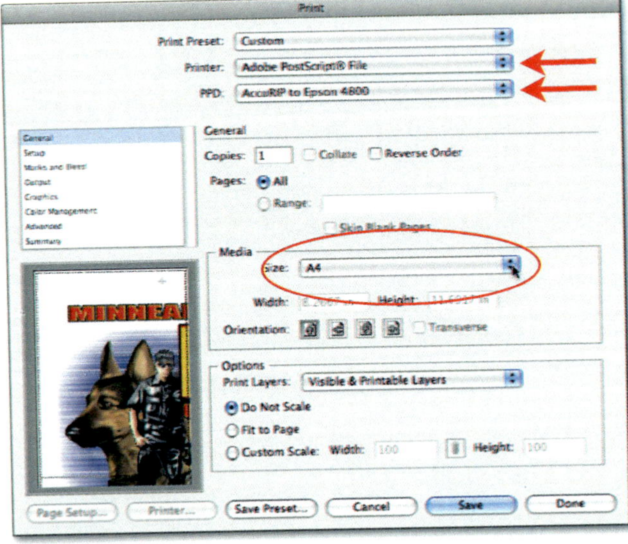

Step 1: Illustrator CS3 - CS5

Go to FILE > PRINT

Step 2:

I'm going to print my separations to an Adobe Postscript® File instead of printing them with a printer, because I don't have a printer hooked up to my computer at the moment. It is possible to print to a file and print the job later, or at an output service. Choose the printer needed in the Printer drop down menu.

Choose the PPD for your printer.

In the Media box area, Click on the Size: drop down menu.

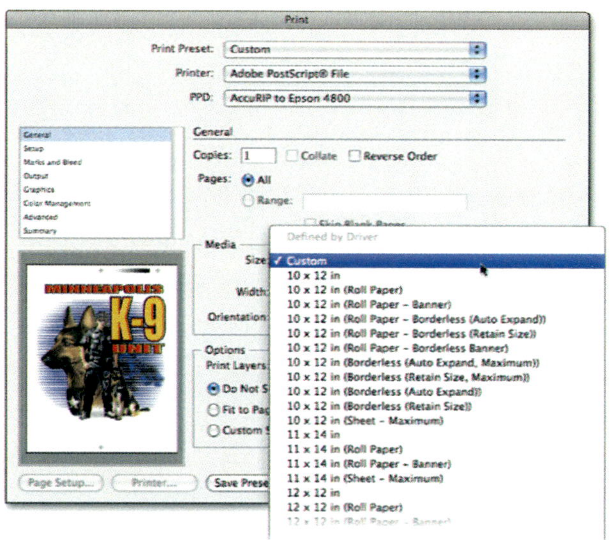

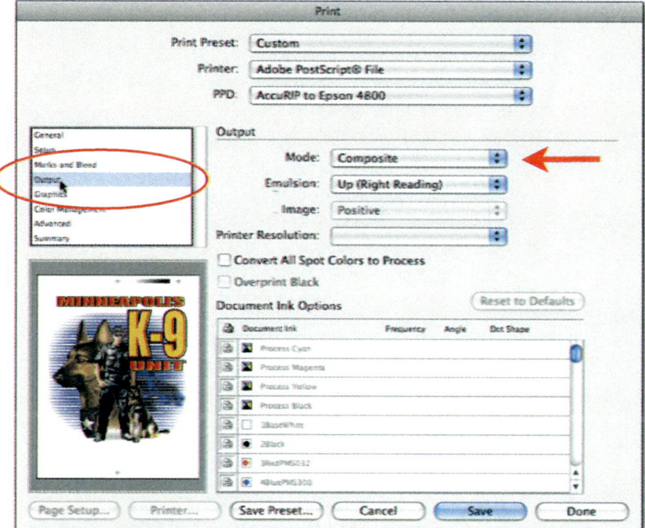

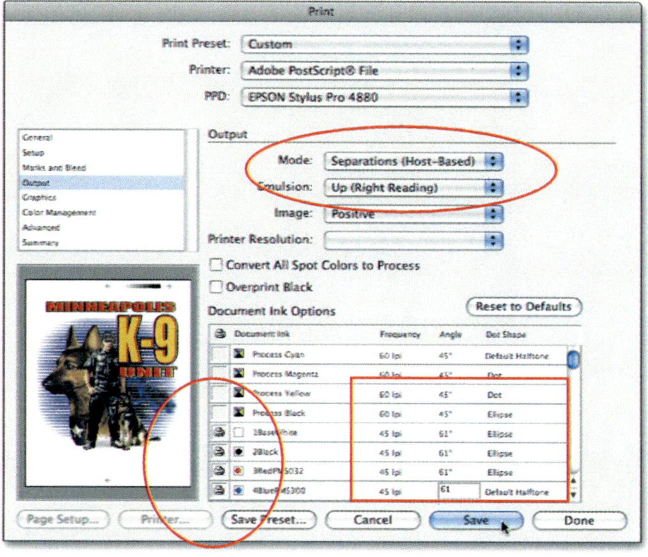

PRINTING OUT SEPARATIONS continued

Step 3:
Choose Custom (or whatever size the job requires).

Step 4:
In the box to the left, choose Output. This changes the options on the right.

Step 5:
In the Output section, change the Mode to Separations (Host-Based).

Uncheck any small Printer icons to the left of the color names. This turns those colors off, and they will not print. Only the colors needed should have little printer icon's next to them.

Change the Frequency, Angle, and Dot Shape for each of those colors. In this example, I chose to print at 45 lines per inch frequency, 61° angle and an Elliptical Dot Shape.

I'm going to click Save, you would click Print.

Why go through the trouble?

The reason I "go through the trouble", as someone once called it, referring to creating vector text on a raster image is shown below. It is to get the best possible final print.

I personally don't think it's any extra trouble to create the artwork the correct way the first time around. I try to create and produce the best art possible for any given job. In my opinion, this is the way to do that.

The two images below are sample films printed out two different ways. The one on the left is text created right in Photoshop. While this is fine if we are printing something digitally ie: Direct to Garment, Dye-sublimation etc., it's just not what should be done for

screen printing. When screen printing this type of job, it is necessary to print films using halftones in order to reproduce it correctly. Those halftones will cause the edges of the text to look bumpy or rough. Small type will be really bad.

If the edges of the type or the vector shapes are to be clean and crisp, do the art by combing both techniques.

Look at the image on the left. Notice the rough edges. Now look at the image on the right. It is perfectly clean and crisp. This one will print much better.

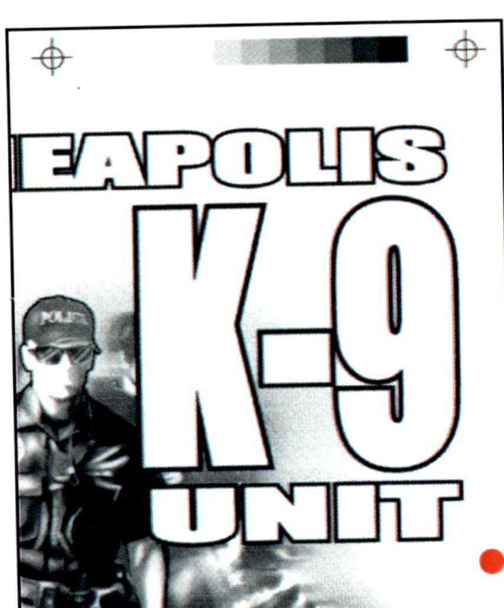

Left:
Sample of the separated films with type created from Photoshop.

Right:
Detail of the same film to show close up of edges.

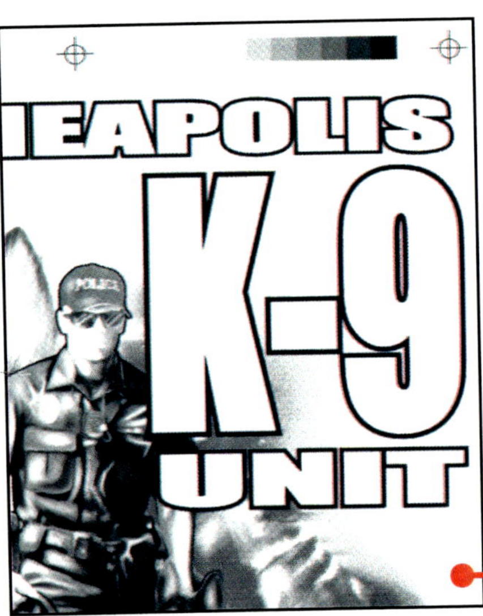

Left:
Sample of the separated films with type created using vector shapes in Illustrator.

Right:
Detail of the same film to show close up of edges.

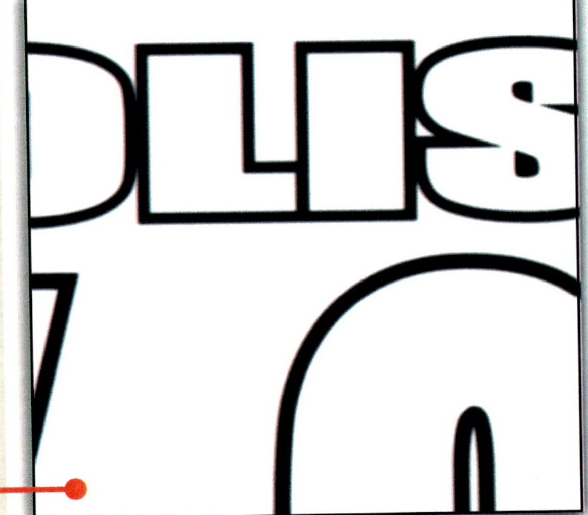

Printing Vector Separations

Printing out your separations is very easy provided the Artwork is created correctly. One of the most important functions required to create the art correctly is the use of Spot Colors.

Build images using Spot Colors, and half the battle is done.

Here's how it works!

PRINTING VECTOR SEPS

Step 1:Illustrator CS3 - CS5

Open the image. For this lesson I'm going to use the Green Scene Art that was created from a customer's business card scan back in Chapter 4.

Step 2:

Go to the FILE MENU > PRINT.

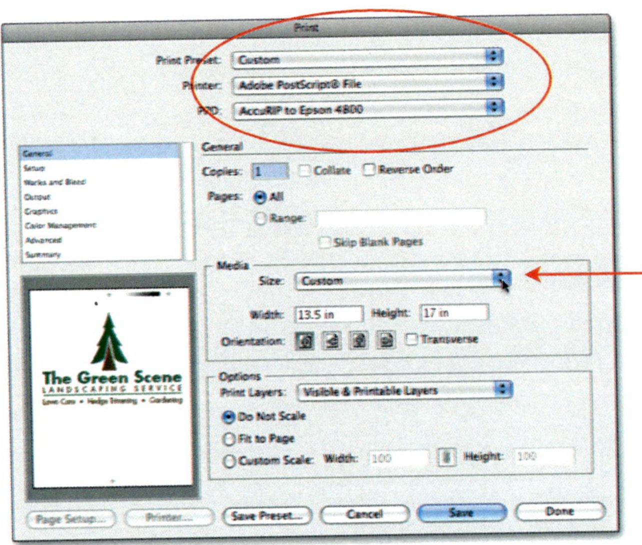

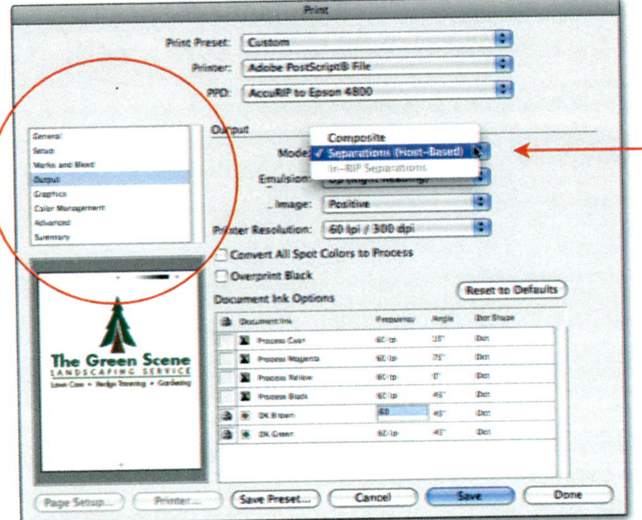

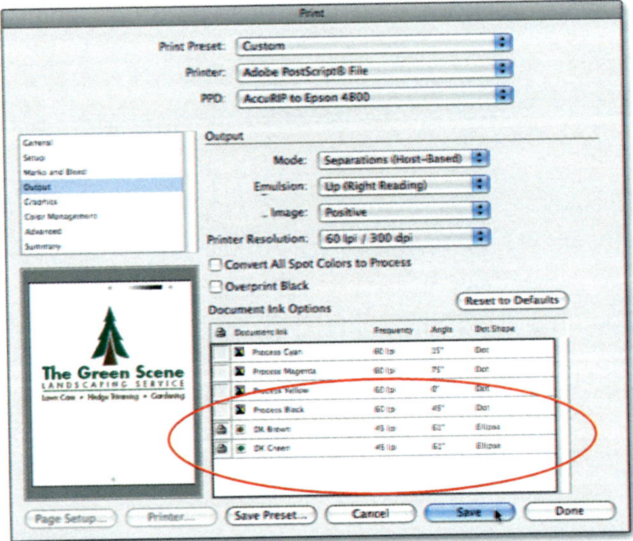

PRINTING VECTOR SEPS continued

Step 3:

In the Print window choose the Printer.
In my case I will print to a PostScript file and not an actual printer. You can choose your printer.

Select the PPD of the printer.

Verify the Media size, and correct it if necessary.

Step 4:

Click on the "Output" word in the list to the left.

Change the Output Mode to Separations (Host-Based).

Step 5:

Turn off the Process Colors. Turn off the little printer icons for the 4 process colors, Cyan, Magenta, Yellow and Black.

Even though this particular job does not have halftones, I would still recommend setting the file up as if it does.

This is good practice.

Use a Frequency of 45 lpi, and an angle of 61° and an Elliptical Dot Shape.

Do this for each Spot Color in the file.

I'm clicking "Save". You will click "Print".

GLOSSARY & INDEX

Glossary

A

Alpha Masking A technique that uses alpha channels to create selections, used to mask certain areas of an image.

Asymmetrical Balance A design that is not identical on both sides of a center line.

AI File Adobe® Illustrator native file format.

B

Backup The act of saving / archiving your artwork off off the computer. On an external hard drive, CDs or DVD disks for instance.

Balance The composition or placement of elements, shapes, objects, images or colors that form an aesthetically pleasing harmonious whole.

Banding Striping in the direction of the movement of the digital print head. Usually caused by a misfiring head or clogged nozzles in the head.

Bit Depth Describes the number of bits used to store information about each pixel in an image. The higher the depth, the more colors that are stored.

Bitmap A digital image made up of individual pixels of various colors. A set of bits that represent a graphic image.

Burning Screens The term used for exposing or imaging screens for screen printing.

BUTT Registration Two colors are printed next to each other with no overlap or gap in between.

C

CDR File Native file format for Corel® Draw software application.

Channel A part of an image file that contains color data. When all colors are previewed, it builds a full color image. Channels are often used to separate colors for screen printing.

Character Palette A palette in most software applications that allow you to adjust and modify characters in a word. It allows you to control size, spacing, kerning, leading and other aspects of a word.

Clip Art Usually simple vector stock designs used as a starting point to create a design.

Color Cast An imperfection in a photograph that tends to have more of one color in it than any other.

Color Scheme The colors selected to work together in a design.

Color Gamut The range of color that can be reproduced or captured using the various printing techniques.

Color Wheel An image or chart that displays the entire color spectrum at one time. Usually shows the relationship or closeness of one color to the next.

Complementary Color Scheme Two colors that are opposite each other on a color wheel.

Composition The arrangement and layout of elements in a design.

Contract Artists An artist used and paid on a per piece basis. See also freelance artist.

Continuous Tone Images that appear to have an infinite range shade and color blended together. It is used to describe full color photographic type of images and generally reproduced using traditional halftone dots.

Copyright The exclusive legal right to a piece of artwork to use for sale or reproduction.

CMYK Cyan, Magenta, Yellow, Black. Four colors used in process printing.

Creative Meeting A meeting of employees to discuss current jobs and to brainstorm about possible design ideas.

Cropping Cutting off or utilizing only part of an image. Often used to show a portion of an image larger than otherwise possible.

Color Separations The process of splitting or pulling apart a full color image using separate channels. These channels are then combined on press to create the final print.

Cutting a Path The act of tracing around a shape in an image using a pen tool to create an outline of the object.

D

DCS 2.0.eps File A file format created by Adobe. It stands for desktop color separation file. It's a "fancy" eps file that contains spot color, alpha channel separations inside.

DPI Screen or printer resolution. Usually determined by the number of dots per linear inch both horizontally and vertically.

Descreening Filter A filter in Photoshop and scanning software that removes the appearance of moiré when scanning something that was already printed using halftones.

Digital Printing The process of printing using a digital print head. As in Direct to Garment Digital Printing.

Digital Underbase The white ink that is printed on a dark shirt before the colors are printed on top. This is a necessary for us to be able to actually see the colors.

Digitizing Tablets Cordless, pressure sensitive surface which uses a stylus pen to help you draw and paint much more naturally in a computer.

Distortion Tools Various tools or envelope commands that allow you to alter or distort part or all of the design.

Distressed Effect The act of making part or all of an image look old and worn out.

Dot Shape The shape of the dot used with halftone screens. The two most popular shapes used in screen printing are round and elliptical.

Drawing Station A work station set up in an art department with a drawing table, lights and tools for an artist to create artwork at.

Drop Shadow Normally a gray soft, fuzzy blur placed beneath an object to represent distance or mass.

Dye-Sublimation A printing process using heat to evaporate pigments from a transfer print and embedding them into a media.

E

Elliptical Dots Oval shaped dots used with halftone screens.

Encapsulated Postscript (EPS) A PostScript vector file format that can include PostScript level, fonts and a preview of the image.

Enhancing Your Type The act of adding special effects or additional elements to type to dress it up.

F

FPO Means, For Position Only.

Flash Curing The process of applying heat to the underbase in screen printing that "gels" or partially dries the ink in order to print the other colors on top.

Film The clear or frosted thin plastic sheet that screen printing separations are printed on.

Focal Point The point of interest in a design that initially attracts the attention of your eye.

Font The group of letters, numbers and other typographical elements all created in the same shape and style.

Four Color Process Printing The basic method for reproducing a broad spectrum of colors using only Cyan, Magenta, Yellow and Black ink.

Freelance Artist An artist used and paid on a per piece basis. See also Contract Artist.

Frequency The measurement of a halftone. How many dots are lined up in one row within one inch. If you have 45 dots per linear inch, the frequency is 45 lpi (lines per inch).

G

GAP Registration Two colors are printed next to each other with a small gap in between to allow for any expansion of ink.

Gesture Drawing An extremely quick rendering of an object meant to convey the general idea of the image being drawn.

Graduations The process of creating art that gradually blends one color into another.

Grayscale An image consisting of no color, only ranges of tones from black to white.

Grayscale Bar A series of small squares filled with incremental amounts of black. Usually created in 10% increments. Starting at 0 up to 100%. Used in production templates for screen printing.

H

Halftone A series of dots, lined up in rows set to a specific angle. It's used to create images or create different percentages of colors.

Halftone Frequency The way the computer defines a line screen. See also Line Screen.

Hard Drive A hardware device used to store digital data either contained in a computer internally or external.

Hue A tint or color of something.

I

Illusion of Space The effect of adding dimension to a piece of artwork.

Image Editor A software application that allows you to manipulate black and white or color images.

Image Setter A raster output device that prints to clear film. A processor and chemistry are necessary to develop the film. These are phasing out for our industry being replaced by inkjet printers.

Image Size The actual dimensions of a document created in Photoshop.

Indexed Color A separation technique that uses from 1 to 256 colors. You can convert RGB files to Indexed files in order to reduce the amount of colors in an image. In order to have a successful looking graduations of colors, a larger press is necessary.

J

JPG or JPEG Stands for (Joint Photographic Experts Group) It is a raster file using a "lossy" compression technique. This means to have losses to the image. When saving the file, image data is disregarded and the image loses quality. Once the loss occurs, it can not be recovered.

Job Order Form A form used to contain all the pertinent information for a particular job. Usually one job form is used per job.

K

Kerning The way to control the amount of space between letters in a word. Some letters look farther apart when placed next to others, use kerning to squeeze them or open them up.

L

Large Format Printing A form of printing large images. Our industry may use it for banners and displays, the sign industry uses it for billboards and larger prints.

Laser Printer A desktop printing device that uses heat to fuse / adhere toner to vellum paper or mylar film.

Layer Think of layers as invisible planes which contain data. The data on one layer can be moved and manipulated independently of the others. Imagine a sheet of glass over a photo. Draw something with a marker on one piece of glass. Now place another sheet of glass over that. Draw something else. Now you can move the three different levels around without touching the others.

Layer Styles One button effects that can be applied to text, shape, or raster layers in Photoshop. When you open the Layer Styles dialog box, you have a bunch of effects you can change and control.

Lightness Channel The channel in a Lab color mode file that contains the luminosity or tonal information in an image. It is a very accurate grayscale of an image.

Light Table A table with a light beneath a glass that is used in production to check film registration. Also used in an art department to trace things.

Line Art Outline style artwork. Often referred to as clip art.

Line Screen The elements of a printing screen, usually determined by the halftone dots per inch. The higher the line screen the more dots contained within the linear inch. Also referred to in the computer as the Frequency.

Inkjet Printer A printer that sprays droplets of ink onto a substrate. Used to print screen printing separations with a RIP software.

M

Magic Wand Tool A tool in Photoshop that selects colors. To determine what color is selected, simply click the tool on the color you want.

Masking a Photo The technique of hiding or revealing only parts of an image. Photoshop does this in many different ways.

Mesh The loosely woven fabric that is tightly stretched over frames in screen printing and to which an image is adhered so that it can be reproduced.

Monitor Calibration The act of reading and controlling color on a monitor which will help ensure quality colors when printed. Once the colors are measured on screen software curves adjustments are then applied to push the colors closer to where they should be.

Moiré A pattern of visible waves or lines caused by printing halftones whose angles aren't aligned properly.

Monochromatic Color Scheme A color scheme that contains colors form one color family. Example, blue, blue violet and blue green are all from one family.

Morgue File A compilation of reference material for illustrators. Usually filed magazine photos of anything that can be used as reference. Also known as a Scrap File.

Multiple Outline Effect An effect created by adding multiple outlines of color around type or a shape in varying widths.·

N

O

Optical Resolution The real maximum resolution that a scanner can render a bitmap image. As opposed to interpolated resolution.

Optimizing Photos The act of taking an original raw photo and applying certain digital processes to it in order to make the photo the best image possible.

P

PDF File (Portable Document Format) Modified PostScript file format used by the Acrobat document exchange system. Fonts and images are usually embedded into the file. Usually used to give to a printer for the purpose of printing the file like it was intended to be, without allowing manipulations to the file.

PSD File Native file format for Adobe Photoshop that supports transparency, alpha channels and embedded color profiles.

Painting Software Software that simulates natural art media such as Corel® Painter.

Pantone® A system for identifying colors. It's the most commonly used system in the world.

Paragraph Palette A palette in most software applications that allow you to adjust and modify text. You can control the alignment of the text either left, center, right or justified. It also lets you control the amount of indent a new paragraph uses.

Photo Template A pre-made layout created with design elements where photos can simply be placed in position to complete the design.

Pixel Picture Element. A single point in a raster image.

Plastisol Ink Is the most commonly used ink in the screen printing industry. It does not dry in the screens, it must reach 325° to cure. The ink is designed to wrap around the fibers of a shirt and form a mechanical bond with the fabric. It will not adhere to non-porous substrates such as plastic and glass.

Postscript A programming language optimized for printing graphics and text. Known as a page description language.

Printing Out Separations The act of printing film or vellum positives for the individual colors needed to reproduce a color image.

Printing Spec Sheet A form used in screen printing that lists all the specific details that pertain to the printing of a certain job, such as ink color, halftone screen, and mesh count.

Process Color The printing of four colors to simulate "full" color. The four colors used are Cyan, Magenta, Yellow and Black.

Q

R

Raided Hard Drives Two hard drives that are mirrored together. When you copy files to one drive it is automatically copied to another. These are used as redundant backup solutions.

RAM Stands for Random Access Memory. This is the memory used in computers specifically for running software.

RGB Color A system for describing colors based on a combination of values of Red, Green and Blue, the additive primaries. This is what makes up the colors we see on a computer screen.

RIP Software Meaning Raster Image Processor. Is software that interpolates artwork for printing on certain printers.

Raster a file format that contains pixels. An example would be a photograph or full color painting.

Red Eye In photos, the red that appears in the eye area due to the reflection of the flash in the retina of the eye which contains blood.

Registration Color A default color located in the color swatches palette of software programs. It is used to color items such as registration marks, so when placed on a layout to be separated, they will print out on every color separation.

Registration Marks A small circle with cross hairs through it. Used to aid in lining up or "registering" multiple colors on press.

Removing Art from Black Background The act of removing the artwork portion of a digital image that has been merged with a black background.

Removing Art from White Background The act of removing the artwork portion of a digital image that has been merged with a white background.

Resolution: Measured in pixels per inch (or centimeter). The higher the resolution, the more pixels and detail in an image.

S

Scanner A device used to scan and copy images digitally into a computer.

Scanning Station A computer area set up in an art department meant solely for use with a scanner allowing for the need for only one scanner meant to be used by multiple artists.

Scrap File A compilation of reference material for illustrators. Usually filed magazine photos of anything that can be used as reference. Also known as a Morgue File.

Screens Device used in screen printing with either a metal or wooden frame with mesh stretched over it which the image to be printed will be burned into.

Screen Angle The orientation of a halftone screen as measured from the horizontal axis.

Screen Printing The process of printing images on a t-shirt or other substrate using screens, mesh and ink. The image is transferred by the pulling or pushing of a squeegee.

Separations The decompiling of the colors in an image into individual screens. Once printed

Separation Software Software that decompiles the colors in an image. It converts the colors to an alpha channel. One channel for each color to be printed.

Simulated Process Color The technique of printing spot colors using halftones to create or simulate the full color look of true process color.

Spot Color A specific or single color applied to individual graphic items. The most popular form of screen printing technique. One color per screen.

Squeegee A tool with a handle and blade used in screen printing to help spread and push ink through a mesh screen to reproduce an image.

Stock Art Usually full color images / illustrations used as a starting point for a design.

Swatches Palette The palette used in drawing and painting programs that show the various colors available for use in a design as small colored squares.

Symmetrical Balance Artwork that is exactly the same on both sides of a visual centerline.

T

Production Template The basic shell of a file that controls image area, registration marks, a grayscale bar and separation name information. These are created once and used over and over again. It saves time and ensures accuracy in setting up a screen printed job.

Thermal Device A desktop printing device that uses heat to develop information on film. It is capable of creating very dense blacks without the need for a processor or chemistry.

TIFF (Tagged Image File Format) A standard raster format used for graphic files. Very commonly used and recognized by most graphic software.

Time Sheet A work form used by employees to log in time spent on a specific job so that a total time can be determined when the job is complete for billing purposes.

Tone On Tone A type of image created using colors that vary only slightly in hue and value and printed on a substrate of a similar color.

Tracing Software Software that is used to automatically trace or outline the shapes or edges of a digital image.

Tracing Services Companies that will take your original art or photos and convert them to vector files for you.

Trap Registration One color printed next to another with a stroke around one of the colors that overprints the color next to it.

Transparency Artwork that is viewed by light passing through it rather than reflecting off it. Elements on a transparent layer in Photoshop will allow other elements or layers beneath it to be seen.

Triadic Color Scheme A color scheme that is created using 3 colors that are equally spaced on the color wheel.

Type on a Path The act of joining a straight line of text copy with a vector shape so the line of the type follows the line of the shape.

U

Underbase The initial color, usually white, printed on colored substrates in order to provide a light colored base for the additional colors to be printed on top of allowing the additional colors to be truer

Unsharp Mask A filter in Photoshop used to sharpen image detail.

V

Vector Art Artwork that is defined by mathematical relationships of lines and shapes. Vector files are resolution independent, which means they can be scaled to any size without losing detail or clarity.

Vellum Thin translucent sheets of paper or film used for printing out color separations to create positives for screen printing.

W

WARP Command An Edit command in Photoshop that allows you to push, pull and mold an image. Used to make an image look as if it was already printed on a mug for instance.

Work For Hire Agreement A form completed between a commissioning party and a contract artist stating that the copyright of any artwork created by the artist will belong to the commissioning party.

X

Y

Z

ZIP File Any file that is compressed using the algorithms developed by PKware. used for loss less compression of files for storage or transfer.

Index

I

illusion of space 14
image adjustment 167
image editing software 28
image size 14
Image setters 31,32
image type 167
include halftone screen 199
include transfer function 199
indexed color 185
Inkjet Printers 31,32
inverse 115
invert 127,139,175

J

JPG or JPEG 20,41,169
job order form 40

K

kerning 76,95

L

Lab color 139,145,152
Laptop 25
Laser Printers 31
layer mask 113
layers palette Illustrator 73,81
layers palette Photoshop 95,99,101
125,133,135,136
layer styles 90,91,92,99,102,110,112
116,117
levels 144,148,151,152,175
light table 33
lightness channel 139,145,152
line art 167,170
line screen 187
links 202
load selection 124
load selection dialog box 125

M

Macintosh 27
magic wand tool 104,120,136
make envelope 48
Managing the art process 35
marching ants 125,132,160,176
marquee tool 114,134,162
masking 178
match color 147
merge layers 139
moiré pattern 187

Monitor 27
monochromatic color scheme 17
morgue file 37
move tool 90,156
multichannel 196
multiple outline effect 67
mylar 31

N

new layer 82

O

object menu 85
optical resolution 28,166
optimizing your files 143,169
outer glow 100

P

PDF file format 21
PSD file format 20
painting software 30
Pantone Matching System 20
paste 132
paste into 181
paths palette 94,130,131
pen tool 74,94,129,132
photo frames 169,178
photo templates 159
Photoshop Import Options 81
Photoshop layered files 41
piecing together multiple scans 155
placement to create focal point 13
placing a DCS into Illustrator 200
plastisol ink 19,28
Postscript 29,31,204,208
preview eyeball 176
printers 31
printers default functions 199
printing 13
printing out separations 204
process color 19,185,208
production template 190

Q
R

RAM 27
RGB 19,87,143,146,196,197
RIP software 19,29,30,120,138,195
196
Raster artwork 26, 35,45,80,87,88
127,184,206

raster image 36,195,200
recreating exiting art 72
rectangle tool Illustrator 193
red eye 153
registration 186,189,201
registration color 189,190,193,194
registration marks 189,191,193,194
remove black matte 128
remove white matte 126
removing artwork from background
120,122
resizing an image 89
resolution 166,167,168,170
reverse type 15
RIP Software 26,27,28

S

save as template 190
saving a DCS 2.0 195,196
scan a FPO logo 171
scan a logo 170
scan a photo 168
scan station 37
scanner 28
scanning software 166,167,168,170
171
scrap file 37
screen angle 187
screen button 197
screen printers 42,120,184
screen printing 13, 17,43,206
screens 184
select all 160
select all unused 200
select menu 176
selective color 143,148,152
separation software 28,29,142,184
separations 19,184,185,195,203
separations host based 205,208
separating your artwork 184
setting up a template 189,190
shape tool 191
simple one color design 46
simulated process color 19,43,185
size to create focal point 13,108
smart object 117
soft photo edge 162
Software 25,26,27,28
split channels 195
spot color 18,49,54,56,59,68,71,185
186,194,196,203,204,207
spot healing tool 153
Spot Process 29,184
staffing your art department 36
starting your artwork 24
stock art 39,108
stroke 57,69,83,203

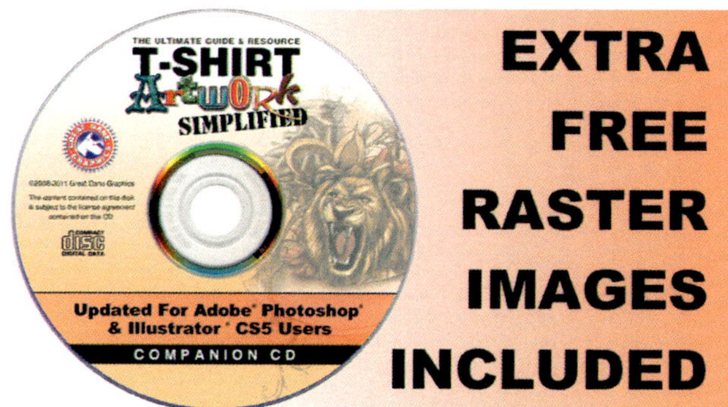

BOBCAT • MA30081

3/4 FOOTBALL HELMET • FB20003

BUCK MAGIC • WL60031

BASKETBALL WITH NET • BK40006

HOCKEY CHECK • HKY40007

MARGARITA PARROT • FD10006

COMPANION CD CONTENT

Raster files and movie files are zipped to conserve space on disk. Unzipping will be required before viewing!

FREE RASTER STOCK ART

Images From Book:

Explosive Soccer Ball • sc50075
Fashion Tiger • ma30077
Roar Lion • ma30054
Baseball Eruption • bb30048
Alien Head • sf90002
K-9 • fp70019
Spike Soccer Ball • sc50032
Iron Cross • mc90004

Extra Free Images:

Bobcat • ma30081
3/4 Football Helmet • fb20003
Buck Magic • wl60031
Basketball with Net • bk40006
Hockey Check • hky40007
Margarita Parrot • fd10006

FREE VECTOR CLIP ART

Images From Book:

Metal Devil • cama50032
Parrot on Wall • caan20019
Monster Basketball • cabk90026
Spike Basketball • cabk90039
Elephant • cawl80004
One Fish • casm40004
Metal Lion • cama50035
Basketball Jam • cabk90025
Spike Soccer Ball • casc40035
Spike Baseball • cabb30029

Extra Free Images:

Football Player Run • cafb70016
Fire Mask • cafp40006
Classic Car • caau30001
Tiger • cama50045
Hockey Player • cahky50004

QUICK TIME TUTORIAL MOVIES

(Over 34 minutes)
Removing Art from White Background (12:42)
Changing Colors (6:33)
Printing Out Seps (6:31)
Type on a Path (8:39)

LESSON FILES

Amber Beer Mug
Business Card Scan
Distressed Texture
Tiger Photo
T-Shirt Template

SOFTWARE TRIAL VERSIONS

Spot Process • AccuRIP
*Text file with links to download
the latest trials included on disk*

LAYER STYLES

GREAT DANE GRAPHICS
LAYER STYLES V.1

w w w . g r e a t d a n e g r a p h i c s . c o m